Morning Time

MORNING TIME: A LITURGY OF LOVE

By Cindy Rollins © 2021

Portions of this book were previously published in 2016 as *A Handbook for Morning Time* by CiRCE Institute.

Cover Design: © 2021 Blue Sky Daisies

Cover image (floral mason jar and lavender) Tati Bordiu via Creative Market
Cover image (watercolor paper) Julie Campbell via Creative Market
Interior recurring image (floral mason jar) Tati Bordiu via Creative Market

ISBN: 978-1-944435-16-5

Morning Time

A LITURGY OF LOVE

Cindy Rollins

Author of *Mere Motherhood*

BLUE SKY
DAISIES

TABLE OF CONTENTS

WHAT ELSE DO I NEED?

CINDY'S ANTHOLOGY

PREFACE

When I originally wrote *The Morning Time Handbook,* it was a series of 30 blog posts based on a theme of "Thirty Days to Morning Time." It helped me clarify what Morning Time was, what it could and even what it could not be. Later, I was asked to turn those posts into a brochure or booklet. I am now returning to my original vision and expanding this heartfelt project to make it accessible to more families. I happen to think Morning Time is the perfect way to reset when you first bring your child home from traditional school or virtual school. Therefore, I am hoping to get it into the hands of new homeschoolers everywhere.

On the other hand, I also believe that having a Morning Time would benefit most schools, and I know of a few which have incorporated it as a morning assembly. Morning Time is a perfect way to create bonds across the school, just as it can create lifelong bonds in a family. We hear a lot about "community" today. I believe Morning Time offers us a unique and organic way to begin the process of community building in our homes, families, schools, churches, and even care homes or assisted living facilities.

Cindy Rollins
2021

FOREWORD

This gloriously satisfying hour together, day in and day out, came almost without fail at home, on vacations, when we had just moved, in happy contented times, and in sad, distressed times of family life.

When there is general upheaval going on, this normal routine is a helpful rhythm. Depression sometimes lightens as people lose themselves in the story. A dawn of interest and even some joy thus entering into a mind can help dispel darkness. Sometimes the spirit of the rebellious child or the ruffled adult gets soothed. Selfish introspection can be turned into concern for other people who lived different kinds of lives, those dealing with other circumstances.

—Susan Schaeffer Macaulay

In reflecting on the practice of Morning Time in our homeschool and how it has blessed our family, I realized that the "gloriously satisfying hour together" that Susan Schaeffer Macaulay wrote of in her book *For the Family's Sake* also describes our experience. She depicts the evening ritual of books, music, and conversation at her parents' home at L'Abri and how she and her husband later made this gathering time a central part of their home as well.

When I first read about the rich family culture the Schaeffers cultivated around books, I knew that was what I wanted for my own family. But a romantic ideal often clashes with real life and the practical outworking of lofty ideas can be a challenge. I had a compelling picture of what gathering my children together might look like in our homeschool, but I wasn't quite sure how to build the practice. I chose my curriculum and had specific books and subjects that I wanted to study together, but

I still struggled to see how to unite my rose-colored vision with my love of practical systems.

When my oldest child was five years old, I discovered Cindy Rollins' blog where she described her family's Morning Time practices. She would explain how she went about planning a year of Morning Time subjects and how, little by little, she led her family through books, poetry, Shakespeare's plays, and other delightful things. Our family had already started a little morning meeting time for reading the Bible, memorizing Scripture and poetry, and singing songs together. Cindy helped me see how the lovely vision cast by Susan Schaeffer Macaulay could be woven into a homeschool day (though we kept bedtime stories as well!).

As my children grew older and more numerous, Morning Time became the center of our homeschool day. Following Cindy's principles and using AmblesideOnline as our primary curriculum, I saw some of the fruits that Macaulay described in her book begin to ripen. We laughed until we cried over Tom Sawyer's antics and we cried until we laughed over the death of several beloved characters. I chose books that I wanted to read for my own education and brought the children along with me. This made homeschooling and Morning Time a feast for my soul as well as theirs. I saw attitudes shift as we sang hymns and folksongs together and wonderful friendships form as we shared inside jokes from our readings. The children recited poetry for one another and argued plenty over literary characters. Morning Time gave us an anchor for our long-haul plan for homeschooling. Many homeschooling mothers look for a curriculum which will allow their students to study the same books or historical period to foster closeness and connections with one another. But I found I didn't need to adapt a curriculum to accomplish those things, I just had to be faithful to this daily hour of books, songs, poetry, and Scripture.

While we never took Morning Time on vacation as the Schaeffers did their reading, we did gather together day in and day out over the weeks, months, and years. It offered us stability in those "happy contented times" when siblings were getting along well and everyone cooperated and loved school and in those "sad, distressed times" when we grieved hard things or I was ready to just be done with all of it in the deeper trenches of parenting.

When my two oldest children were close to the end of high school, they were often too busy to fit our Morning Time into their schedules. And this was almost as hard a loss for me as graduating them a year or two later. I tried to pick books they couldn't resist listening in on or Shakespeare plays in which I knew they'd want to take a part. There are just three of us now and we each have to take more parts in the plays and sing as best we can with fewer voices; but this continues to be as central a part of our homeschool as math and grammar; perhaps even more so.

I believe that this book will inspire you and provide some practical help for establishing a time for sharing songs, books, art, poetry, and anything else that is an important part of your family culture. Morning Time may offer a place to include some of the subjects that often get pushed aside or overlooked more often than you'd like. Cindy has inspired many of us to see the work of the homeschooling mother as a gift of leisure and to view Morning Time as a liturgy for our days. It is an opportunity to set a feast of ideas before our children and partake of that feast with them.

Jami Marstall
2021

Part I

A LITURGY OF LOVE

WHAT IS MORNING TIME?

When I began having "Morning Time" with my children, I didn't imagine that it would become the hallmark of my homeschool.

My oldest son Timothy was four years old, and I was pregnant with our fourth child. We had just moved to New Jersey, and it was time to start homeschooling. I had been reading about homeschooling for years, and now that Timothy was four, finally the time had come to dive in.

The book that stayed with me through all that mass of reading was *For the Children's Sake* by Susan Schaeffer Macaulay. The vision she laid out in her book introducing Charlotte Mason captured my imagination. I wanted that for my children. I wanted that for myself.

You may be wondering, "Who is Charlotte Mason?" Charlotte Mason was a British educator who lived from 1847-1923. She started a movement which spread around the world based on her 20 principles. Two of these principles are key:

- Children are born persons.
- Education is the science of relations.

"Children are born persons."

"Education is the science of relations."

Her principles were a radical departure from modern educational theory of both her time and ours. She summed her philosophy up with the sentence,

Education is an atmosphere, a discipline, and a life.

Charlotte left us with her life's work of six volumes which are available online at AmblesideOnline.[1] AmblesideOnline is a free site dedicated to helping parents implement Charlotte's philosophy, "however imperfectly," and as inexpensively as possible.[2]

As I was discovering Charlotte Mason, four-year-old Timothy was in Awana, a church program with an emphasis on Scripture memory, at our new church. His weekly memory verses became a part of our mornings. We would have breakfast, clean up, sit on the couch, read nursery rhymes and picture books, and recite his verses. This time with Timothy was so perfect. It was working so well, I naturally wanted to do more. First, I added the reading aloud of chapter books. Next, because I have always loved poetry, I started reading poetry in Morning Time too, in addition to the nursery rhymes. I expanded our Bible time. Not only did we work on Awana memorization, but we also started the day with Bible reading. These were the bones of Morning Time.

As our memorization increased quite easily, since Timothy loved to memorize, I started to wonder how we could retain old memory work while continuing to memorize new items. I remembered the memorization system that my college roommate Pam Woerner taught me. This system consisted of reading a Bible verse daily for about two weeks and then moving that verse to a review pile. Every day you read your new Bible verse and reviewed one verse from the review pile. The review pile grew, but you were always cycling back through everything you had already memorized. This was the perfect solution to my worries. Each day, for however many days or weeks it took, Timothy and I worked on a new Bible passage and we reviewed one old passage in rotation. Of course, this worked just as well for poetry, speeches, or other memory pieces. Each day we were learning something new and reviewing something old in each category.

Later I would expand Morning Time to make room for other categories, other important "subjects" that didn't quite make the regular school day cut. These subjects were important to me but were easily shuffled out of the day—things like composer study, picture study, Plutarch, Shakespeare, and nature notebooks. As you can guess, Morning Time became my way of implementing a Charlotte Mason education. Morning Time was an atmosphere, a discipline, and a life. I almost effortlessly filled it up with the elements of education that Charlotte Mason advised. All I had to do was step back and watch the years roll by.

And the years did roll by. My children grew up, every single one of them. But after thirty plus years of Morning Time, I realized that I couldn't just stop. I still wake up each morning and have my own little Morning Time. This reminds me of Charlotte Mason principle that "children are born persons." That means that we all learn in

Morning Time became my way of implementing a Charlotte Mason education.

humane ways, whether we are a young person or an old person. We all feed on ideas. If Morning Time gave us all a chance to feed on ideas for thirty years, there was no reason why I could not keep the power of that habit going even though the children had the audacity to grow up.

These days, my Morning Time consists of reading through the Bible (I just pick a Bible-in-a-year plan and make adjustments to the schedule if I fall behind, that way I am continually reading through the whole Bible), devotional reading, a logic puzzle, sometimes a sentence to diagram, some poetry, and a maybe a few other short readings, sometimes Shakespeare. Morning Time is addicting.

Moms often ask me if they *have* to have Morning Time and I think, "My goodness, of course not!" But I also think there are very few things we do in this life that bear as much fruit as Morning Time.

People often wonder whether or not Morning Time is part of a Charlotte Mason education. Did Charlotte Mason say to do something like that? Morning Time was my way of implementing Charlotte's words long before there were so many helps available. Charlotte herself did not speak of it. You can construct a perfectly fine Charlotte Mason day without Morning Time or group time of any flavor. But Morning Time was my organic way of imparting a Charlotte Mason education to my children. It endured and produced most of the fruit my homeschool enjoyed. Morning Time is not some untested, fly-by-night idea I came up with and am quickly making money off of before realizing it doesn't work. (I have fallen for many of those in my day.) I know from the experience of my own life that this practice can bring peace, joy, and family camaraderie over many long years.

I am happy to see the idea growing and flourishing in all kinds of places by all kinds of names. If you want to have Morning Time in your home, this book will help. I can almost guarantee you will never regret the hours spent in Morning Time. If you don't want to have Morning Time, don't. I still think you will like all the poems, songs, and lists we have added to this book. What is Morning Time? It is capturing the hours of your day before they flit away. It is making sure the most beautiful things happen first. It is impossible to regret that.

Perhaps you are coming to this book as a newly-minted, and possibly reluctant, homeschooler. You could be longing for your child to escape screen learning. You sense there is something off with a child sitting in front of a computer all day, but you also fear that traditional school knows something about education that you don't know. I believe this book will give you a living alternative, that it will empower you to try something fresh and lasting, and that it may help you rethink what it means to be educated in a way that brings joy to your family and lifelong learning to your children.

You may be rethinking so many things that it is hard to figure out what to do.

What is Morning Time? It is capturing the hours of your day before they flit away. It is making sure the most beautiful things happen first. It is impossible to regret that.

Morning Time can start very small. As you have success with a short Morning Time, you will begin to see how you can add things to it to increase your time together and your learning capacity. This book goes over all the things I used and tried in Morning Time, but there is no reason for you to feel pressure to do it all. Maybe you will be inspired to come up with new things I never even considered.

MORNING TIME: A LITURGY OF LOVE

A few years ago, after the publication of *Desiring the Kingdom* by James K. A. Smith, "liturgy" became a buzzword among some of us. As I was thinking about the word, I suddenly realized that what I had called "Morning Time" for so many years was a liturgy. It was a liturgy offering my children tethers from the past which they could carry far into the future to places I am unable to even imagine. I did not understand why Morning Time worked, although I knew it had, but as I read more about liturgy it began to make sense. Liturgy is a form. We think of it usually as the form worship takes on. Because it is a form, it is tied to memory or remembrance. Communion, or what is sometimes called the Lord's Supper, is a form for remembrance—the ultimate form for the ultimate remembrance. We not only remember what Christ did for us on the cross by shedding his blood, but we also are reminded that there is a feast day coming in the future for the bride of Christ.

I like to think of it as a stalk carrying life from the root to the outer parts of a plant. The stalk is not important in itself, it is just a form, but what it carries is precious to the plant.

Some people worry that liturgy is a dead form—lifeless and cold—but I like to think of it as a stalk carrying life from the root to the outer parts of a plant. The stalk is not important in itself, it is just a form, but what it carries is precious to the plant. *Truth*, *goodness*, and *beauty* are roots attached to the soil of the past. Our liturgies are the stems carrying life-giving properties into the future.

The liturgy of Morning Time reminds us there is no separation between the sacred and the secular. We sing both sacred hymns and secular folk songs; we read both sacred Scriptures and secular books in Morning Time. We are not forced to divide our time with God from our other pursuits. We are Christians made in the image of God—image-bearers. We are filled with the Holy Spirit. The form of Morning Time is a reminder that *everything* we do is for the glory of God.

We memorize and we remember in Morning Time. We memorize Psalm 23 or "An English Country Garden" folksong. We remember King Alfred and Sam Gamgee. Morning Time is a liturgy of love, and because of that, it organically works with the way we are made by our Creator.

MORNING MEETING

Our Morning Time always began with a morning meeting. This was a time to take care of family logistics. In a large family like ours, this step was crucial. It also gave me a chance to nag. I never kept chore charts because the upkeep of the chart became the focus. I found that tedious. Better to assign permanent chores than have a constant, confusing rotation. Generally new job assignments were given out at the beginning of the school year. Other habits were incorporated into our regular morning routine, which stayed the same for almost twenty years.

Our mornings generally looked like this: Rise, make bed, read Bible, eat breakfast, do chores, start math. At some point in the morning, generally around 8:30 a.m., but sometimes as late as 10:30, I would announce, "Morning meeting in ten minutes." This gave the kids time to wrap up whatever they were doing.

As we gathered on the couches, I would start asking various questions to individual children. "Did you read your Bible?" "Did you sweep the kitchen?" Or as a group I might say, "Who brushed their teeth?" The response was often discouraging (meaning I had to wait while everyone went off to brush their teeth). I am not completely sure this was the best plan, but it was the simplest.

It was also a time to discuss hygiene and life skills.

We tried to figure out who needed the car for the day and who might have a dentist appointment. I learned that with so many people I could only handle today's problems. The morning meeting gave me a chance to meet that day's logistics without worrying too much about the future, although we could also discuss the week ahead.

The kids and I used to get a kick out of walking around in Costco and hearing the announcement to employees that it was time for the Morning Meeting. They had a Morning Meeting, too!

MORNING TIME STRUCTURE

For our family Morning Time started very simply with just a couple categories and lots of reading aloud, but over the years I realized that it was a great place to add all sorts of categories. It was the perfect time for all those ideas that got squeezed out of the regular school day, things like composer study and art, Plutarch and Shakespeare, but it was also a good place to start teaching more traditional subjects in very short lessons, Charlotte Mason style—a few minutes of grammar or Latin each day. The possibilities are truly endless.

There are so many resources now to help you with pursuing a Charlotte Mason education. It can be completely overwhelming. Many of them are not necessary and

> . . . the perfect time for all those ideas that got squeezed out of the regular school day, things like composer study and art, Plutarch and Shakespeare, but it was also a good place to start teaching more traditional subjects in very short lessons, Charlotte Mason style—a few minutes of grammar or Latin each day.

can make mothers feel inadequate. My journey included the help and reading lists of AmblesideOnline and I still heartily recommend the resources found there.[3] I have also included some other recommendations in the Resources and Recommendations section at the back of this book. Throughout my Morning Time story and in my sample plans you will often see "AmblesideOnline Selections," which refers to time spent with artist and composer studies, Plutarch, and Shakespeare.

Morning Time took anywhere from one to two hours in our house. Generally, I would say about an hour and a half. Over the years I developed organizational strategies which cut down on the time I spent looking for materials. For many years I wasted precious minutes searching for this book or that version of the Bible every single day.

Eventually I learned to have them all beside me when I started. In the early years, every day was an adventure of trying to find this song and that poem. I finally spent one summer making up a memory notebook, a Morning Time notebook, and family hymnbooks. I kept a basket in the living room with teacher's editions of textbooks and Morning Time books and materials. Certainly, technology added to the ease. I could quickly google a verse or a song in the latter years. This was often quicker than turning to the page in our family poem book, but then again you miss the fun of looking over other poems as well. I've put many of these things into the anthology in this book.

Life sends interruptions. They are inevitable—the baby wakes up, the dryer beeps, the phone rings. Interruptions are chances to take short breaks. I tried not to let interruptions throw me off completely. I learned to pick right up wherever we were after a phone call or other problem. I learned not to quit just because my plans were delayed. The children learned to come to Morning Time with their own reading materials so if there was an interruption, they could get some of their list done during the timeout or even do a math problem or two. Sometimes I even let them continue Morning Time without me. Giving over the reins to an older child for a few minutes can be refreshing for the whole family.

I didn't make the kids sit completely quietly, either. After Bible time they were allowed to play silently on the floor. I don't suggest letting the toddlers wander off unless you want to find they have ironed several big patches of carpet in a far room. I have heard of this happening. Wink.

If you have a clear understanding that Morning Time is valuable for the long haul you won't be as likely to skip it or stress over how much time it takes but being flexible is helpful.

A sample of my weekly Morning Time sheet is on the facing page. I've included some blank planning pages for you on pages 67 and 71.

> If you have a clear understanding that Morning Time is valuable for the long haul you won't be as likely to skip it or stress over how much time it is taking, but being flexible is helpful.

SAMPLE MORNING TIME PLANNING WORKSHEET

Date: _____   New Poem: "Sea Fever"

Bible Passage: I Peter 5:5-11   Shakespeare: *The Tempest* (movie this week)

New Hymn: "When I Survey"   Plutarch: Numa Pompilius

Composer: Vivaldi   Grammar: *The Mother Tongue* sentences

Artist: Dürer   Other: _____

Morning Time Element	Monday	Tuesday	Wednesday	Thursday	Friday
Prayer Focus (*Requests, Praises, Thanksgivings*)					
Bible Time	Daily Proverb		W. Catechism Q. 5		W. Catechism Q. 6
Review	Books of the OT	Books of the NT	Psalm 33	Eph. 6:10-18	Psalm 42
Hymn Singing	"When I Survey"				
Review	"A Mighty Fortress"	"Come, Thou Fount"	"Crown Him with Many Crowns"	"Be Thou My Vision"	"All Creatures of Our God and King"
Poetry	"Sea Fever"				
Review	"The Creation"	"The Pasture"	"Dutch Lullaby"	"Clouds"	"Nobility"
Misc. Memory	Civics Question of the Day Presidents Bee	Heidelberg #1	Planets Oceans	West Point Cadet Prayer	"Contem-plate" by Sam Adams
Reading Aloud	*Carry On, Mr. Bowditch* *The Marsh King*				

Visit blueskydaisies.net for a printable version of this sample worksheet.

Part II

ELEMENTS OF MORNING TIME

PRAYER AND BIBLE READING

Here we are at the beginning of Morning Time. We have had our Morning Meeting. Now we move into the Bible portion of our time together. This section has a structure like all the other sections, but it is also a category that can cover everything from worship to theology to Christian living.

It makes sense to begin with prayer. Ideally, it is nice to write down prayer requests and then have everyone pray. But when time is short a quick beginning prayer at least sets the tone for the day. I left a row on my planning sheet for prayer because I could write in prayer requests as they came up in the boxes. Writing them down also allowed us to remember when they were answered.

Usually even before prayer we sang two hymns. I will cover that in the singing section (see page 24).

I began by reading a passage from the Bible. Sometimes we worked our way through the whole Bible, but often I read a Proverb for the day. If it was October 8, we read Proverbs 8. I do not think you can read Proverbs too often. Just be careful, Mom, not to try and drive every lesson home, which is one of the biggest dangers of Morning Time. Let the Holy Spirit work on your children as you put truth before them.

I very much love the King James Version (KJV) of the Bible, and I think that children benefit greatly from using that version because of its beautiful English. I made the mistake of adapting our translation to that of the churches we attended over the years, which meant we started out memorizing in the New International Version

I do not think you can read Proverbs too often. Just be careful, Mom, not to try and drive every lesson home, which is one of the biggest dangers of Morning Time.

(NIV), moved to the KJV, and later to the New KJV, which I probably would have stayed with if it had not fallen out of use. Now I often read from the English Standard Version (ESV). But you can't go wrong with the old Authorized King James Version for beauty of language.

In the section of my Morning Time sheet titled "Bible," I put in passages to read, passages to review, and any read-alouds which cover Bible, theology, or Christian living.

We were always working on learning a new passage from the Bible, reading it every day for weeks, and reviewing a previous passage each day. You can see how I organized that on my weekly planning chart (see page 19).

For instance, on the sample chart you can see we were memorizing I Peter 5:5-11 by reading it each day. I much prefer memorizing passages as opposed to isolated verses, even for young children. That week we reviewed the books of the Old Testament, the books of the New Testament, Psalm 33, Ephesians 6:10-18, and Psalm 42. I alternated reviewing Old Testament and New Testament selections. I put recently memorized pieces on our review list more frequently, going from daily to weekly before adding them to the longer review list.

This is also a good place for a devotional read-aloud, especially if you have teens who are only staying for part of the time (more on that later). You may want them to hear a book such as *Grace Unknown* by R.C. Sproul or *Fifty Reasons Why Jesus Came to Die* by John Piper.

My philosophy has always been that my job, since I am *not* the Holy Spirit, is to give the children lots of hooks in their hearts so that when the Holy Spirit is working on them, he will have something to bring to their remembrance.

I used to tell them all this memory work was for the time when they were in prison (for righteousness's sake) and the rats were nibbling their toes. I am not recommending you do that.

My original goal was to memorize something from every book in the Bible. We didn't quite pull that off. Here is the list of information, verses, and passages we memorized over the years. The "Bible Information to Memorize" and the "Best Bible Passages to Start Memorizing" are collected in the anthology for you (see page 114).

> . . . give the children lots of hooks in their hearts so that when the Holy Spirit is working on them, he will have something to bring to their remembrance.

BIBLE INFORMATION TO MEMORIZE

The Books of the Old Testament

The Books of the New Testament (We sing these, but the song is pretty terrible.)

The Lord's Prayer

The 12 Apostles

The 12 Tribes of Israel

The 14 Judges of Israel

BEST BIBLE PASSAGES TO START MEMORIZING

FIVE FROM OLD TESTAMENT

Genesis 1:1-5
Exodus 20:1-7
Deuteronomy 6:4-9
Psalm 1
Isaiah 40:28-31

FIVE FROM NEW TESTAMENT

Matthew 5:3-16
Luke 2:1-21
John 1:1-14
John 14:1-7
I Corinthians 13

OTHER PASSAGES WORTH MEMORIZING

OLD TESTAMENT

Deuteronomy 28:1-17
Ruth 1:16-17
I Samuel 16:6-7
I Chronicles 4:9-10
Psalm 8
Psalm 15
Psalm 19
Psalm 20
Psalm 23
Psalm 24

Psalm 27:1-7
Psalm 33
Psalm 42
Psalm 100
Psalm 104
Psalm 121
Psalm 127
Psalm 128
Psalm 139
Psalm 150

Proverbs 4:20-27
Proverbs 20:11
Isaiah 9:6
Isaiah 11:1-2
Isaiah 53:1-6
Jeremiah 9:23-24
Daniel 1:17
Micah 6:8
Habakkuk 3:17-19

NEW TESTAMENT

Matthew 6:19-34
Matthew 11:28-30
Matthew 16:24-28
John 6:47-51
John 14:21
Romans 6
II Corinthians 4:16-18
II Corinthians 10:5

Ephesans 6:10-18
Philipians 4:4-8
Colossians 3
I Thessalonians 4:13-18
II Timothy 2:15
I Peter 5:5-11
Hebrews 11:1-6
Hebrews 12:1-7

I John 4:1-11
III John 1:4
Jude 1:20-25
Revelation 3:20
Revelation 21:1-8

SINGING

After we finished the Morning Meeting we moved into worship. I described our prayer and Bible reading in the previous section. Another important part of worship is singing, and we often sang psalms, hymns, or spiritual songs even before our prayer time.

This singing was not as easy as it sounds. It began because I wanted the kids to know the hymns that we were singing in church even before they could read the hymnal. In fact, you could say that before we added music, Morning Time was just a jumble of morning events, but after we added music our time together had definition. I am not sure why music works like this, but it does.

When we had a lot of people at home, this singing time was good—melodious. Then we went through a few dry years after two of our better singers grew up. We muddled through a couple dismal years of singing and then I deleted singing from Morning Time. We were running to shut the windows every day before we sang, and no one was happy.

After I spoke at a conference and mentioned our singing failure, a couple of old friends came up to me and gently rebuked me for not scheduling singing just because we sounded awful. I heeded their advice, bucked myself up to work through our family hymnbook one more time and, in fact, finished one last round through the hundred-plus hymns in our family hymnbook. The children left at home were not happy about this, but I was impervious.

Eventually, we started to enjoy singing again. Now that I understand Morning Time to be a liturgy, I cannot see my way clear to quit singing, even if we only sing the Gloria Patri or the Doxology each day or even if I am all alone having my own Morning Time.

To create our family hymnbook, we started by learning one hymn. We sang that hymn every day for weeks, adding one more verse each week. In week one, we would sing the first verse of the hymn. Week two would have us singing verses one and two each day. We did this until we had learned all the appropriate verses.

Then we moved that hymn to our review list. Eventually, each day we were working on our new hymn, singing it daily over several weeks, and we were reviewing one old hymn each day. That had us singing two hymns a day for years and years and years.

If you look at our hymnbook, you can follow us on a theological journey from traditional lighter hymns to more complex hymns to Psalms to newer music from people like the Gettys. It has been a musical and theological journey.

For years and years, I scrambled around the house each day trying to remember which hymnbook had which hymn. My husband and I both grew up using the Christian & Missionary Alliance hymnbook *Songs of the Christian Life*. Later we added other

. . . we started by learning one hymn. We sang that hymn every day for weeks, adding one more verse each week. In week one, we would sing the first verse of the hymn. Week two would have us singing verses one and two each day. We did this until we had learned all the appropriate verses.

denominational hymnbooks to our collection, and psalters, too. This scrambling began taking up too much time, so I began to develop strategies to avoid the morning scramble in the area of music. I printed out four copies, in one form or another, of every hymn we had ever learned. I made up a table of contents and *voila!* We had our own family hymnbooks which only required us to turn to the next page each day. Many of our favorite hymns' words are included here in the anthology so that you don't have to scramble. It's also helpful to find versions on YouTube or Spotify to give you music to sing along with.

I think the first hymn we learned in Morning Time was "Blessed Assurance." I remember going to church one Wednesday night and hearing our pastor's children singing that without the hymnbook. I went home and added hymns to our morning meeting. I think Timothy was six. Some of these songs I don't even like anymore, but some will never grow old.

One of our family favorites is "My Anchor Holds," but we have not found many people who know it. I've included it in the anthology.

Let me repeat: We are terrible singers, not counting my dear husband. We rarely sing in public anymore, although Tim used to sing with the kids at church when they were little. They did a pretty awesome rendition of Judy Rogers's "Listen My Son."

One year, I tried to talk the children into singing "Coram Deo," another Judy Rogers song, at the annual Reformation Party, but after one practice I conceded that we still sounded awful. Tim actually left the room in the middle of our practice.

Another time, during the Reformation Day[4] skits at church, poor little Andrew turned to me with fear in his eyes and said, "We aren't doing the 'Modern Major-General,' are we?" We all got a kick out of that.

Our family hymnal eventually numbered 119 pages, but rather than overwhelm you with that, here is a list of my top ten favorites. The anthology includes the lyrics for these, plus for a number of other great hymns I recommend. There are so many hymns that we love. Find the full list in the anthology which begins on page 75.

TOP TEN FAVORITE HYMNS

1. "A Mighty Fortress"
2. "All Creatures of Our God and King"
3. "Be Still My Soul"
4. "Be Thou My Vision"
5. "Come Thou Fount"
6. "Crown Him with Many Crowns"

7. "Fairest Lord Jesus"
8. "Great Is Thy Faithfulness"
9. "When I Survey"
10. "Immortal, Invisible"

MORE THAN HYMNS

But hymns are not the only songs worthy of Morning Time. Patriotic and folk songs should have an honored place because they are an important part of passing on a culture of remembrance to our children. The words of these old songs carry with them a remembrance of times and people past. I believe the words carry a DNA in them that connects us to the past. We learn about history in a way that is absorbed into our hearts.

Music is the response of patriotism, too. Who can forget the scene in *The Sound of Music* when the Von Trapp family sings the national anthem of Austria at a festival even though the Nazis had outlawed the song "Edelweiss"?

In Scottish history, the bagpipes played an important role. The English ruled Scotland for many years as oppressors and, in fact, they outlawed the bagpipes. Why? The bagpipes were not lethal weapons. You could not shoot bullets from the bagpipes and yet, the English knew the bagpipes had the power to stir the hearts of men to overthrow their oppressors. Music is a powerful force! Morning Time is often the only time we have to sing together as a family.

Folk songs don't just add a nostalgic element to Morning Time, they are a vital element in passing down culture. They are key reminders that our thoughts and our way of knowing did not begin with us and perhaps there are ways of living and treating one another we have forgotten.

AmblesideOnline has a great selection of folk songs that bring just plain fun to Morning Time, but also help us transfer culture to our children. I like their list, but here are ten favorites to get you started. The lyrics for them are found in the anthology beginning on page 106.

> Folk songs are key reminders that our thoughts and our way of knowing did not begin with us and perhaps there are ways of living and treating one another we have forgotten.

TEN FAVORITE FOLK AND POPULAR SONGS

1. "The Ash Grove"
2. "The Drinking Gourd"
3. "An English Country Garden"
4. "The Happy Wanderer"

5. "Molly Malone" (Cockles and Mussels)
6. "The Three Ravens"
7. "Scarborough Faire"
8. "Simple Gifts"
9. "Star of the County Down"
10. "Swing Low, Sweet Chariot"

I am older now and usually alone in the morning. It is probably hard for a mom in the thick of it to even imagine this, but my mornings are quiet now. For the last several years I haven't had any time outside of church to sing. This year I noticed that my voice was getting increasingly weak. One day, seemingly from out of nowhere, I knew that I should be singing every single day, out loud, all by myself. Since that day I have faithfully been singing songs of praise or even songs just for fun. Truly this has changed both my voice, making it much stronger, and my life, making it much richer. Having mentioned this in my newsletter "Over the Back Fence" and online, people have been sending me articles and excerpts from books about this very thing. Singing is vital to humanity. One of the greatest tragedies of modernity is that we have pro-fessionalized singing. It is something only talented people do. And yet, when we sing, we even breathe differently, more deeply. It's life-giving.

Before my epiphany of singing, I was a guest on a podcast and just as we were signing off the host asked me what the most important thing to do in Morning Time was. I started to say, "Bible" like a child in Sunday School, but I heard myself saying, "Singing." Where did that come from? The minute I said it though, I knew that it was true. Singing is the most important way to build a family culture based on joy and worship, which are two things we desperately need in these tough times.

> One day, seemingly from out of nowhere, I knew that I should be singing every single day, out loud, all by myself.

POETRY

Some people do not like poetry which makes them quick to underestimate its value. Some people think it has some value, but that the time spent memorizing poetry would be better spent memorizing more useful information.

To the first group I say: Do not let your own lack of love for poetry cause you to dismiss it. I am almost convinced that poetry may be the most important thing we do in our homes apart from those things which draw us to Christ such as Bible study and singing. Still, we do not want to be guilty of separating the sacred and secular. Poetry can draw us to Christ too, and it can draw us to our fellow men. It can open our eyes to the world around us.

> Do not let your own lack of love for poetry cause you to dismiss it.

POETRY IS A WAY OF SEEING

Poetry is the highest form of language. It requires a level of thinking that cannot easily be taught. It must be caught. As your children hear and hear and hear poetry, they will gradually begin to think in the form of connections or metaphors. I have heard it said that a genius is someone who makes connections that other people miss. The more connections a person can make between seemingly unlike things, the more the world opens up to them. Poetry is almost our only tool for teaching this kind of thinking. It is far more valuable to memorize poetry than to memorize lists of information. In fact, when in doubt, err on the side of poetry.

> It is far more valuable to memorize poetry than to memorize lists of information. In fact, when in doubt, err on the side of poetry.

There are many ways we can introduce poetry into our homes. Some ways will include memory, and some will just involve hearing. Poetry is perfect for memorization, because the lessons it has for us come slowly.

Often the first time we read a poem it is gibberish to us, but as we read it day after day after day, it slowly begins to make sense and come alive. We gradually begin to see what the poet is sharing. It is magic. Pure magic.

This is why I recommend reading the same poem for weeks on end when memorizing it. We are going for quality not quantity. It is okay to talk about a few elements of the poem at first, but I would keep it to a minimum. Don't steal all the "ahas" from your children. After you have read the poem for a week or so then start asking your children what they think it means and maybe discuss some of the vocabulary. Maybe just bring up one word a day to discuss, or one metaphor, or none.

This is the best way to spend time with a poem, over a few weeks. But poetry has other values and other lessons to teach us that aren't quite so in depth. It can teach us to feel rhythm or meter. It can teach us to grasp for meaning.

Therefore, we approach poetry each day in three ways. First, we listen to the poem we are memorizing every day for weeks. Second, each day we review one poem from the past. Finally, I read a new poem and we talk about the author and the rhyme scheme. This is like a short calisthenic to work the metaphoric muscles. This daily reading will not help us get to know a certain poem, but it will help us become people who think poetically. The key to this kind of learning is to avoid overkill. Don't tear the poem apart, just look for delights.

Warning: If you choose to memorize a long poem like "Paul Revere's Ride," your mind will never forget it and if ever, in passing, you say a line from that poem your brain will immediately insist on reciting the whole poem back to you. You will not be able to turn the poem off, especially if you are just getting ready to go to bed.

A list of poems that I recommend is on the following pages and the poems themselves are included in the anthology which begins on page 75.

TEN FAVORITES FOR YOUNGER CHILDREN

(Don't forget lots of nursery rhymes)

1. "The Creation" by Cecil Frances Alexander (1818-1895)
2. "The Pilgrim" by John Bunyan (1628-1688)
3. "Little Things" by Julia Abigail Fletcher Carney (1823-1908)
4. "Dutch Lullaby" by Eugene Field (1850-1895)
5. "The Pasture" by Robert Frost (1874-1963)
6. "Clouds" by Christina Rossetti (1830-1894)
7. "Who Has Seen the Wind?" by Christina Rossetti (1830-1894)
8. "Lullaby of an Infant Chief" by Sir Walter Scott (1771-1832)
9. "Bed in Summer" by Robert Louis Stevenson (1850-1894)
10. "Whether the Weather" by Unknown

FAVORITES FOR MIDDLE SCHOOL AND UP

(Not including Shakespeare. He is in a class by himself. See page 40 for a list of suggested Shakespeare memory passages.)

1. "Be Strong" by Maltbie D. Babcock (1858-1901)
2. "The Tyger" by William Blake (1757-1827)
3. "The Lamb" by William Blake (1757-1827)
4. Sonnet 43, "How do I love thee?" by Elizabeth Barrett Browning (1806-1861)
5. "Out in the Fields with God" by Louise Imogen Guiney (1861-1920)
6. "To a Mouse" by Robert Burns (1759-1796)
7. "A Red, Red Rose" by Robert Burns (1759-1796)
8. "The Destruction of Sennacherib" by George Gordon, Lord Byron (1788-1824)
9. "Jabberwocky" by Lewis Carroll (1832–1898)
10. "Nobility" by Alice Cary (1820–1871)
11. "The New-England Boy's Song about Thanksgiving Day" ("Over the river and through the woods . . .") by Lydia Maria Child (1802-1880)
12. "Kubla Khan" by Samuel Taylor Coleridge (1772–1834)
13. "How Did You Die?" by Edmund Vance Cooke (1866-1932)
14. "The Listeners" by Walter de la Mare (1873–1956)
15. "There is no Frigate like a Book" by Emily Dickinson (1830–1886)
16. "'Hope' is the thing with feathers" by Emily Dickinson (1830–1886)
17. Sonnet X, "Death, be not proud" by John Donne (1572–1631)
18. "Mending Wall" by Robert Frost (1874-1963)
19. "The Road Not Taken" by Robert Frost (1874-1963)

20. "Stopping by Woods on a Snowy Evening" by Robert Frost (1874-1963)
21. "Modern Major-General's Song" by W. S. Gilbert (1836-1911)
22. "Weathers" by Thomas Hardy (1840-1948)
23. "Easter Wings" by George Herbert (1593–1633)
24. "Easter" by Gerard Manley Hopkins (1844–1889)
25. "God's Grandeur" by Gerard Manley Hopkins (1844–1889)
26. "Pied Beauty" by Gerard Manley Hopkins (1844–1889)
27. "Trees" by Joyce Kilmer (1886-1894)
28. "If—" by Rudyard Kipling (1865-1936)
29. "Recessional" by Rudyard Kipling (1865-1936)
30. "The New Colossus" by Emma Lazarus (1849-1887)
31. "The Arrow and the Song" by Henry Wadsworth Longfellow (1807-1882)
32. "Paul Revere's Ride" by Henry Wadsworth Longfellow (1807-1882)
33. "The Village Blacksmith" by Henry Wadsworth Longfellow (1807-1882)
34. "Horatius at the Bridge" by Thomas Babington, Lord Macaulay (1800-1859)
35. "Sea Fever" by John Masefield (1878-1967)
36. "In Flanders Fields" by John McCrae (1872-1918)
37. "Columbus" by Joaquin Miller (1837-1913)
38. "Sonnet on His Blindness" by John Milton (1608-1674)
39. "Invocation to Light" by John Milton (1608-1674)
40. "In the bleak midwinter" by Christina Rossetti (1830-1894)
41. "Ozymandias" by Percy Bysshe Shelley (1792-1822)
42. "The Fool's Prayer" by Edward Rowland Sill (1841-1887)
43. "Opportunity" by Edward Rowland Sill (1841-1887)
44. "Keep a' Goin'" by Frank Lebby Stanton (1857-1927)
45. "Autumn Fires" by Robert Louis Stevenson (1850-1894)
46. "Requiem" by Robert Louis Stevenson (1850-1894)
47. "Where Go the Boats" by Robert Louis Stevenson (1850-1894)
48. "Whole Duty of Children" by Robert Louis Stevenson (1850-1894)
49. "Windy Nights" by Robert Louis Stevenson (1850-1894)
50. "The Charge of the Light Brigade" by Alfred, Lord Tennyson (1809-1892)
51. "Crossing the Bar" by Alfred, Lord Tennyson (1809-1892)
52. "English War Song" by Alfred, Lord Tennyson (1809-1892)
53. "Casey at the Bat" by Ernest Lawrence Thayer (1863-1940)
54. "Awaken" by Lawrence Tribble (c. 18th century)
55. "Four Things" by Henry Van Dyke (1852-1933)
56. "Love Between Brothers and Sisters" by Isaac Watts (1674-1748)
57. "How doth the little busy bee" by Isaac Watts (1674-1748)
58. "The Sluggard" by Isaac Watts (1674-1748)

59. "Obedience to Parents" by Isaac Watts (1674-1748)
60. "I wandered lonely as a cloud" by William Wordsworth (1770–1850)
61. "My heart leaps up" by William Wordsworth (1770–1850)
62. "The world is too much with us" by William Wordsworth (1770–1850)
63. "The Lake Isle of Innisfree" by William Butler Yeats (1865-1939)
64. "The Second Coming" by William Butler Yeats (1865-1939)

HOW I MIGHT TEACH A POEM

Just so we are clear, there are three ways to enjoy poetry.

1. We can read it for pleasure.
2. We can memorize it for the future.
3. We can study it to understand how it means.

1. Read.
2. Memorize.
3. Study.

Let's take a look at "Stopping by Woods on a Snowy Evening."

STOPPING BY WOODS ON A SNOWY EVENING
By Robert Frost

Whose woods these are I think I know. (a)
His house is in the village though; (a)
He will not see me stopping here (b)
To watch his woods fill up with snow. (a)

My little horse must think it queer (b, this hearkens back to the above stanza)
To stop without a farmhouse near (b)
Between the woods and frozen lake (c)
The darkest evening of the year. (b)

He gives his harness bells a shake (c, there it is again)
To ask if there is some mistake. (c)
The only other sound's the sweep (d)
Of easy wind and downy flake. (c)

The woods are lovely, dark and deep. (d, still looking back to the last stanza)
But I have promises to keep, (d)
And miles to go before I sleep, (d)
And miles to go before I sleep. (d)

Here we have a simple poem which may be somewhat understood after one reading. First, we will read the poem through once slowly, enjoying the flow. If it doesn't flow too well, try reading it again until you get the feel of the rhythm. At this point you could ask the kids if anyone understands what is happening in the poem or you could even narrate the poem together (retell it in your own words).

You could also work through the rhyme scheme. Just add a letter of the alphabet to every new sound at the end of a line. I have added the rhyme scheme above. This poem ends with a quatrain rhyme. Often poems of various schemes end with couplets. This quatrain is really just two couplets, in a way, especially as the last two lines repeat the same thing.

You could talk about why the poem ends with a repeated line.

You could talk about how many syllables are in each line. In this poem we have lines of eight syllables each.

Since each stanza has four lines, they are called *quatrains*.

What about that word "queer"? Did your children giggle when you read that? If they did, now would be a great time to talk about the changing nature of words. A child raised on poetry learns the nuances of words and begins to understand something about the transitory meaning of words. This is an important skill.

You could also ask the children for word pictures describing what the poem evokes in their own words. None of this need last more than a few minutes. We are not dissecting the poem; we are learning how to understand how the poem means.

If we were going to be memorizing this poem, I would do none of this until we had read the poem for at least a week. But I would talk about some of this if I was just reading the poem for one day. As I said, but will say again, this is helping us to think poetically.

Of course, there can be much more to poetry than just those things I mentioned. You can also get into which syllables are stressed and other more difficult feats, but as I said, we don't want to tear the poem apart. We want only to start to think. The beauty of poetry is that the brain works to figure it out long after we have set it aside.

RESOURCES FOR TEACHING POETRY

Need help learning to do this? Here are a few of my favorite resources:

Perrine's Sound and Sense: An Introduction to Poetry by Thomas R. Arp and Greg Johnson

How Does a Poem Mean? by John Ciardi. This is the best book that I know of on poetry. This is not for the kids, but is for mom.

The Classic Hundred Poems by William Harmon. This book will hold your hand through all of the above.

Rules for the Dance: A Handbook for Writing and Reading Metrical Verse by Mary Oliver.

Of course, you will want to have many poetry books around your home, beginning with nursery rhymes. You will soon begin to find poems you love on your own and might not even need lists of ideas. I found Thomas Hardy when my children were small; he remains a favorite.

BEYOND POETRY: WHAT ELSE TO MEMORIZE

If we keep in mind Stratford Caldecott's definition of the grammar stage as "remembering," we can avoid making the mistake of looking at memorization as something to help us keep information sorted in our mind.[5] Of course, that is one way of using memorization, but it is the least useful way for our purposes of training the affections of our children.

So far, we have talked about memorizing Psalms, Bible passages, hymns and songs, and poetry. In a way, that is just the beginning. Before we ever break out the periodic table of elements or the math flashcards, there are still myriads of things which will order our children towards truth, beauty, and goodness.

> There are myriads of things [to memorize] which will order our children towards truth, beauty, and goodness.

HISTORICAL DOCUMENTS AND SPEECHES

The most obvious choices come from history.

Primary source documents can be memorized. Every American child should know the Bill of Rights.

Speeches of great men such as Winston Churchill, Martin Luther King, Jr., and Patrick Henry can be memorized.

Parts of pamphlets can be memorized, such as "These are the times that try men's souls . . ." by Thomas Paine, or "Contemplate the mangled bodies of your countrymen . . ." by Samuel Adams.

The Declaration of Independence is a document so rich in the use of language that just memorizing it will inform the minds of your children in ways I cannot even begin to explain; it may teach them logic, too.

This is how these words seep into our hearts and come out again in our own speech and writing.

> This is how these words seep into our hearts and come out again in our own speech and writing.

OTHER MEMORY WORK

There are lists of information that are worth our time. We particularly loved memorizing the presidents. Every other week or so we had a presidents bee to see how many we could name. This is the kind of information that the children love to have because they run across it in life and can make connections.

The names of the planets, the oceans, and the continents are also things that can help in the science of relations.

I have found if something can be learned by way of flashcards or the computer, it might not be something we need to cover in Morning Time. I am thinking of things like the states and capitals. But memorizing the list of presidents is something else altogether. Each time we have a presidents bee it gives us a chance to discuss different presidents. I often give hints such as, "He was considered one of the worst presidents," or, "His wife was called Lemonade Lucy." It becomes a way to play with a timeline and picture the past as it moves towards where we ourselves stand in time.

We are not memorizing these things as a utility, but rather as a way of being connected to the past and in being connected to truth, goodness, or beauty. This sort of information should not puff us up as know-it-all smart-alecks but will humble us as we apply it to the future.

Each day, after we had worked on poetry, we moved into our last memorization category, which I have ingeniously called "Miscellaneous Memory." There I put all those extra things I wanted us to remember and contemplate. As with the other categories, we always had a selection we were working on over many weeks repeating it daily, and a review selection we read or recited from the past. Our miscellaneous memory list is not long but it does contain some of the most important things for ordering our minds that we have memorized.

CREEDS AND CATECHISMS

The Apostles' Creed

The Nicene Creed

The Westminster Shorter Catechism

The Heidelberg Catechism

Prayer of Confession

The West Point Cadet Prayer

HISTORICAL DOCUMENTS

The Bill of Rights (the first ten amendments). You can also use Morning Time as a time to read through all the amendments, one a day with discussion. We found this to be enlightening.

The Declaration of Independence (I recommend memorizing to the first "He
has." See anthology page 201.)

The Preamble to the Constitution

SPEECHES

The Gettysburg Address by Abraham Lincoln

"The War Inevitable" by Patrick Henry (The boys love this!)

"We Shall Fight" by Winston Churchill

Farewell Address by George Washington

"The Man in the Arena" by Theodore Roosevelt

"I Have a Dream" by Martin Luther King, Jr.

PAMPHLETS, ETC.

Thomas Paine's "These are the times that try men's souls . . ."

Samuel Adams's "Contemplate the mangled bodies . . ."

OTHER MEMORY IDEAS

Planets

Continents and oceans

States and capitals

Presidents

U.S. CIVICS TEST QUESTIONS AND ANSWERS

I used this document in Morning Time to teach my children the basics of American
civics. It's not a complete government course, but it did help me cover the fundamen-
tals of American government and civic life. The most current Civics Test is included
in the anthology on page 217.

SHAKESPEARE

After reading Susan Schaeffer Macaulay's *For the Children's Sake* for the first time
when my oldest was around three, I was most excited by the idea of someday reading
Shakespeare to my children. Susan Macaulay's descriptions of her little girls returning home from school joyously playing Shakespeare melted my heart. That is what I
wanted for my children.

I had already developed my own love of Shakespeare. In high school we had stud-
ied the 1968 Franco Zeffirelli *Romeo and Juliet* film. One summer I bought one of those
huge volumes of *The Complete Works of Shakespeare* and read with delight *The Taming*

of the Shrew. After I went to college, I forgot about Shakespeare until I picked up Macaulay's book and recalled the joy I found in the meter of *The Taming of the Shrew.* No one had told me that Shakespeare was often written in meter. I stumbled onto the meter on my own and that discovery filled me with joy. I wanted my children to have that from an early age.

And yet, year after year after year went by and I wasn't able to incorporate the reading of Shakespeare into our Morning Time. This was one of life's disappointments.

When my oldest was around twelve, a group of ladies began what was called PUO or Parents' Union Online. You know it today as AmblesideOnline. This awoke in me a fresh desire to introduce my children to Shakespeare and so that summer we set up our lawn chairs in the back yard each afternoon and began reading *A Midsummer Night's Dream* one scene at time. It was the perfect play to start with. The children laughed in all the right places.

Since that time I have continued to read Shakespeare one scene at at time to my children and the scenes turned into acts and the acts turned into plays until we have now read together almost the entire canon.

And that is it, really. One scene. Another scene. An act. A play.

No lesson plans. No fancy resources. It can be *that* simple. I will be giving you hints and helps here, but never forget that all you really need to do is pick up a play and start reading.

That is my story, but you might be wondering why you should read Shakespeare. Here is what Charlotte Mason says,

> To become intimate with Shakespeare in this way is a great enrichment of mind and instruction of conscience. Then, by degrees, as we go on reading this world-teacher, lines of insight and beauty take possession of us, and unconsciously mould our judgments of men and things and of the great issues of life.[6]

Simple and lovely: the instruction of conscience and the molding of our judgments—truth, beauty and yes, goodness, all within the canon of the plays of William Shakespeare.

Then, of course, there are the added utilitarian benefits to vocabulary and cultural literacy.

I want to address one more aspect of reading Shakespeare—inappropriate material. It is true that sometimes Shakespeare is coarse. He does not shy away from presenting coarse people as coarse. He never feels the need to sanitize his characters. He shows them to us as they are.

> ...the scenes turned into acts and the acts turned into plays until we have now read together almost the entire canon.

You can handle this in many different ways:

- You can read the plays out loud skipping awkward sections. I am quite good at reading ahead and skipping parts.
- You can avoid plays that are too mature such as *Pericles* or *The Merry Wives of Windsor.*
- You can read the parts without comment since they will most likely not be understood by the immature anyway.
- You can read them and use them as a chance to talk about mature themes.

While most plays will have at least a little bit of uncomfortable material, overall these inappropriate parts are rare. Most families will be able to work around them without too many issues or giggles.

THE REALITY

Right up front I will tell you that for all of our reading of Shakespeare my children do not love him as I do. That is okay. This is another instance where I am counting on the long haul and, in this case, it is the extra-long haul. I say that so that you don't think that the value of reading Shakespeare is measured by what your child says about it today, next year, or even in a few years. Even though education is the training of the affections, it is often a future hope. Some of you will have a certain temperament of child who will revel in Shakespeare. Great. But if reading Shakespeare is good, and it is, then you can afford to read it even when it is unappreciated—just keep it short. Do not weary the children with pushing through too much material.

I read from Shakespeare and/or Plutarch immediately after our initial prayer, singing, and part of our Bible time. I did this for the sake of the upper high school students who left after that.

THE READING

My system for reading Shakespeare was quite simple. I usually read a synopsis or story form of the play from either *Tales from Shakespeare* by Charles and Mary Lamb or *Beautiful Stories from Shakespeare for Children* by E. Nesbit. This took around one to three Morning Times.

I then spent one day reading through the cast of characters. This was very helpful as we started reading. I might, more often with the historical plays, have pulled out a reference book and read more for my own benefit. That way I could pass on tidbits of information as we went. By far my favorite Shakespeare reference is Isaac Asimov's

But if reading Shakespeare is good, and it is, then you can afford to read it even when it is unappreciated—just keep it short. Do not weary the children with pushing through too much material.

Guide to Shakespeare. This book is so well-written that you can read it for pleasure. Asimov is opinionated, but I am guessing that is what makes the book so fascinating.

I began reading the play with Act I, Scene I and almost always just read one scene a day, even if it was just a tiny scene. Sometimes if the scene was super-short or we were almost finished with the play, I would read two, but that was rare. Some plays have extra long scenes that are best broken up into two readings. *Antony and Cleopatra* is Shakespeare's longest play and it shows in the scenes.

Being a minimalist, for years I read the plays aloud by either pausing and changing voices slightly between speakers or deadpanning the name of the speaker before saying the part. Each way depended on the scene. It was easy to do separate voices if the scene was between a man and a woman. My accents are so bad I got into trouble very quickly if I tried to give each character a separate accent.

THE MOVIES

As we were getting into the play I began thinking about watching a version of it. There are many ways to approach this:

- You could watch one version of the play before you read it and a different version afterwards. This works well with plays which have many excellent movie adaptations such as *Hamlet* or *Julius Caesar*.
- You could watch the play midway through the reading, which is often the best way. This gives the benefit of approaching the movie with some familiarity with the play, and the viewing of the movie and the reading of the play begin to work symbiotically.
- You could cap off your reading of the play with a movie.

When you do watch a production, you may want to just use up a whole Morning Time for that purpose. I have found that in a busy family, it is hard to carve out time to watch something together. Skipping a regular Morning Time to watch Shakespeare is a good compromise. Depending on the ages of your children and the quality of the movie, you may want to break up the movie into two days. *Yay* for intermissions!

It is also valuable to watch plays randomly, plays you haven't gotten to yet, or plays you would like to review. Some Shakespearean movies are so well-done they are enjoyable as entertainment and there are many plays which have quirky but fun adaptations. Some plays will be shot as stage productions and some as regular movies.

Warning: Do your research before turning on the movie. I turned on a 1960s BBC production of *A Midsummer Night's Dream* once only to find none of the female fairies wore blouses and then there was our famous *King Lear* fiasco. It was years before I had the heart to read *Lear* again after that gruesome movie with the bloody eyes and naked Lear. Often theater companies will take a stance on interpreting every innuendo with zeal. This is frustrating, so read reviews!!

USING TECHNOLOGY

In later years I tried to buy an audio version of the play we were be reading. I prefer the Arkangel Productions and hope to collect them all someday. I liked for everyone to read along as we listened, so I accomplished this by pulling up the text on my laptop and mirroring my computer screen to the TV so everyone could see. You could do something similar, or you could pick up very inexpensive paperbacks at your local used bookstore. The Folger's Shakespeare has inexpensive paperbacks, as well.

The downside of this was that if we wanted to discuss as we went I had to pause the audio. When reading Shakespeare I would often ask the kids what they thought something meant, especially metaphors. I didn't do this for every metaphor but once a day I would usually ask a question as we read. If a scene was especially confusing I would stop, explain what just happened, and then read it again. Once again, I didn't do this for every confusing scene. The kids quickly caught on that Shakespeare uses nuances of language and they began to stretch for them.

MEMORIZING SHAKESPEARE

I highly recommend memorizing passages from any play you are enjoying. For some plays there are a wealth of passages worth remembering and for others you have to dig deep into the text to find one passage you'd like to memorize, but I think memorizing Shakespeare is worth the effort.

Over the years I have come to prioritize the memorizing of Shakespeare over other poetry just because it is rare to find better meter or meaning. It was not unusual for four out of five poems in our memory work to have come from Shakespeare. When in doubt, pick Shakespeare.

HOW TO MEMORIZE SHAKESPEARE

One thing I failed to mention in the earlier memory sections is how we went about memorizing poems. For the most part we just read the poem every day and gradually begin to leave out words. After about two weeks of this, I assigned the poem as copywork, and then in a couple more weeks, I did it again. When I thought we almost had it, I would set an end date and push to leave out more and more. Finally, when we learned the poem, I put in on my review list every week for a while.

A FEW OF SHAKESPEARE'S FINEST MEMORY PASSAGES

These passages are included in the anthology. See page 227.

1. "The quality of mercy" from *The Merchant of Venice*
2. "To be or not to be" soliloquy from *Hamlet* (This is quite delightful with its odd words.)
3. Marc Antony's "Friends, Romans, countrymen" from *Julius Caesar*
4. "All the world's a stage" from *As You Like It*
5. St. Crispin's Day speech from *Henry V* (Every boy should know this!)
6. "How sweet the moonlight" from *The Merchant of Venice*
7. "The man that hath no music" from *The Merchant of Venice*
8. "Fear no more" from *Cymbeline*
9. "When icicles hang" from *Love's Labour's Lost*
10. "Tomorrow and tomorrow and tomorrow" from *Macbeth*
11. Kate's speech "Thy husband is thy lord, thy keeper" from *The Taming of the Shrew*
12. "But, soft! what light through yonder window breaks" from *Romeo and Juliet*
13. "The lunatic, the lover and the poet" from *A Midsummer Night's Dream*
14. Othello's death speech, "Then you must speak of one who loved not wisely" from *Othello*
15. "Farewell to His Greatness" soliloquy from *Henry VIII*
16. Polonius's famous advice to Laertes "Give thy thoughts no tongue" from *Hamlet*
17. "This royal throne of kings, this scepter'd isle" from *Richard II*
18. "If we shadows have offended" from *A Midsummer Night's Dream*
19. Sonnet 29
20. Sonnet 18

PLUTARCH

Our family came to enjoy reading Shakespeare together after years of longing. It was a heart's desire of mine that became a reality over time. Not so with Plutarch and his *Lives*. When I first read how some Charlotte Mason cottage schools (Parents' National Education Union—known as PNEU schools) in Britain read Plutarch's *Lives* in class, I barely gave it a thought. One reason was my own dismal education. Plutarch who? It took many years of hearing the name and the book mentioned before I had the faintest stirring in that direction. To tell the truth, I wasn't ready to appreciate the author at all. But as time went by, I began to trust Charlotte Mason and her ideas; this inevitably led to reading Plutarch's *Lives* aloud to my children.

My first faltering attempts to read "Pericles," one of the Greek lives, were tarnished by my own inability to read long sentences correctly. (When it comes to long sentences, Plutarch beats Thomas Jefferson hands down.) Over time I began to get the hang of it and now I find it an absolute joy to trip through phrase after phrase of Plutarch's long thoughts. This density of thought makes Plutarch perfect for short readings, appropriate for homes and schools.

Our students benefit from hearing these long sentences; their minds are forced to attention and they begin to absorb the purposes of the English phrase. I say English because, at least around here, we generally read Arthur Hugh Clough's revision of John Dryden's translation.

The old PNEU schools used Plutarch to teach citizenship.

> Citizenship becomes a definite subject rather from the point of view of what may be called the inspiration of citizenship than from that of the knowledge proper to a citizen, though the latter is by no means neglected. We find Plutarch's *Lives* exceedingly inspiring. These are read by the teacher (with suitable omissions) and narrated with great spirit by the children.[7]

Certainly, we find ourselves in need of teaching citizenship in these dark days.

Plutarch can provide us with a way out of the red state–blue state divide into the clear air of individual responsibility and the consequences of ideas.

Reading Plutarch is an excellent tool for training the judgment. The book is set up to compare the lives of the Greeks and the Romans, alternating between them.

> [Children] learn to answer such questions as,—'In what ways did Pericles make Athens beautiful? How did he persuade the people to help him?' And we may hope that the idea is engendered of preserving and increasing the beauty of their own neighbourhood without the staleness which comes of much exhortation . . . Plutarch is like the Bible in this, that he does not label the actions of his people as good or bad but leaves the conscience and judgment of his readers to make that classification. What to avoid and how to avoid it, is knowledge as important to the citizen whether of the City of God or of his own immediate city, as to know what is good and how to perform the same.[8]

This is a beautiful thing. When presented with the facts, children allowed to come to their own conclusions will be forced by nature to make their own judgments, thus developing their consciences in ways that cannot be easily uprooted. Long sentences, citizenship, and judgment are hefty reasons for persevering as a teacher in learning to read aloud Plutarch's *Lives* in a quality translation. A word of warning here: While we do want our children to learn judgement and discernment, we must be careful not to be heavy-handed. Let them learn these things organically without too much forcing or questioning on our part. When we over-moralize in our zeal to make our children "good" we are really harming our child. We are puffing him up and that puts our children in grave spiritual danger.

Long sentences, citizenship, and judgment are hefty reasons for persevering as a teacher in learning to read aloud Plutarch's *Lives* in a quality translation.

41

HOW DO I GO ABOUT READING PLUTARCH?

In our family, I read one or two of the long paragraphs a day, stopping along the way frequently to discuss the meaning of the vocabulary or to deconstruct a sentence, figuring out what is being said. It can be a fun exercise, almost like doing a group puzzle. The *Lives* do not need to be rushed; we usually read only three lives a year. Take your time and enjoy the ramble. They are not the type of book you read through once and call it a day. The greatest profit is gained by a lifelong friendship with the work.

Plutarch is not easy, but I can now say with Charlotte that it should not be skipped.

Unlike with Shakespeare, you will not find a long list of books available for sale dedicated to helping you teach Plutarch. To tell the truth, that is good. As with most things it is better to do something than to read about doing it. I believe that so much that I would be happy if you stopped reading this right now and instead picked up Plutarch and began reading a paragraph or two to your children.

> It is better to do something than to read about doing it.

But there are quite a few articles online from the Charlotte Mason community about reading Plutarch. These articles can inspire you and give you hints about how to go about it.

When I first started, I used Anne White's notes from AmblesideOnline. I printed off all of her notes and the text of the Life and put them in my Morning Time notebook. This was very helpful, and I highly recommend doing this. Anne now has Plutarch guides you can purchase, and her notes are still available at AmblesideOnline.

After I got the hang of Plutarch, I found it easier to just pick up the volume and read, marking my copy of the book wherever we stopped.

Personally, I don't really like to read children's versions of Plutarch because what I really like is the way he says what he says. The stories, of course, are beneficial for picturing virtue and citizenship, but the language of the John Dryden (Arthur Hugh Clough, editor) version is superior. It is beautiful and worthy to sit on a shelf beside Shakespeare and the King James Bible. A child who hears this language is a fortunate child.

And yet, I would not begin my small children on the full Plutarch's *Lives*. I started later when I already had older kids, but the small children who do sit in while you are reading to the older children will still benefit from hearing this, I believe.

> This is the cheesecake of literature.

So I would say that children's versions serve a good purpose, but don't let them keep you from eventually reading the real thing.

I did not read more than a page and half a day and often much less. The ideas are packed densely. This is the cheesecake of literature.

Plutarch throws a lot of names around. I only stopped to comment on the main ones: "Who was Aristomache again? Oh, yeah she is Dionysius' wife and Dion's sister."

If I was confused, I assumed the kids were too, and I stopped and figured out what was going on out loud. If I came across something that I had a background in, I would stop and explain what I was bringing to the table. I stopped often and asked the kids what just happened. I stopped to note interesting word choices and we discussed them.

"What if Heraclides be perfidious, malicious and base . . ." Perfect place for a vocabulary lesson and one where the kids can figure out what perfidious means from the context.

I didn't bog down every reading with every possible discussion, but I only read small amounts with lots of discussion along the way. Usually, once we got the hang of the direction of the Life, our comprehension went way up, which is why using Anne White's study guides could be a good idea for newbies.

COMPOSERS AND ARTISTS

Keeping with the idea that it is the little things we do often which add up to an education, Morning Time is a great place to add composer and artist studies. This is *not* the place to do big composer or artist projects.

COMPOSERS

The easiest way to study a composer is set your pieces for the term (I usually went with AmblesideOnline choices, which you could do, or you could use the list I am including at the end of this chapter), create a playlist on an app like Spotify, and then set the music playing each morning, mentioning which piece is playing when possible.

You can easily add a biography of the composer, such as those by Opal Wheeler, to read aloud during the term. When I read *Beethoven and the Chiming Bells* by Opal Wheeler to one of my students last year, we liked to look up any pieces referred to in the book on YouTube. In that way he came to love *Rage Over a Lost Penny*, op. 129, and frequently asked me to play it again.

Before the beginning of the school year I worked on term selections for our three Terms. Our Term 1 was August-November. Term 2 was January-March and Term 3 was April-June. Often Term 3 was our weakest term. I was somewhat serendipitous about these selections. Often I followed along with the AmblesideOnline terms, but just as often I made a different decision. I always used the month between Thanksgiving and Christmas for Advent devotions using Handel's *Messiah*, which you can also do with my book *Hallelujah: Cultivating Advent Traditions with Handel's Messiah*.

> Set the music playing each morning, mentioning which piece is playing when possible.

Here is a sample of my Term 1 composer selections for a past year, in which I relied heavily on AmblesideOnline. I generally compiled all my AmblesideOnline selections in a three-term file for the year.

Composer: Franz Josef Haydn (1732-1809) Classical
String Quartet op. 76 no. 3 ("Emperor")
or
String Quartet op. 76 no. 4 ("Sunrise")
Symphony no. 104 ("London") (4 weeks)
The Creation (4 weeks)
A horn concerto

ARTISTS

Artist study is equally as simple. I collected prints of the works we wanted to study (either printing them on my own computer when funds were short or ordering a set from either Simply Charlotte Mason or Riverbend Press). In later years I found I could upload the images to a photo-printing website and get prints, usually small individual ones and larger ones for the wall. We then looked at one picture a week, discussing it and then trying to recall and describe it from memory. I either spent a couple of days reading an online biography of the artist or picked a longer biography selection such as Joyce McPherson's *Artist of the Reformation: Albrecht Dürer*.

> We then looked at one picture a week, discussing it and then trying to recall and describe it from memory.

If you participate in a local Charlotte Mason co-op, this is fun to do in a group. The children enjoy the competition of seeing who can "see" the most. We liked to have them look at the picture for several minutes and then try to describe it from memory.

PUTTING IT ALL TOGETHER

Here is a sample of my plans one year using the AmblesideOnline selections.

TERM 1

Artist: Jan Van Eyck (1395-1441) Flemish Northern Renaissance (also composers Camille Saint-Saëns and Hector Berlioz, Early Romantic)
The Crucifixion, 1425-30 or *Birth of John the Baptist*, 1422
The Last Judgement, 1425-30 or *Madonna with Child Reading*, 1433
Adoration of the Lamb (from the *Ghent Altarpiece*, 1425-30)
The Annunciation, 1434–1436
Arnolfini Wedding, 1434
Man in a Red Turban, 1433

Composer:	Edvard Grieg (1843-1907) and Jean Sibelius (1865-1957) Nationalists
	Peer Gynt, Suite no. 1 (Grieg)
	Piano Concerto in A (Grieg)
	Norwegian Dances no. 2 (Grieg)
	Finlandia (Sibelius)
	Symphony no. 1 *or* no. 2 (Sibelius)
Plutarch:	Aristides/Coriolanus
Shakespeare:	Finish *Cymbeline/Coriolanus*
Folk Song:	"The Old Oaken Bucket"

TERM 2

Artist:	John Singer Sargeant (1856-1925) American
Composer:	Franz Liszt (1811-1886) Early Romantic
	Piano Concerto no. 1
	Hungarian Rhapsodies (especially no. 2)
	Les Preludes
	Liebestraum
	Piano Sonata in B Minor
	"Mephisto Waltz"
Plutarch:	Cato the Censor
Shakespeare:	*A Midsummer Night's Dream*
Folk Song:	"The Jam on Gerry's Rocks"

TERM 3

Composer:	Maurice Ravel (1875-1937) Impressionist
	Daphne et Chloe - selections
	Bolero
	Mother Goose suite
	Pavane pour une infante dufunte
	Piano Concerto in D for left hand
	Rhapsodie espagnole
Artist:	Claude Monet (1840-1926) French Impressionist
Plutarch:	Romulus
Shakespeare:	*Titus Andronicus*
Folk Song:	"Farewell to Nova Scotia," "Land of the Silver Birch"

LANGUAGE ARTS

We didn't always do a bit of grammar in Morning Time, but it became one of my favorite sections.

I am not a grammarian. I want to be, and I have tried to be, but it has been a slow road. I noticed it was a slow road for the children, too. We could study, fill out worksheets, and take tests, but if I randomly asked someone what part of speech a word was, they invariably got it wrong. Sometimes they could not remember the most basic words. This led me have a deep mistrust of programs which taught grammar repetitively. It also led me to realize that Charlotte Mason was right about grammar being best taught in context through narration and dictation with short lessons.

Several years ago, I began reading aloud *The Mother Tongue,* an out-of-print grammar series by George Lyman Kittredge and Sarah Louise Arnold, which was recommended to me by people who knew grammar. This reading worked well in Morning Time. We would read a tiny section and discuss it. I still had trouble holding concepts in my head, but I was making progress and as I did the kids did too.

This book has recently been updated for modern students with answer keys and student workbooks by Blue Sky Daisies and reissued as *The Mother Tongue: Adapted for Modern Students (The Mother Tongue Set).*

After we finished reading aloud those books, I was looking for other ways to incorporate grammar into Morning Time. I have every grammar resource known to man around my house! If money could make me a grammarian, I would be teaching English in a university.

I had purchased a pile of Michael Clay Thompson (MCT) books but was having trouble fitting them into our regular school time.

> Diagramming one sentence and breaking down another sentence takes less than five minutes a day. Very doable and so rewarding.

We began diagramming, one sentence a day, in Morning Time. This went very well. I added studying one sentence a day using MCT's *Practice* books. Michael Clay Thompson breaks down each sentence four ways. This simple idea has gone a long way in untangling grammar for me. First, break down each word into its part of speech. Second, find out what job the words or phrases are performing, such as subject, predicate, or direct object. Next, look for phrases and clauses. Finally, discuss the poetics of the sentence. We began doing this one sentence at a time and loved it. Best of all, grammar was starting to make sense. For this type of group study, you only need the teacher's edition.

Diagramming one sentence and breaking down another sentence takes less than five minutes a day. Very doable and so rewarding. This way of teaching grammar in very short lessons, with much discussion and application, works.

DIAGRAMMING IN MORNING TIME

I used a whiteboard. First, I read a small section of the diagramming book and then I put up a sample sentence. The next day, I let one of the boys diagram a similar sentence from the book and then the next day the other boy did it. Then if all was well, we moved to the next sentence type.

I wrote the sentence of the day taken from the MCT practice book on the white board. Next, we wrote under each word what the part of speech it was, adding parentheses to prepositional phrases or infinitives. Following that, we identified the subject and verb and any other things, such as direct or indirect objects. Finally, we discussed whether there was a dependent or independent clause and finished clearing up any confusing vocabulary words. We didn't always stick to the script. Sometimes we discussed the vocabulary first. In the end, I was quite happy to drop diagramming for the Michael Clay Thompson way of parsing sentences.

My only regret is that it took me so many years to figure out this very simple, effective answer to what for me had always been a daunting problem.

READING ALOUD

I can hardly think of anything I have enjoyed more these last thirty years than reading aloud. When life was less complicated and didn't include a television, we read aloud morning, noon, and night. As time went by, Morning Time became a way for me to cling to this habit for a few more years. Morning Time was a small way to stand against the rising tide of technology, even as technology had made some parts of it much easier.

There is nothing so simple as picking up a book and reading it. Morning Time provides the time and the place; you provide the will.

There is nothing so simple as picking up a book and reading it.

I asked each member of our family to name their five favorite read-alouds. They each answered me remarkably quickly. Some of these are included in the lists below.

Here I have assembled a list of general favorites. In the anthology, I have commented on each title, explaining more about why I love that particular book (see page 239).

FAVORITE FAMILY READ-ALOUDS
1. *The Adventures of Huckleberry Finn* by Mark Twain
2. *The Adventures of Tom Sawyer* by Mark Twain
3. *Alice's Adventures in Wonderland* and *Through the Looking-Glass* by Lewis Carroll
4. *American Tall Tales* by Adrien Stoutenburg
5. *The Arthurian Trilogy: The Sword and the Circle, The Light Beyond the Forest*, and *The Road to Camlann* by Rosemary Sutcliff

6. *Beautiful Stories from Shakespeare for Children* by E. Nesbit
7. *The Black Arrow* (Scribner Classic) by Robert Louis Stevenson
8. *Black Fox of Lorne* by Marguerite De Angeli
9. *The Blue Fairy Book* and others by Andrew Lang
10. *The Book of the Ancient Greeks* by Dorothy Mills
11. *Caddie Woodlawn* by Carol Ryrie Brink
12. *Carry On, Mr. Bowditch* by Jean Lee Latham
13. *Cheaper by the Dozen* by Frank B. Gilbreth and Ernestine Gilbreth Carey
14. *A Christmas Carol* by Charles Dickens
15. *The Complete Winnie-the-Pooh* by A. A. Milne
16. *Family Grandstand* by Carol Ryrie Brink
17. *Farmer Giles of Ham* by J. R. R. Tolkien
18. *The Fellowship of the Ring, The Two Towers*, and *The Return of the King* by J. R. R. Tolkien
19. *The Gospel Story Bible: Discovering Jesus in the Old and New Testaments* by Marty Machowski
20. *Hans Brinker, or The Silver Skates* by Mary Mapes Dodge
21. *Heidi* by Johanna Spyri
22. *The Hiding Place* by Corrie Ten Boom
23. *The Hobbit* by J. R. R. Tolkien
24. *House of Arden Series: The House of Arden* and *Harding's Luck* by E. Nesbit
25. *The Iliad* by Homer (trans. by Richmond Lattimore or Robert Fagles)
26. *The Iliad and the Odyssey: The Heroic Story of the Trojan War and the Fabulous Adventures of Odysseus* by Jane Werner Watson (illus. by Alice Provensen and Martin Provensen)
27. *Johnny Tremain* by Esther Forbes
28. *Kidnapped* (Scribner Classic) by Robert Louis Stevenson
29. *King Alfred's English* by Laurie J. White
30. *The King of Ireland's Son* by Padraic Colum
31. *Koshka's Tales: Stories from Russia* by James Mayhew
32. *Lassie Come-Home* by Eric Knight
33. *The Last of the Mohicans* (Scribner Classic) by James Fenimore Cooper (illus. by N. C. Wyeth)
34. *Little Britches* series by Ralph Moody
35. *Little Pilgrim's Progress: From John Bunyan's Classic* by Helen L. Taylor
36. *Little Women* by Louisa May Alcott
37. *Lives of the Noble Greeks and Romans* by Plutarch (trans. by John Dryden)
38. *The Marsh King* by C. Walter Hodges
39. *Men of Iron* by Howard Pyle
40. *The Merry Adventures of Robin Hood* (Scribner Classics) by Howard Pyle

41. *The Odyssey* by Homer (trans. by Richmond Lattimore or Robert Fagles)
42. *The Outsiders* by S. E. Hinton
43. *The Passion of Jesus Christ: Fifty Reasons Why He Came to Die* by John Piper
44. *The Pilgrim's Progress* by John Bunyan
45. *The Princess and Curdie* by George MacDonald
46. *The Princess and the Goblin* by George MacDonald
47. *Roll of Thunder, Hear My Cry* and sequels by Mildred D. Taylor
48. *The Sign of the Beaver* by Elizabeth George Speare
49. *Smoky the Cowhorse* (Scribner Classic) by Will James
50. *The Story of King Arthur and His Knights* (Scribner Classics) by Howard Pyle
51. *The Story of Rolf and the Viking Bow* by Allen French
52. *Swallows and Amazons* by Arthur Ransome
53. *Treasure Island* (Scribner Classic) by Robert Louis Stevenson
54. *Treasures of the Snow* by Patricia St. John
55. *Understood Betsy* by Dorothy Canfield
56. *The Wheel on the School* by Meindert DeJong
57. *The Wind in the Willows* by Kenneth Grahame
58. *With Wolfe in Canada* by G. A. Henty
59. *The White Company* by Sir Arthur Conan Doyle

BELOVED BOOK SERIES

The Chronicles of Narnia by C. S. Lewis (listed in publication order)
    The Lion, the Witch, and the Wardrobe
    Prince Caspian
    The Voyage of the Dawn Treader
    The Silver Chair
    The Horse and His Boy
    The Magician's Nephew
    The Last Battle

Little House books by Laura Ingalls Wilder (listed in publication order)
    Little House in the Big Woods
    Farmer Boy
    Little House on the Prairie
    On the Banks of Plum Creek
    By the Shores of Silver Lake
    The Long Winter
    Little Town on the Prairie
    These Happy Golden Years
    The First Four Years

NATURE NOTEBOOKS

The way I used nature notebooks over the long haul is a little bit different than the normal method of taking a nature hike and either bringing home a specimen to record in the nature notebook or actually drawing or painting in the wild. We did all of those things, but the most successful way I found of doing nature notebooks was to have the children draw in them during Morning Time read-alouds.

I had many field guides on hand and books with lovely nature pictures, too. While I read, each child copied a picture from the nature book into their nature notebook, usually using Prismacolor pencils. In this way, each child completed a couple of notebooks during their childhood at home. Sometimes they would draw specimens they had found outside, but usually they stuck to copying from field guides. Perhaps this isn't the ideal way to do a nature notebook, and yet I have no regrets about it.

A little nature notebooking every day adds up over the long haul and contributed to a way of seeing, which is the whole point of the nature notebook, after all.

Hand-in-hand with this is the idea that even when we didn't take formal nature hikes, the children still spent hours and hours outdoors. Also, remember that any and every walk is a nature hike—in city or country we can open our eyes to the world God has made.

... the most successful way I found of doing nature notebooks was to have the children draw in them during Morning Time read-alouds.

Part III

IMPLEMENTING MORNING TIME

SCHEDULING TIPS

I always had two school schedules in place, which I ingeniously called Plan A and Plan B. Plan A days were days with no scheduled interruptions—days with Morning Time in place. Plan B days were the default minimum. On Plan B days, the children worked independently through their daily lists, which included math, written narration, and reading for at least two hours, usually three. Realistically speaking, during a good year we had Morning Time about two-thirds of the year; in a bad year, we only had it about half of the time.

While I kept five-day schedules for Morning Time, I just did whatever day was next. When a sheet was completely filled out, I started a new one.

Here are a couple of examples of Morning Time planning structures, followed by narratives of actual days where I recorded what happened during Morning Time.

For a brief two years, I had an afternoon time with my sixth and seventh children which I called "Ambleside Time." It gave me a chance to have an extra mini-Morning Time more geared to younger children. My philosophy for regular Morning Time was to always gear it towards the oldest child in the room. Samples of my Morning Time schedules begin on the following page.

MORNING TIME SCHEDULE SAMPLE ONE

Composer: Beethoven's 5th Symphony (4 Weeks)

Artists: Hudson River Valley Artists

Shakespeare: *Much Ado About Nothing*

Plutarch: Timoleon

Folk Song: "The Outlandish Knight"

Bible Time: *The Book of Life* (KJV Bible readings with supplements, photographs, fine art, and poetry)

Review:

I Corinthians 13

II Corinthians 4:16-18

Psalm 42

II Corinthians 10:5

Psalm 100

Ephesians 6:10-18

Hymn Singing: "More Secure Is No One Ever" (Sung to the tune "Children of the Heavenly Father")

Review:

Psalm 148 and Psalm 46 C (from the Psalter [a book of Psalms similar to a hymnal])

"Beneath the Blood-Stained Lintel"

Navy Hymn ("Eternal Father, Strong to Save")

"Great Is the Lord Our God"

Psalm 98

Poetry: "Modern Major-General's Song" (Gilbert & Sullivan)

Review:

"Keep a' Goin'"

"The Gift Be Strong"

"Trees"

"How Did You Die?"

"Opportunity"

Misc. Memory: *Polite Moments*

Review:

Presidents

Planets

States

"We Shall Fight" by Winston Churchill

The Apostles' Creed

Reading Aloud: *Our Island Story* (Finish this week)
Then begin *English Literature for Boys and Girls*
The Story of the Romans
The Story of Mankind ("Conquest" part 2)
How's Inky
The Wheel on the School
Story of the World volume 1

Younger Kids Time: *Trial and Triumph*
Tanglewood Tales
Fifty Famous Stories
Winnie-the-Pooh

MORNING TIME SCHEDULE SAMPLE TWO

Artist: Johannes Vermeer
Composer: Henry Purcell
Folk Song: "An English Country Garden"
Shakespeare: *A Winter's Tale*
Plutarch: Aemilius Paulus
Bible Time: Psalm 33
The Book of Life
Proverbs

Review:
Books of OT
Deuteronomy 17:1-28
Matthew 5:3-16
Ruth 1:16-17

Hymn Singing: Review:
"O God, Our Help in Ages Past"
"Great Is Thy Faithfulness"
"Hallelujah, What a Saviour"
"Higher Ground"

Poetry: "Horatius at the Bridge"
Review:
Hamlet's soliloquy

History Poem: "Noblity"
"Solitude"
Marc Antony's speech

Misc. Memory: Review:
"We Shall Fight"

The Apostles' Creed

Continents and oceans

Heidelberg Catechism

Ambleside Creed

Reading Aloud: *The Story of the Romans*

English Literature for Boys and Girls

Ludwig Beethoven and the Chiming Tower Bells by Opal Wheeler

Fiction:

Hostage to Alexander

Huguenot Garden

MORNING TIME SCHEDULE SAMPLE THREE

Composer: Rimsky-Korsakov

Folk Song: "Go Get the Ax," "Star of the County Down"

Shakespeare: *Measure for Measure*

Plutarch: Demetrius

Bible Time: *The Book of Life*

Bitesize Theology by Peter Jeffery

Proverbs

To Relearn Daily:

John 1:1-14

Review:

Isaiah 40:28-31

John 1:4

Isaiah 40:28-31

Jude 1:20-25

Hymn Singing: "Arise, Arise" (last week, sing daily)

Review:

"Brethren, We Have Met to Worship" (Ok, I realized as we sang this today that I don't LIKE this song. Do you?)

"Bringing in the Sheaves"

"Brother's Keeper" (old Promise Keepers chorus)

"Christ the Lord Is Risen Today"

"Come, Thou Fount"

Poetry: "The Second Coming" (repeat daily)

Review:

"Autumn Fires" by Robert Louis Stevenson

"The New Colossus" by Emma Lazarus

"The Creation" by Cecil Frances Alexander
"Obedience to Parents" by Isaac Watts
Misc. Memory: Preamble (daily)
<u>Review:</u>
"Contemplate" by Samuel Adams
Declaration of Independence
Bill of Rights, amendments #1, #2, and #3
Civics: Question of the Day from the Civics Test
Reading Aloud: *English Literature for Boys and Girls*
Famous Men of the Middle Ages
A Little History of the World by Gombrich
<u>Fiction:</u>
Just David
Younger Kids Time: *My Book House* volumes 1 and 2
Russian Fairy Tales
Little Pilgrim's Progress
Hans Christian Andersen's fairy tales
Asking Father

MORNING TIME DIARY

MORNING TIME IN REAL LIFE: EXAMPLE ONE

This is a detailed (read: boring) account for those with a need to know. It is recorded in real time.

First of all, I got up later than usual. For some reason I have failed to wake up at my usual 6:30 a.m. the last couple of days. That did not stop the children from getting up and beginning their school lists. Finally, around 10:00 a.m. I called everyone to come to our Morning Meeting.

I began by telling the children about a new idea I had. When I have an extra odd job, I am going to look around the house at the clutter, count the items left about, find who has left out the most, and give the job to that person. It won't work, but it really does sound like a good idea. [In hindsight, it didn't work out.]

Then my husband came in and discussed a few logistical things with the children.

The boys give him 30 minutes a day in the yard or on projects. We almost always start the Morning Meeting with family logistics. Even on non-school days, we have a Morning Meeting.

Time to take prayer requests. This morning we focused on Nicholas since he has been sick. Usually we all pray, but this morning James (not a student) needed something, so I just prayed for sake of time.

We began saying the books of the Old Testament, and then the phone rang. Tim, my husband, now running errands, had a question. The kids went on without me.

Christopher read Ephesians 6:10-18; Nathaniel read Psalm 100.

Because this is our first week to relearn "A Mighty Fortress" we only sang one verse. We will add a verse every week. It is the first hymn in our family hymnal.

Next, we sang Psalm 148, changing keys with each verse. Smile.

I got out the *Bitesize Theology: An ABC of the Christian Faith* book and read two short paragraphs titled "God is Holy."

This led to a discussion on whether a four-point Calvinist (no L for "Limited Atonement"), isn't actually a three-point Calvinist (no U for "Unconditional Election") or not a Calvinist at all. I didn't bring up the topic, but we followed through with it anyway. [I won't tell you what we concluded, lest I hurt your feelings.]

At this time, I finish up the things the older boys need to stay for. We haven't started a new Shakespeare yet, so I just read a couple pages in *The Ballad of the White Horse* by G. K. Chesterton, and we discussed some of the allusions.

Big boys departed. They don't go too far away though and frequently shout in their answers to questions I ask the younger children.

Andrew recited "Who Has Seen the Wind?" and Alex begged to do "Clouds." Emily recited "The Creation" and Benjamin "The Charge of the Light Brigade." I had to excuse myself for a few seconds while they recited. They must have them completely memorized by next Friday. I am doing things a little differently in this area than I used to because the younger children did not have some of the older poems memorized and they were going to grow up missing some very good poetry.

I reviewed the poem "The Whole Duty of Children" by Robert Louis Stevenson and discussed it at length with Alex, who told me he doesn't always say what's true. He said that James had just told him that if you crossed your fingers it was still lying. He was distressed.

Apparently he had been using the crossing the fingers ploy frequently.

Emily read the Declaration of Independence through the first "He has . . ." This is a wonderful piece of prose and worth memorizing for its supreme use of argument and language.

I recited the Preamble to the Constitution. Then I read Civics Test questions for their civics lesson.

"What do we call the first ten amendments to the Constitution?"

"What is the capital of your state?"

"Who is your governor?" Andrew answered George Bush [he was president at the time]. Alex answered John Quincy Adams and Benjamin and Emily swore they knew the answer after I told them.

I got out *The Book of Life* and we read about David's jaunt living with the Philistines. *The Book of Life* is basically a KJV Bible with notes and pictures.

Then I had to take a break. I had not eaten breakfast and it was after 11:00 a.m. I told everyone to do something else until after I had eaten. I returned nourished and ready to read.

I read two pages of Plutarch's "Antony." In this particular section, we ended with Antony decimating his own troops for failure to keep watch on a fortification. We learned that "decimation" meant killing one out of every ten soldiers. [I never knew that, did you?] The remaining soldiers had to eat corn and barley instead of wheat. We argued over whether this was a wise way to deal with your own army. Finally, we had to move on without agreeing.

Next up was *English Literature for Boys and Girls*. I read about Shakespeare's final years living in Stratford. Andrew was the only one to remember that Shakespeare had died in April.

Moving on to *The Story of the Middle Ages*, we read about the towns and villages of medieval times and discussed the lack of freedoms and feudal lordships.

Finally we got to *The Princess and Curdie*. My husband came in to listen (obviously home from running errands), and we read two chapters.

As Morning Time ended we began our Latin lesson and finished up in time for lunch. During lunch we listened to "Minstrel Boy," our folk song. Andrew had played our Schumann pieces earlier in the morning. Hopefully we can have a time for the older kids' AmblesideOnline readings after Alex's phonics this afternoon.

MY PLAN FOR THAT WEEK ON PAPER

Artist:	John Constable
Composer:	Robert Schumann
Folk Song:	"Minstrel Boy"
	[The boys are enjoying this far more than "An English Country Garden" (my favorite) or "Scarborough Faire." I bought the Homestead Pickers' album years ago. It greatly simplifies this subject.]
Shakespeare:	*Henry VIII*
	[We will be reading *Henry VIII* this term if we ever finish our current Plutarch reading. I think we all enjoyed *Richard III* and his name has become a new byword in our house (which according to Josephine Tey's *The Daughter of Time*, he doesn't deserve).]

Plutarch: Antony

[This is a long life and it is taking us a long time. I find I can only read two pages of Plutarch at a time. The good thing about Antony is that his life is very familiar to all of the children so they get more out of it.]

Bible Time: *The Book of Life* (vol. 3, *The Life of David*)

Bitesize Theology

Passage to memorize: Ephesians 6:10-18

[Last week we worked on Psalm 100, and this week we will work on Ephesians 6:10-18. I have been plowing through new passages with my younger children, but I finally had to realize I needed to start all over with this group, as if they had never learned our review passage—because they never had. I really struggled with making this decision, but I have conceded the point for all of our memory work.]

Review: Psalm 100, Psalm 104, Psalm 100, Philippians 4:4-8, Psalm 121.

Hymns: Gloria Patri (last week), "A Mighty Fortress" (this week).

Review: Psalm 148

"Beneath the Blood-Stained Lintel"

Navy Hymn ("Eternal Father, Strong to Save")

"Great is the Lord our God"

Poetry: Andrew & Alex: "Who Has Seen the Wind?" by Rossetti

Emily: "The Creation" by Cecil Frances Alexander

Benjamin: "The Charge of the Light Brigade"

Colloquy with everyone: *The Ballad of the White Horse* by G. K. Chesterton

Misc. Memory: The Declaration of Independence

Civics: Civics Test questions

Review: Preamble to the Constitution

"Contemplate" by Samuel Adams

West Point Cadet Prayer

Bill of Rights

Read Alouds: *English Literature for Boys and Girls.*

[We are on the Shakespeare chapters. Wonderful.]

The Story of the Middle Ages. [Almost finished.]

The Princess and Curdie

MORNING TIME IN REAL LIFE: EXAMPLE TWO

Today was our first day back at Morning Time after over a week-long break. I spent last week visiting two families of grandchildren, and the children and I attended an out-of-town funeral. Plenty of learning took place in these breaks, including at the funeral. The hardest part about the break was getting back on schedule. I returned from Florida in the wee hours of Wednesday morning, so even though I was up at my normal time, and I had hoped to have Morning Time, it didn't happen. Today (Thursday), I woke up and was faced with another choice. We are headed out of town again on Saturday, and we will be gone early next week, too. I was sorely tempted to just say, "Let's resume Morning Time when we get back on schedule next week," but in the end I decided to make myself have one today. It was a difficult decision, but I am happy I went for the plodding success rather than giving in to the desire to wait until all my ducks were in a row. Even as we started Morning Time, I told myself we could always cut it short, but in the end we took our time and read both Plutarch and Shakespeare.

At 10:30 a.m. I screwed my courage to the sticking place and called, "Ten minutes until Morning Time." Andrew yelled out that he needed to finish a chapter, so we waited for him. I gathered all my books and notebooks and put them on the love seat where I sit, and at around 11:00 we finally sat down for Morning Time. Both boys had grabbed a snack, and we had spent a little time setting up the laptop on the television. We immediately looked at a few paintings by Copley on the big screen, and I read a tiny bit about him from Wikipedia.

As we settled in, I started singing the Gloria Patri and the boys sat down and joined in. After Alex prayed, I then tried to sing our song of the day without the hymnbooks, but ended up googling "Come, Ye Thankful People" and looking at the lyrics on the TV while we sang. We didn't sound too great, but we all tried hard and sang all the verses. Singing all the verses was a moral victory.

I began reading the story in *The Gospel Story Bible: Discovering Jesus in the Old and New Testaments* [which may surprise you since my boys are not little]. We have been reading through this for about three years and I want to finish it. I like how it ties all the Bible into the **one** story. We rotate who reads each day.

Today we read about Paul's letter to the Romans and it was a good chance to talk about grace, works, and Christ's sacrifice. I did not go on and on, but I did point out how most religions, if not all, are based on the good works of the believer while Christianity rests solely on the completed work of Christ. The boys joined in the discussion, which is one way I gauge whether or not I am moralizing.

I picked up the Bible to go over our review verse (I actually picked up my phone with the Bible app). It turns out our review verse for the day was Isaiah 53:1-6, which repeated the lesson we had heard from Romans about Christ bearing our sins. This sort of thing happens so often that I would be afraid to organize my school too thoroughly, lest I miss these serendipitous instances of the science of relations.

All of this led very nicely into the Prayer of Confession which we are repeating daily rather than learning a new Bible passage (see page 123).

At this point, I decided to read both Plutarch and Shakespeare to keep the flow going during this busy time of traveling. I read about one-and-a-quarter pages of Plutarch's "Dion." This story has been quite interesting with a tug of war between Dion and Dionysius which ended in mayhem and fire today.

For *Macbeth*, I pulled up the text of the scene on the TV, and we listened to it using the *Macbeth* (Arkangel Shakespeare) production, which I like because they all have Scottish accents. Alex asked a question when this section started:

> MACBETH [*Aside*]
> The Prince of Cumberland! that is a step
> On which I must fall down, or else o'erleap,
> For in my way it lies. Stars, hide your fires;
> Let not light see my black and deep desires:
> The eye wink at the hand; yet let that be,
> Which the eye fears, when it is done, to see.

I paused the audio so we could talk about who the Prince of Cumberland was and why he was a threat to Macbeth. We listened to this part again and finished the scene which took less than five minutes.

I started to pull out our white board to go over our daily grammar sentences, but my poet-son Alex had written yet another poem on the board. I wanted him to transcribe it before I erased the board, so I read aloud while he transcribed his poem. First, we reviewed our new memory passage: "Tomorrow and tomorrow and tomorrow" from *Macbeth*. I was happy to see that the boys knew this short passage fairly well for only hearing it for a couple of weeks.

We also reviewed the first amendment. Andrew did especially well on that. Then I pulled out *The Classic Hundred Poems* and saw we were reading "Mending Wall" by Robert Frost. Before I read it, I asked the boys what other poems they knew that Robert Frost wrote (they should know three). They kept saying, "Wait, wait, I know," but they couldn't think of them. When I said "Two roads diverged . . ." they were rightly disgusted with themselves. I explained a bit about the New England winter and read the first few lines of "Mending Wall," then asked what was going on in the poem, and what two things had messed up the wall so far in the poem. Andrew correctly said, "Weather and hunters." We all enjoyed this poem.

I then pulled out *The Book of the Ancient Greeks* by Dorothy Mills. We read about the Ionians, Lydians, and Croesus. We especially enjoyed hearing how the Oracle had tricked Croesus. This did not surprise us as we have learned not to trust oracles by reading Plutarch. Poor Macbeth should have read Plutarch.

I then pulled out *Science Matters: Achieving Scientific Literacy* by Robert M. Hazen and James Trefil, a book I cannot recommend highly enough for middle school and up. Today we read three sections, which ended up being about a page and a half. We read about ultra-violet light, X-rays, and gamma rays. We spent a lot of time trying to find examples of ultra-violet light. The boys had never seen a black light. We finally remembered that one of the caves at Rock City had ultra-violet light. Then Alex wondered about how weird it was that the X-ray was discovered accidentally.

The white board was available now, so I pulled out our two grammar books. First, I talked to the boys for a second about compound direct objects. Then we diagrammed together the sentence:

Brandon caught the new ball and dropped his favorite mitt.

I told them tomorrow I would assign one of them to diagram this type of sentence. I use *Digging Into Diagramming* by Tamela Davis.

Next, I wrote our Michael Clay Thompson sentence on the board. Today we did sentence 27 from *Practice Voyage*. I only need the teacher's edition for this. I wrote this sentence on the board:

Oh, who can understand the doleful cry of the white seagulls?

Alex yelled out that there was a prepositional phrase, so we wrote the parts of speech under that phrase, and continued on to write out the parts of speech under each word. Then we talked about the verb, found the subject, and identified the direct object. Finally, we talked about the meaning of the word "doleful."

Our Kindle battery had died, so we did not read *King Alfred's English*, but we did read a long chapter in *Huckleberry Finn* to end our day. At one point, we discussed the difference in Missouri and Illinois for a runaway slave named Jim.

I forgot to say, "The Lord be with you." I forget that a lot.

It was around 12:30 p.m. as we finished up. Today we had a special treat afterwards as Andrew is watching the mini-series *John Adams* for his American history class and Alex has joined him.

TODDLERS, TEENS, AND TROUBLEMAKERS

This book outlines a somewhat idealized picture of Morning Time—all the things we long to do. We visualize it as beautiful, but then reality hits. The toddler screams and throws a temper tantrum, the fifteen-year-old sulks, the nine-year-old dominates the conversation, and you are feeling more than a little tired. Morning Time is not how you dreamed it would be. What to do?

The first thing we must do is recognize that it is always going to be this way. For every idyllic morning there will five okay mornings and three terrible ones. Here is where the plodding comes in. I assure you that plodding pays off. That is why I am here to remind you to take the next step.

The next thing is to recognize that some children might not need to be in Morning Time. Once a child reaches high school level, usually in tenth grade, I let him leave right after Shakespeare. In fact, I moved Shakespeare and Plutarch to right after prayer and Bible reading just so I could let those older students go earlier.

If you only have older students then you can gear Morning Time to them and then judge for yourself how long it needs to be. I enjoyed reading aloud *The Iliad* and *The Odyssey* to Alex and Andrew our last two years of Morning Time.

In a larger family, a sulking high school student can ruin Morning Time for everyone, so it is best to let that child see that you are trying to accommodate his more strenuous school schedule by letting him leave Morning Time. Eventually you may have to excuse him altogether. This is very difficult for a mother to do this but part of the process of letting our children grow up.

Another hint is to make sure the talkative child does not ruin Morning Time for everyone else. Don't call on him too much. Don't be afraid to ask him to be quiet. Learning to commune with other people without dominating is a good skill. Hand in hand with that is making sure the quiet child is drawn into the conversation, too.

Learn to enjoy what you can do with your children without getting too depressed that the ideal cannot be reached. Morning Time, as with most truly good things, is about the long haul. You have to have faith that it will bear fruit in a far-off future. It does not provide the immediate rewards of a completed worksheet or satisfying test score, but the fruit of Morning Time will last long after the worksheet has crumbled and the test score forgotten.

Let me add here that I usually do the history and other reading from their specific AmbelsideOnline year, early in Morning Time, sometimes even as a part of the Morning Meeting. As I said, I usually do Shakespeare and/or Plutarch immediately after Bible time so that the older high school students can leave. Eleventh and 12th

I assure you that plodding pays off.

Learning to commune with other people without dominating is a good skill. Hand in hand with that is making sure the quiet child is drawn into the conversation, too.

grade students can benefit from Morning Time, but often their work load requires they leave early. It is hard to let them go, but it usually must be done.

If you have a high school student who has not learned to love Morning Time, then you may want to compromise with them and let them leave early. Morning Time is more fun without the sulkers, and bad attitudes can infect the rest of the family. Learn to enjoy what you can with your children without getting too depressed that the ideal cannot be reached.

THE FUTURE OF MORNING TIME

When people are together for any purpose, day after day, week after week, they generally have a schedule they want to follow. But when that schedule becomes organic and tuned into everything that makes us human—body, soul, and mind—then it is a liturgy. At church, our soul cries for liturgy and when we see the same people on Monday as we do on Sunday, it is natural to form bonds of love and practices of love that follow a pattern of love, a give and a take. This is especially powerful when we are looking outside of ourselves, which is why it begins at church. Morning Time began as a way to bring some of the practices of church to our home, such as Bible memorization and hymn singing. But it grew into something bigger, and that brought it right back to church. Liturgy is a circle of life, a pathway from spirit, to body, to mind, and back again. It is no great surprise that it happened in our home and many other homes, too.

And it is no great surprise that it works in other places. I have heard stories of people having Morning Time in care homes. To me this is the ultimate use of Morning Time: bringing remembrance to people who are struggling to maintain it. I have been hoping to start a little Morning Time in the residential care home my mother lives in. A little singing, a little poetry, a little Bible reading, a story or two, and maybe sometimes a chance to let *them* tell *their* stories.

I once went to an event at a care home which was a story contest. The residents wrote stories of their childhoods to share. The lady who won was as good a writer as any Marilyn Robinson or Laura Ingalls Wilder. "Some unknown Milton" may be sitting in front of a TV somewhere, knitting or dreaming. Morning Time might be a chance to capture something fleeting. If you do decide to start a Morning Time in a care home, please let me know how it goes. Maybe we can share ideas.

Another place just begging for Morning Time is Sunday School. We really need someone to write a Charlotte Mason Sunday School program, because while it would be as simple as a series of short lessons like Morning Time, it would need to be explained in detail to those whose paradigm would have to shift. When I taught Sunday

School a couple of years ago, I read the passage from the Bible rather than from the lesson, and I asked for narrations. The kids loved it. We led up to that moment with a few Morning Time-like activities. The nice thing about this approach is that it involves the students in the process without making it all about them. Let us get our Sunday School kids out of themselves, not into themselves. Why? Because the road inward is a prison, a Castle Despair. The road to freedom is a wide-open door out of our own heads. Try it and watch how children naturally thrive when they are free from carrying the burden of self. If you do try a Morning Time Sunday School please let me know how you did it. I would love to put together an idea forum for those endeavoring to offer the children solid food and not the sickly, over-digested material most of us use for Sunday School. No wonder children grow up bored with church.

All that brings us to other places and areas where the short, varied lessons of Morning Time would work. Morning Time concepts would work in almost any setting where people meet regularly—Bible studies, Vacation Bible School, club meetings, prisons, etc. All the places where we give lessons that tend to be boring, or we are tempted to dumb down God's word with entertainment, are potential places to implement a Morning Time education.

So don't hesitate to contact me with your ideas. Don't contact me for my ideas though. I have put those here in this book. Wink.

May the Lord bless you as you venture to wake up the minds of your children with living ideas and a shared culture.

GETTING STARTED WITH YOUR MORNING TIME

Getting started with *your* Morning Time shouldn't be overwhelming. I strongly believe that Morning Time should not become something so elaborate that it requires enormous preparation. And don't feel intimidated by all the Instagram-beautiful Morning Times, so perfectly photographed, filtered, and hashtagged. If doing that inspires you, go for it, but don't let any of that stand in the way of your children's education.

Keep your preparation simple and suitable to your personality. This book is intended to help anyone dive into Morning Time—the anthology will give you most everything you need for a solid start. Just jump right in!

One of the biggest stumbling blocks to Morning Time can be to make it too thematic. This is problematic in two ways. First, I see moms going to great lengths to set up a theme and make it appealing. I have seen them setting out books in beautiful, thematic ways and generally just working too hard to bring it all together. This is a lot of work and whenever something is too much work it loses it staying power. But there is even a bigger problem going on when we turn Morning Time into a unit study or theme and it is somewhat hard to explain because themes seem so perfect for Morning Time. How could a theme be a problem? And yet they are a problem, a big problem. When we do all the work of creating a theme we are stealing relationship-building from our children. We are building all the relationships so that they don't have to and when they don't build the relationships they don't learn. Eclectic groupings in Morning Time open the doors for all sorts of unthought of connections between the child and the material. One of Charlotte Mason's main points, and you can read Karen Glass's *In Vital Harmony* to explore this more, is that education is the science of relations. Themes quite simply make the relations for the child and hence they are stumbling blocks to learning, not doors to go through. Perhaps mom learns a lot while setting up a theme but since she has done all the work, she is the only one learning. Learning is what happens when the child does the work of the mind. I know this is a hard idea to comprehend but the older I get the more sure of it I am. That is one reason I find it valuable to read about different time periods simultaneously. You will be pleasantly astounded at the connections formed when you don't make the connections for the child. A good teacher opens doors with the right books and gets out of the way so the child can walk through. The following pages have tools to help you get started.

GETTING STARTED

1. Gather:

___ This book

___ Morning Time Planning Worksheet (see page 67 or use the printable available at blueskydaisies.net)

___ A Bible story book such as *The Book of Life*

___ A Mother Goose collection

___ Coloring pages and colored pencils or crayons

___ LEGOs, blocks, or KEVA planks

2. Plan for your first week by choosing and jotting down into the weekly planning sheet:

___ Bible passage

___ Hymn

___ Composer for the week (choose a piece to play during breakfast)

___ Artist for the week (choose a painting to look at online if you don't have prints)

___ Poem for the week

___ Read-aloud picks (start a basket with a fairy tale collection, several picture books, and a chapter book)

3. Plan for your other subjects.

Morning Time covers a lot of ground in the early years, but you don't want to neglect things like math and reading. Math, reading, and narration should be done every day. Sometimes the narration subject was my students' choice, and sometimes I chose for them. They will be doing grammar with a few resources and spelling practice through continuing daily narration. Refer to "What Else Do I Need?" on page 69.

4. Considerations for having Morning Time with older kids, or a wide range of ages.

If you have kids in a wide range of ages, aim your Morning Time toward your older children. Younger children, even those not yet school age, can listen quietly and color, draw, play with playdough, or build with LEGOs or blocks.

Depending on how your first week goes, you might want to add in a folk song, some catechism questions, or some grammar sentences. Or, maybe you will want to back off a little and do less. Most likely you will want to continue for a few weeks at the same pace before you add more. Don't forget: Plodding along, even just a little, will add up to more than you can imagine over time.

Don't forget: Plodding along, even just a little, will add up to more than you can imagine over time.

MORNING TIME PLANNING WORKSHEET

Date: _____   New Poem: _____

Bible Passage: _____   Shakespeare: _____

New Hymn: _____   Plutarch: _____

Composer: _____   Grammar: _____

Artist: _____   Other: _____

Morning Time Element	Monday	Tuesday	Wednesday	Thursday	Friday
Prayer Focus (*Requests, Praises, Thanksgivings*)					
Bible Time *Review*					
Hymn Singing *Review*					
Poetry *Review*					
Misc. Memory					
Reading Aloud					

Visit blueskydaisies.net for a printable version of this planning worksheet.

Part IV

WHAT ELSE DO I NEED?

OTHER CORE SUBJECTS

Morning Time can be part of a complete education for your children. Some of you might be adding Morning Time to your existing educational plan; others of you might be seeking to build a complete educational plan around Morning Time. If you are one of the latter, here are some suggestions to help you create a complete educational plan with Morning Time as a foundation.

Young Children. Children in their early years of schooling need to learn to read with regular phonics instruction and to become proficient at arithmetic, although research has shown that delaying formal math until 10 years old will contribute to better future outcomes in math. Be sure to have a plan for accomplishing this in addition to Morning Time. I also highly recommend daily oral narration in the early years. If you aren't doing nature notebooks in your Morning Time, make time for that.

Middle Elementary Children. After children are able to read, be sure to give them plenty of reading practice, both out loud and independent reading. Elementary children also need spelling and writing practice. I recommend narration and suggest using Karen Glass's *Know and Tell* as your guide. Continue to be faithful in daily math lessons.

Middle Schoolers. This is a time of developmental transition for kids as they move from concrete to abstract thinking. They will be likely beginning pre-algebra and algebra. They will be doing grammar and spelling practice, and continuing daily narration. They may be studying Latin. This is the time to begin thinking about preparing for high school success. If your oldest is in middle school, looking ahead to high school curriculum will help you access if you are preparing your student well.

High Schoolers. High school can be intimidating for homeschool parents, particularly those new to homeschooling, but there has never been a better time to take on homeschooling high school. There are so many resources and supports available for you through online courses, local co-ops, and community college dual credit opportunities. It's important that you check with your local state requirements for high school, as well as look ahead to what the college-bound student needs for college admissions (a good start for this is to look at your state Board of Regent requirements). I also highly recommend AmblesideOnline's high school web page: https://www.amblesideonline.org/HighSchool.shtml.

Don't be dismayed. You can still pursue a Charlotte Mason education with a Morning Time component for high schoolers—and even integrate that learning into their transcript. On the other hand, depending on your family situation (younger children's needs, for instance), high school may be a time for your teen to transition out of Morning Time after about 30 minutes (refer to "Toddlers, Teens, and Troublemakers" on page 62). Your choices about this will depend on your family circumstances and your teen's needs.

CORE SUBJECTS PLANNING WORKSHEET

This worksheet is set up to give you space to jot down your year goals for core subjects for all your children.

Child's Name -->				
Math				
Phonics **Reading** **Spelling** **Grammar**				
Narration				
Science				
History *(If you are not covering this in Morning Time)*				
Literature *and/or Independent Reading*				
Other *What other goals do you have, especially for high schoolers?*				

Part V

CINDY'S ANTHOLOGY

ANTHOLOGY CONTENTS

POETRY: FAVORITES FOR MIDDLE SCHOOL AND UP

OTHER MEMORY WORK

CIVICS QUESTIONS

SHAKESPEARE MEMORY PASSAGES

TEN FAVORITE HYMNS

**A MIGHTY
FORTRESS**

Martin Luther
(1483-1546)
Translated by Friedrich
Hedge (1805-1890)

A mighty fortress is our God,
a bulwark never failing;
our helper he amid the flood
of mortal ills prevailing.
For still our ancient foe
doth seek to work us woe;
his craft and pow'r are great;
and armed with cruel hate,
on earth is not his equal.

Did we in our own strength confide,
our striving would be losing;
were not the right man on our side,
the man of God's own choosing.
Dost ask who that may be?
Christ Jesus, it is he,
Lord Sabaoth his name,
from age to age the same,
and he must win the battle.

And though this world, with devils filled,
should threaten to undo us,
we will not fear, for God hath willed
his truth to triumph through us.
The prince of darkness grim,
we tremble not for him;
his rage we can endure,
for lo! his doom is sure;
one little word shall fell him.

That Word above all earthly pow'rs,
no thanks to them, abideth;
the Spirit and the gifts are ours
through him who with us sideth.
Let goods and kindred go,
this mortal life also;
the body they may kill:
God's truth abideth still;
his kingdom is forever.

ALL CREATURES OF OUR GOD AND KING

Francis of Assisi
(1182-1226)
Translated by William
H. Draper (1855-1933)

All creatures of our God and King,
lift up your voice and with us sing
alleluia, alleluia!
Thou burning sun with golden beam,
thou silver moon with softer gleam,
O praise him, O praise him,
alleluia, alleluia, alleluia!

Thou rushing wind that art so strong,
ye clouds that sail in heav'n along,
O praise him, alleluia!
Thou rising morn, in praise rejoice,
ye lights of evening, find a voice,
O praise him, O praise him,
alleluia, alleluia, alleluia!

Thou flowing water, pure and clear,
make music for thy Lord to hear,
alleluia, alleluia!
Thou fire so masterful and bright,
that givest man both warmth and light,
O praise him, O praise him,
alleluia, alleluia, alleluia!

And all ye men of tender heart,
forgiving others, take your part,
O sing ye, alleluia!
Ye who long pain and sorrow bear,
praise God and on him cast your care,
O praise him, O praise him,
alleluia, alleluia, alleluia!

Let all things their Creator bless,
and worship him in humbleness,
O praise him, alleluia!
Praise, praise the Father, praise the Son,
and praise the Spirit, three in one,
O praise him, O praise him,
alleluia, alleluia, alleluia!

BE STILL MY SOUL

Kathrina von Schlegel
(1697-1797)
Translated by Jane
Borthwick (1813-1897)

Be still, my soul: the Lord is on thy side;
Bear patiently the cross of grief or pain;
Leave to thy God to order and provide;
In every change He faithful will remain.
Be still, my soul: thy best, thy heavenly Friend
Through thorny ways leads to a joyful end.

Be still, my soul: thy God doth undertake
To guide the future, as He has the past.
Thy hope, thy confidence let nothing shake;
All now mysterious shall be bright at last.
Be still, my soul: the waves and winds still know
His voice who ruled them while He dwelt below.

Be still, my soul: when dearest friends depart,
And all is darkened in the vale of tears,
Then shalt thou better know His love, His heart,
Who comes to soothe thy sorrow and thy fears.
Be still, my soul: thy Jesus can repay
From His own fullness all He takes away.

Be still, my soul: the hour is hastening on
When we shall be forever with the Lord,
When disappointment, grief and fear are gone,
Sorrow forgot, love's purest joys restored.
Be still, my soul: when change and tears are past
All safe and blessèd we shall meet at last.

Be still, my soul: begin the song of praise
On earth, believing, to Thy Lord on high;
Acknowledge Him in all thy words and ways,
So shall He view thee with a well pleased eye.
Be still, my soul: the sun of life divine
Through passing clouds shall but more brightly shine.

BE THOU MY VISION

Ancient Irish poem
(c. 8th century)
Translated by Mary E.
Byrne (1880-1931)

Be thou my vision, O Lord of my heart;
naught be all else to me, save that thou art.
Thou my best thought, by day or by night,
waking or sleeping, thy presence my light.

Be thou my wisdom, and thou my true word;
I ever with thee and thou with me, Lord;
thou my great Father, I thy true son;
thou in me dwelling, and I with thee one.

Be thou my battle shield, sword for my fight;
be thou my dignity, thou my delight,
thou my soul's shelter, thou my high tow'r;
raise thou me heav'n-ward, O Pow'r of my pow'r.

Riches I heed not, nor man's empty praise,
thou mine inheritance, now and always:
thou and thou only, first in my heart,
High King of Heaven, my treasure thou art.

High King of heaven, my victory won,
may I reach heaven's joys, O bright heav'n's Sun!
Heart of my own heart, whatever befall,
still be my vision, O Ruler of all.

COME, THOU FOUNT

Robert Robinson
(1735-1790)

Come, thou fount of every blessing,
tune my heart to sing thy grace;
streams of mercy, never ceasing,
call for songs of loudest praise.
Teach me some melodious sonnet,
sung by flaming tongues above;
praise the mount! I'm fixed upon it,
mount of God's unchanging love.

Here I raise my Ebenezer;
hither by thy help I'm come;
and I hope, by thy good pleasure,
safely to arrive at home.
Jesus sought me when a stranger,
wand'ring from the fold of God:
he, to rescue me from danger,
interposed his precious blood.

O to grace how great a debtor
daily I'm constrained to be;
let that grace now, like a fetter,

bind my wand'ring heart to thee.
Prone to wander—Lord, I feel it—
prone to leave the God I love;
here's my heart, O take and seal it,
seal it for thy courts above.

CROWN HIM WITH MANY CROWNS

Matthew Bridges
(1800-1894)
Altered by Godfrey
Thring (1823-1903)

Crown him with many crowns,
the Lamb upon his throne;
hark! how the heav'nly anthem drowns
all music but its own:
awake, my soul, and sing
of him who died for thee,
and hail him as thy matchless King
through all eternity.

Crown him the Lord of love;
behold his hands and side,
rich wounds, yet visible above,
in beauty glorified:
no angel in the sky
can fully bear that sight,
but downward bends his burning eye
at mysteries so bright.

Crown him the Lord of peace;
whose pow'r a scepter sways
from pole to pole, that wars may cease,
absorbed in prayer and praise:
his reign shall know no end;
and round his pierced feet
fair flow'rs of paradise extend
their fragrance ever sweet.

Crown him the Lord of years,
the Potentate of time;
Creator of the rolling spheres,
ineffably sublime:
all hail, Redeemer, hail!
for thou hast died for me:
thy praise shall never, never fail
throughout eternity.

FAIREST LORD JESUS

Anonymous
(17th century)

Fairest Lord Jesus, Ruler of all nature,
  Son of God and Son of Man!
Thee will I cherish, thee will I honor,
thou, my soul's glory, joy, and crown.

Fair are the meadows, fair are the woodlands,
robed in the blooming garb of spring:
Jesus is fairer, Jesus is purer,
who makes the woeful heart to sing.

Fair is the sunshine, fair is the moonlight,
and all the twinkling, starry host:
Jesus shines brighter, Jesus shines purer
than all the angels heav'n can boast.

GREAT IS THY FAITHFULNESS

Thomas O. Chisholm
(1866-1960)

Great is Thy faithfulness, O God my Father;
  There is no shadow of turning with Thee,
Thou changest not, Thy compassions they fail not,
As Thou hast been, Thou forever wilt be.

Great is Thy faithfulness!
Great is Thy faithfulness!
Morning by morning new mercies I see
All I have needed Thy hand hath provided
Great is Thy faithfulness, Lord unto me!

Summer and winter and springtime and harvest,
Sun, moon, and stars in their courses above;
Join with all nature in manifold witness,
To Thy great faithfulness, mercy, and love.

Pardon for sin and a peace that endureth,
Thine own dear presence to cheer and to guide;
Strength for today, and bright hope for tomorrow
Blessings all mine, with ten thousand beside.

WHEN I SURVEY

Isaac Watts
(1674-1748)

When I survey the wondrous cross
on which the Prince of glory died,
my richest gain I count but loss,
and pour contempt on all my pride.

Forbid it, Lord, that I should boast
save in the death of Christ, my God!
All the vain things that charm me most,
I sacrifice them through his blood.

See, from his head, his hands, his feet,
sorrow and love flow mingled down.
Did e'er such love and sorrow meet,
or thorns compose so rich a crown?

Were the whole realm of nature mine,
that were a present far too small.
Love so amazing, so divine,
demands my soul, my life, my all.

IMMORTAL, INVISIBLE

Walter C. Smith
(1824-1908)

Immortal, invisible, God only wise,
in light inaccessible hid from our eyes,
most blessed, most glorious, the Ancient of Days,
almighty, victorious, thy great name we praise.

Unresting, unhasting and silent as light,
nor wanting, nor wasting, thou rulest in might;
thy justice like mountains high soaring above
thy clouds which are fountains of goodness and love.

Great Father of glory, pure Father of light,
thine angels adore thee, all veiling their sight;
all praise we would render; O help us to see
'tis only the splendor of light hideth thee!

OTHER GREAT HYMNS

BLESSED ASSURANCE

Fanny Crosby
(1820-1915)

Blessed assurance, Jesus is mine!
Oh, what a foretaste of glory divine!
Heir of salvation, purchase of God,
born of his Spirit, washed in his blood.

Refrain:
This is my story, this is my song,
praising my Savior all the day long.
This is my story, this is my song,
praising my Savior all the day long.

Perfect communion, perfect delight,
visions of rapture now burst on my sight.
Angels descending bring from above
echoes of mercy, whispers of love. [Refrain]

Perfect submission, all is at rest.
I in my Savior am happy and bless'd,
watching and waiting, looking above,
filled with his goodness, lost in his love. [Refrain]

COME, YE THANKFUL PEOPLE, COME

Henry Alford
(1810-1871)

Come, ye thankful people, come,
Raise the song of harvest home!
All is safely gathered in,
ere the winter storms begin:
God our Maker doth provide
for our wants to be supplied!
Come to God's own temple, come,
Raise the song of harvest home!

We ourselves are God's own field,
fruit unto His praise to yield;
wheat and tares together sown,
unto joy or sorrow grown;
First the blade, and then the ear,
then the full corn shall appear;
Grant, O Harvest-Lord, that we
wholesome grain and pure may be!

95

For the Lord our God shall come,
and shall take His harvest home:
from His field shall in that day
all offenses purge away:
give His angels charge at last
in the fire the tares to cast;
but the fruitful ears to store
in His garner evermore.

Then, thou Church triumphant, come,
Raise the song of harvest home!
All are safely gathered in,
free from sorrow, free from sin:
there forever purified,
in God's garner to abide;
Come, ten thousand angels, come,
Raise the glorious Harvest home! Amen.

HOLY, HOLY, HOLY

Reginald Heber
(1783-1826)

Holy, holy, holy! Lord God almighty!
Early in the morning our song shall rise to thee.
Holy, holy, holy! Merciful and mighty!
God in three persons, blessed trinity!

Holy, holy, holy! All the saints adore thee,
casting down their golden crowns around the glassy sea;
cherubim and seraphim falling down before thee,
which wert, and art, and evermore shalt be.

Holy, holy, holy! Though the darkness hide thee,
though the eye of sinfulness thy glory may not see,
only thou art holy; there is none beside thee,
perfect in pow'r, in love, and purity.

Holy, holy, holy! Lord God almighty!
All thy works shall praise thy name, in earth, and sky, and sea.
Holy, holy, holy! Merciful and mighty!
God in three persons, blessed trinity!

HOW FIRM A FOUNDATION

Anonymous
(18th century)

How firm a foundation, ye saints of the Lord
Is laid for your faith in His excellent Word
What more can He say than to you He hath said
To you who for refuge to Jesus have fled

Fear not, I am with thee; oh be not dismayed
For I am thy God and will still give thee aid
I'll strengthen thee, help thee, and cause thee to stand
Upheld by My righteous, omnipotent hand

When through the deep waters I call thee to go
The rivers of sorrow shall not overflow
For I will be with thee, thy troubles to bless
And sanctify to thee thy deepest distress

When through fiery trials thy pathways shall lie
My grace all sufficient shall be thy supply
The flame shall not hurt thee; I only design
Thy dross to consume and thy gold to refine

The soul that on Jesus has leaned for repose
I will not, I will not desert to its foes
That soul, though all hell should endeavor to shake
I'll never, no never, no never forsake.

IT IS WELL WITH MY SOUL

Horatio G. Spafford
(1828-1888)

When peace, like a river, attendeth my way,
When sorrows, like sea billows, roll;
Whatever my lot, Thou hast taught me to say,
It is well, It is well with my soul.

Chorus:
It is well with my soul,
it is well, it is well with my soul.

Though Satan should buffet, though trials should come,
Let this blest assurance control,
That Christ hath regarded my helpless estate,
And hath shed His own blood for my soul. [Chorus]

My sin—oh, the bliss of this glorious thought—
My sin, not in part but the whole,
Is nailed to His cross and I bear it no more,
Praise the Lord, praise the Lord, oh, my soul. [Chorus]

And, Lord, haste the day when the faith shall be sight,
The clouds be rolled back as a scroll,
The trump shall resound, and the Lord shall descend,
"Even so"—it is well with my soul. [Chorus]

JESUS SHALL REIGN

Isaac Watts
(1674-1748)

Jesus shall reign where'er the sun
does its successive journeys run,
his kingdom stretch from shore to shore,
till moons shall wax and wane no more.

To him shall endless prayer be made,
and praises throng to crown his head.
His name like sweet perfume shall rise
with every morning sacrifice.

People and realms of every tongue
dwell on his love with sweetest song,
and infant voices shall proclaim
their early blessings on his name.

Blessings abound where'er he reigns:
the prisoners leap to lose their chains,
the weary find eternal rest,
and all who suffer want are blest.

Let every creature rise and bring
the highest honors to our King,
angels descend with songs again,
and earth repeat the loud amen.

JOYFUL, JOYFUL WE ADORE THEE

Henry Van Dyke
(1852-1933)

Joyful, joyful, we adore You,
God of glory, Lord of love;
Hearts unfold like flow'rs before You,
Op'ning to the sun above.
Melt the clouds of sin and sadness;
Drive the dark of doubt away;
Giver of immortal gladness,
Fill us with the light of day!

All Your works with joy surround You,
Earth and heav'n reflect Your rays,
Stars and angels sing around You,
Center of unbroken praise;
Field and forest, vale and mountain,
Flow'ry meadow, flashing sea,
Chanting bird and flowing fountain
Praising You eternally!

Always giving and forgiving,
Ever blessing, ever blest,
Well-spring of the joy of living,
Ocean-depth of happy rest!
Loving Father, Christ our Brother,
Let Your light upon us shine;
Teach us how to love each other,
Lift us to the joy divine.

Mortals, join the mighty chorus,
Which the morning stars began;
God's own love is reigning o'er us,
Joining people hand in hand.
Ever singing, march we onward,
Victors in the midst of strife;
Joyful music leads us sunward
In the triumph song of life.

MAY THE MIND OF CHRIST MY SAVIOR

Kate B. Wilkinson
(1859-1928)

May the mind of Christ, my Savior,
Live in me from day to day,
By his love and pow'r controlling
All I do and say.

May the word of God dwell richly
In my heart from hour to hour,
So that all may see I triumph
Only through his pow'r.

May the peace of God, my Father,
Rule my life in ev'rything,
That I may be calm to comfort
Sick and sorrowing.

May the love of Jesus fill me
As the waters fill the sea.
Him exalting, self abasing:
This is victory.

May we run the race before us,
Strong and brave to face the foe,
Looking only unto Jesus
As we onward go.

MY ANCHOR HOLDS

William C. Martin
(1864-1914)

Tho' the angry surges roll
On my tempest-driven soul,
I am peaceful, for I know,
Wildly though the winds may blow,
I've an anchor safe and sure,
That can evermore endure.

Refrain:
And it holds, my anchor holds:
Blow your wildest, then, O gale,
On my bark so small and frail;
By His grace I shall not fail,
For my anchor holds, my anchor holds.

Mighty tides about me sweep,
Perils lurk within the deep,
Angry clouds o'ershade the sky,
And the tempest rises high;
Still I stand the tempest's shock,
For my anchor grips the rock.

I can feel the anchor fast
As I meet each sudden blast,
And the cable, though unseen,
Bears the heavy strain between;
Thro' the storm I safely ride,
Till the turning of the tide.

Troubles almost 'whelm the soul;
Griefs like billows o'er me roll;
Tempters seek to lure astray;
Storms obscure the light of day:
But in Christ I can be bold,
I've an anchor that shall hold.

O, SACRED HEAD

Bernard of Clairvaux
(1090-1153)

O sacred Head, now wounded,
with grief and shame weighed down,
now scornfully surrounded
with thorns, thine only crown!
O sacred Head, what glory,
what bliss till now was thine!
Yet, though despised and gory,
I joy to call thee mine.

What thou, my Lord, hast suffered
was all for sinners' gain.
Mine, mine was the transgression,
but thine the deadly pain.
Lo, here I fall, my Savior!
'Tis I deserve thy place.
Look on me with thy favor,
and grant to me thy grace.

What language shall I borrow
to thank thee, dearest Friend,
for this, thy dying sorrow,

thy pity without end?
Oh, make me thine forever,
and should I fainting be,
Lord, let me never, never
outlive my love to thee.

Be near when I am dying,
oh, show thy cross to me,
and for my rescue, flying,
come, Lord, and set me free!
These eyes, new faith receiving,
from Jesus shall not move,
for one who dies believing
dies safely, through thy love.

O, THE DEEP, DEEP LOVE OF JESUS

S. Trevor Francis
(1834-1925)

O the deep, deep love of Jesus!
Vast, unmeasured, boundless, free,
rolling as a mighty ocean
in its fullness over me.
Underneath me, all around me,
is the current of thy love;
leading onward, leading homeward,
to thy glorious rest above.

O the deep, deep love of Jesus!
Spread his praise from shore to shore;
how he loveth, ever loveth,
changeth never, nevermore;
how he watches o'er his loved ones,
died to call them all his own;
how for them he intercedeth,
watcheth o'er them from the throne.

O the deep, deep love of Jesus!
Love of ev'ry love the best:
'tis an ocean vast of blessing,
'tis a haven sweet of rest.
O the deep, deep love of Jesus!
'Tis a heav'n of heav'ns to me;
and it lifts me up to glory,
for it lifts me up to thee.

ROCK OF AGES

Augustus Toplady
(1740-1778)

Rock of Ages, cleft for me,
let me hide myself in thee;
let the water and the blood,
from thy wounded side which flowed,
be of sin the double cure;
save from wrath and make me pure.

Not the labors of my hands
can fulfill thy law's demands;
could my zeal no respite know,
could my tears forever flow,
all for sin could not atone;
thou must save, and thou alone.

Nothing in my hand I bring,
simply to the cross I cling;
naked, come to thee for dress;
helpless, look to thee for grace;
foul, I to the fountain fly;
wash me, Savior, or I die.

While I draw this fleeting breath,
when mine eyes shall close in death,
when I soar to worlds unknown,
see thee on thy judgment throne,
Rock of Ages, cleft for me,
let me hide myself in thee.

SOUND THE BATTLE CRY

William F. Sherman
(1826-1888)

Sound the battle cry!
See, the foe is nigh,
Raise the Standard high
For the Lord.
Gird your armour on;
Stand firm every one;
Rest your cause upon
His holy word.

Refrain:
Rouse, then, soldiers, rally round the banner!
Ready, steady, pass the word along;
Onward, forward, shout aloud hosanna!
Christ is captain of the mighty throng.

Strong to meet the foe,
Marching on we go,
While our cause we know
Must prevail.
Shield and banner bright,
Gleaming in the light,
Battling for the right,
We ne'er can fail.

O thou God of all,
Hear us when we call,
Help us one and all
By thy grace!
When the battle's done,
And the victory won,
May we wear the crown
Before thy face.

THE CHURCH'S ONE FOUNDATION

S. J. Stone
(1839-1900)

The Church's one foundation
Is Jesus Christ her Lord;
She is His new creation
By water and the word:
From heaven He came and sought her
To be His holy bride;
With His own blood He sought her,
And for her life He died.

Elect from every nation,
Yet one o'er all the earth,
Her charter of salvation,
One Lord, one Faith, one Birth;
One holy Name she blesses,
Partakes one holy food,
And to one hope she presses,
With every grace endued.

Though with a scornful wonder
Men see her sore opprest,
By schisms rent asunder,
By heresies distrest;

Yet saints their watch are keeping,
Their cry goes up "How long?"
And soon the night of weeping
Shall be the morn of song.

'Mid toil and tribulation,
And tumult of her war
She waits the consummation
Of peace for evermore;
Till with the vision glorious
Her longing eyes are blest,
And the great Church victorious
Shall be the Church at rest.

Yet she on earth hath union
With God the Three in One,
And mystic sweet communion
With those whose rest is won:
O happy ones and holy!
Lord, give us grace that we
Like them, the meek and lowly,
On high may dwell with Thee.

WE GATHER TOGETHER

Anonymous (1625)
Translated by Theodore Baker (1851-1934)

We gather together to ask the Lord's blessing;
He chastens and hastens his will to make known;
The wicked oppressing now cease from distressing.
Sing praises to his name; he forgets not his own.

Beside us to guide us, our God with us joining,
Ordaining, maintaining his kingdom divine;
So from the beginning the fight we were winning;
Thou, Lord, wast at our side; all glory be thine!

We all do extol thee, thou leader triumphant,
And pray that thou still our defender wilt be.
Let thy congregation escape tribulation;
Thy name be ever praised! O Lord, make us free!

FOLK AND POPULAR SONGS

THE ASH GROVE ("LLWYN ONN")
Welsh Folk Song

The ash grove, how graceful, how plainly 'tis speaking;
  The harp through it playing has language for me,
Whenever the light through its branches is breaking,
A host of kind faces is gazing on me.
The friends of my childhood again are before me;
Each step wakes a memory as freely I roam.
With soft whispers laden the leaves rustle o'er me;
The ash grove, the ash grove alone is my home.

Down yonder green valley where streamlets meander,
When twilight is fading I pensively rove,
Or at the bright noontide in solitude wander
Amid the dark shades of the lonely ash grove.
'Twas there while the blackbird was cheerfully singing
I first met that dear one, the joy of my heart.
Around us for gladness the bluebells were ringing,
But then little thought I how soon we should part.

My lips smile no more, my heart loses its lightness;
No dream of the future my spirit can cheer.
I only can brood on the past and its brightness;
The dear ones I long for again gather here.
From ev'ry dark nook they press forward to meet me;
I lift up my eyes to the broad leafy dome,
And others are there, looking downward to greet me;
The ash grove, the ash grove again is my home.

THE DRINKING GOURD
African-American Folk Song

When the sun comes back
  And the first quail calls,
Follow the drinking gourd,
For the old man is waiting
For to carry you to freedom
If you follow the drinking gourd.
[Chorus]

The riverbank will make a very good road,
The dead trees show you the way,
Left foot, peg foot traveling on,
Following the drinking gourd.

Chorus:
Follow the drinking gourd,
Follow the drinking gourd,
For the old man is waiting
For to carry you to freedom
If you follow the drinking gourd.

The river ends between two hills,
Follow the drinking gourd,
There's another river on the other side,
Follow the drinking gourd.
[Chorus]

Where the great big river meets the little river,
Follow the drinking gourd,
The old man is waiting,
For to carry you to freedom
If you follow the drinking gourd.
[Chorus]

AN ENGLISH COUNTRY GARDEN
English Folk Song

How many gentle flowers grow in an English country garden?
I'll tell you now, of some that I know, and those I miss I hope you'll pardon.
Daffodils, hearts-ease and flocks, meadow sweet and lilies, stocks,
Gentle lupins and tall hollyhocks,
Roses, fox-gloves, snowdrops, forget-me-knots in an English country garden.

How many insects find their home in an English country garden?
I'll tell you now of some that I know, and those I miss, I hope you'll pardon.
Dragonflies, moths and bees, spiders falling from the trees,
Butterflies sway in the mild gentle breeze.
There are hedgehogs that roam and little garden gnomes in an English
country garden.

How many song-birds make their nest in an English country garden?
I'll tell you now of some that I know, and those I miss, I hope you'll pardon.
Babbling, coo-cooing doves, robins and the warbling thrush,
Blue birds, lark, finch and nightingale.
We all smile in the spring when the birds all start to sing in an English
    country garden.

THE HAPPY WANDERER

Florenz Friedrich
Sigismund (1791–1877)

I love to go a-wandering,
Along the mountain track,
And as I go, I love to sing,
My knapsack on my back.

Chorus:
Val-deri, Val-dera,
Val-deri,
Val-dera-ha-ha-ha-ha-ha
Val-deri, Val-dera.
My knapsack on my back.

I love to wander by the stream
That dances in the sun,
So joyously it calls to me,
"Come! Join my happy song!"
[Chorus]

I wave my hat to all I meet,
And they wave back to me,
And blackbirds call so loud and sweet
From ev'ry green wood tree.
[Chorus]

High overhead, the skylarks wing,
They never rest at home
But just like me, they love to sing,
As o'er the world we roam.
[Chorus]

Oh, may I go a-wandering
Until the day I die!
Oh, may I always laugh and sing,
Beneath God's clear blue sky!
[Chorus]

MOLLY MALONE (COCKLES AND MUSSELS)

Irish Folk Song

In Dublin's fair city
Where girls are so pretty,
I first set my eyes on sweet Molly Malone,
As she wheeled her wheelbarrow
Through streets broad and narrow,
Crying "Cockles and mussels! Alive, Alive Oh!"

Chorus:
"Alive, alive Oh! Alive, alive Oh!"
Crying, "Cockles and mussels! Alive, Alive Oh!"

She was a fishmonger
But sure 'twas no wonder
For so were her father and mother before
And they each wheeled their barrow
Through streets broad and narrow
Crying "Cockles and mussels! Alive, Alive Oh!"
[Chorus]

She died of a fever,
And no one could save her,
And that was the end of sweet Molly Malone,
But her ghost wheels her barrow
Through streets broad and narrow,
Crying "Cockles and mussels! Alive, alive Oh!"
[Chorus]

THE THREE RAVENS

English Folk Ballad

There were three Ravens sat on a tree,
Downe a downe, hey downe, hey downe.
They were as blacke as blacke could be—with a downe.
Then one of them said to his mate,
Where shall we our breakefast take?
With a downe derrie, derry, derry, downe, downe.

Downe in yonder greene field,
Downe a downe, hey downe, hey downe.
There lies a Knight slain under his shield—with a downe.
His hounds they lie downe at his feete
So well do they their Master keepe
With a downe derrie, derry, derry, downe, downe.

His Hawkes they flie so eagerly,
Downe a downe, hey downe, hey downe.
There's no fowle that dare him come nie—with a downe.
Downe there comes a fallow Doe,
As great with yong as she might go
With a downe derrie, derry, derry, downe, downe.

She lifted up his bloody head,
Downe a downe, hey downe, hey downe.
And kiss'd his wounds that were so red—with a downe.
She got him up upon her backe
And carried him to earthen lake.
With a downe derrie, derry, derry, downe, downe.

She buried him before the prime,
Downe a downe, hey downe, hey downe.
She was dead her selfe ere evensong time—with a downe.
God sent every gentleman,
Such hawkes, such hounds, and such a leman
With a downe derrie, derry, derry, downe, downe.

SCARBOROUGH FAIRE
English Ballad

"O, where are you going?" "To Scarborough fair,"
Savoury sage, rosemary, and thyme;
"Remember me to a lass who lives there,
For once she was a true love of mine.

"And tell her to make me a cambric shirt,
Savoury sage, rosemary, and thyme,
Without any seam or needlework,
And then she shall be a true love of mine.

"And tell her to wash it in yonder dry well,
Savoury sage, rosemary, and thyme,
Where no water sprung, nor a drop of rain fell,
And then she shall be a true love of mine.

"Tell her to dry it on yonder thorn,
Savoury sage, rosemary, and thyme,
Which never bore blossom since Adam was born,
And then she shall be a true love of thine."

"O, will you find me an acre of land,
  Savoury sage, rosemary, and thyme,
  Between the sea foam, the sea sand,
  Or never be a true lover of mine.

"O, will you plough it with a ram's horn,
  Savoury sage, rosemary, and thyme,
  And sow it all over with one peppercorn,
  Or never be a true lover of mine.

"O, will you reap it with a sickle of leather,
  Savoury sage, rosemary, and thyme,
  And tie it all up with a peacock's feather,
  Or never be a true lover of mine.

"And when you have done and finished your work,
  Savoury sage, rosemary, and thyme,
  You may come to'me for your cambric shirt,
  And then you shall be a true lover of mine."

SIMPLE GIFTS
Shaker Song
Aaron Copland used
the melody for "Simple
Gifts" in *Appalachian
Spring*.

'Tis the gift to be simple, 'tis the gift to be free
  'Tis the gift to come down where we ought to be,
And when we find ourselves in the place just right,
'Twill be in the valley of love and delight.
When true simplicity is gained,
To bow and to bend we shan't be ashamed,
To turn, turn will be our delight,
Till by turning, turning we come 'round right.

STAR OF THE COUNTY DOWN

Cathal McGarvey
(1866–1927)

Near Banbridge town, in the County Down
One morning last July
Down a boreen green came a sweet colleen
And she smiled as she passed me by.
Oh she looked so sweet from her two bare feet
To the sheen of her nut brown hair
Such a coaxing elf, sure I shook myself
To be sure I was really there.

Chorus:
And from Bantry Bay up to Derry Quay
And from Galway to Dublin town
No maid I've seen like the brown colleen
That I met in the County Down.

As she onward sped I shook my head
And I gazed with a feeling rare
And I said, says I, to a passerby
"Who's the maid with the nut-brown hair?"
He smiled at me, and with pride says he,
"That's the gem of Ireland's crown.
She's young Rosie McCann from the banks of the Bann
She's the star of the County Down."
[Chorus]

I've travelled a bit, but never was hit
Since my roving career began
But fair and square I surrendered there
To the charms of young Rose McCann.
I'd a heart to let and no tenant yet
Did I meet with in shawl or gown
But in she went and I asked no rent
From the star of the County Down.
[Chorus]

At the crossroads fair I'll be surely there
And I'll dress in my Sunday clothes
And I'll try sheep's eyes, and deludhering lies
On the heart of the nut-brown rose.
No pipe I'll smoke, no horse I'll yoke
Though with rust my plow turns brown
Till a smiling bride by my own fireside
Sits the star of the County Down.
[Chorus]

SWING LOW, SWEET CHARIOT

Traditional Spiritual

Swing low, sweet chariot
Coming for to carry me home,
Swing low, sweet chariot,
Coming for to carry me home.

I looked over Jordan, and what did I see
Coming for to carry me home?
A band of angels coming after me,
Coming for to carry me home.

Chorus:
Swing low, sweet chariot
Coming for to carry me home,
Swing low, sweet chariot,
Coming for to carry me home.

Sometimes I'm up, and sometimes I'm down,
(Coming for to carry me home)
But still my soul feels heavenly bound.
(Coming for to carry me home)
[Chorus]

The brightest day that I can say,
(Coming for to carry me home)
When Jesus washed my sins away.
(Coming for to carry me home)
[Chorus]

If I get there before you do,
(Coming for to carry me home)
I'll cut a hole and pull you through.
(Coming for to carry me home)
[Chorus]

If you get there before I do,
(Coming for to carry me home)
Tell all my friends I'm coming too.
(Coming for to carry me home)
[Chorus]

BIBLE INFORMATION

THE BOOKS OF THE OLD TESTAMENT

Genesis
Exodus
Leviticus
Numbers
Deuteronomy
Joshua
Judges
Ruth
I Samuel
II Samuel
I Kings
II Kings
I Chronicles
II Chronicles
Ezra
Nehemiah
Esther
Job
Psalms
Proverbs

Ecclesiastes
Song of Solomon
Isaiah
Jeremiah
Lamentations
Ezekiel
Daniel
Hosea
Joel
Amos
Obadiah
Jonah
Micah
Nahum
Habakkuk
Zephaniah
Haggai
Zechariah
Malachi

THE BOOKS OF THE NEW TESTAMENT

Matthew
Mark
Luke
John
Acts
Romans
I Corinthians
II Corinthians
Galatians
Ephesians
Philippians
Colossians
I Thessalonians
II Thessalonians

I Timothy
II Timothy
Titus
Philemon
Hebrews
James
I Peter
II Peter
I John
II John
III John
Jude
Revelation

THE LORD'S PRAYER Matthew 6:9-13 (KJV)	Our Father which art in heaven, Hallowed be thy name. Thy kingdom come, Thy will be done in earth, as it is in heaven. Give us this day our daily bread. And forgive us our debts, as we forgive our debtors. And lead us not into temptation, but deliver us from evil: For thine is the kingdom, and the power, and the glory, for ever. Amen.

THE 12 APOSTLES Matthew 10:2-3 (ESV)	The names of the twelve apostles are these: first, Simon, who is called Peter, and Andrew his brother; James the son of Zebedee, and John his brother; Philip and Bartholomew; Thomas and Matthew the tax collector; James the son of Alphaeus, and Thaddaeus; Simon the Zealot, and Judas Iscariot, who betrayed him.
Luke 6:13-16 (ESV)	And when day came, he called his disciples and chose from them twelve, whom he named apostles: Simon, whom he named Peter, and Andrew his brother, and James and John, and Philip, and Bartholomew, and Matthew, and Thomas, and James the son of Alphaeus, and Simon who was called the Zealot, and Judas the son of James, and Judas Iscariot, who became a traitor.

TWELVE TRIBES OF ISRAEL

Reuben	Dan
Simeon	Naphtali
Levi	Gad
Judah	Asher
Issachar	Benjamin
Zebulan	Joseph

HALF-TRIBES OF JOSEPH

Ephraim
Manassah

THE 14 JUDGES OF ISRAEL

Othniel	Jephthah
Ehud	Ibzan
Shamgar	Elon
Deborah/Barak	Abdon
Gideon	Samson
Tola	Eli
Jair	Samuel

OLD TESTAMENT SELECTIONS

English Standard Version

GENESIS 1:1-5

In the beginning, God created the heavens and the earth. 2 The earth was without form and void, and darkness was over the face of the deep. And the Spirit of God was hovering over the face of the waters. 3 And God said, "Let there be light," and there was light. 4 And God saw that the light was good. And God separated the light from the darkness. 5 God called the light Day, and the darkness he called Night. And there was evening and there was morning, the first day.

EXODUS 20:1-7

And God spoke all these words, saying,
2 "I am the Lord your God, who brought you out of the land of Egypt, out of the house of slavery.
3 "You shall have no other gods before me.
4 "You shall not make for yourself a carved image, or any likeness of anything that is in heaven above, or that is in the earth beneath, or that is in the water under the earth. 5 You shall not bow down to them or serve them, for I the Lord your God am a jealous God, visiting the iniquity of the fathers on the children to the third and the fourth generation of those who hate me, 6 but showing steadfast love to thousands of those who love me and keep my commandments.
7 "You shall not take the name of the Lord your God in vain, for the Lord will not hold him guiltless who takes his name in vain.

DEUTERONOMY 6:4-9

Hear, O Israel: The Lord our God, the Lord is one. 5 You shall love the Lord your God with all your heart and with all your soul and with all your might. 6 And these words that I command you today shall be on your heart. 7 You shall teach them diligently to your children, and shall talk of them when you sit in your house, and when you walk by the way, and when you lie down, and when you rise. 8 You shall bind them as a sign on your hand, and they shall be as frontlets between your eyes. 9 You shall write them on the doorposts of your house and on your gates.

PSALM 1

Blessed is the man
who walks not in the counsel of the wicked,
nor stands in the way of sinners,
  nor sits in the seat of scoffers;
2 but his delight is in the law of the Lord,
  and on his law he meditates day and night.

3 He is like a tree
  planted by streams of water
that yields its fruit in its season,
  and its leaf does not wither.
In all that he does, he prospers.
4 The wicked are not so,
  but are like chaff that the wind drives away.

5 Therefore the wicked will not stand in the judgment,
  nor sinners in the congregation of the righteous;
6 for the Lord knows the way of the righteous,
  but the way of the wicked will perish.

ISAIAH 40:28-31

Have you not known? Have you not heard?
The Lord is the everlasting God,
  the Creator of the ends of the earth.
He does not faint or grow weary;
  his understanding is unsearchable.
29 He gives power to the faint,
  and to him who has no might he increases strength.
30 Even youths shall faint and be weary,
  and young men shall fall exhausted;
31 but they who wait for the Lord shall renew their strength;
  they shall mount up with wings like eagles;
  they shall run and not be weary;
  they shall walk and not faint.

NEW TESTAMENT SELECTIONS

English Standard Version

**MATTHEW
5:3-16**

Blessed are the poor in spirit, for theirs is the kingdom of heaven. 4 "Blessed are those who mourn, for they shall be comforted.

5 "Blessed are the meek, for they shall inherit the earth.

6 "Blessed are those who hunger and thirst for righteousness, for they shall be satisfied.

7 "Blessed are the merciful, for they shall receive mercy.

8 "Blessed are the pure in heart, for they shall see God.

9 "Blessed are the peacemakers, for they shall be called sons of God.

10 "Blessed are those who are persecuted for righteousness' sake, for theirs is the kingdom of heaven.

11 "Blessed are you when others revile you and persecute you and utter all kinds of evil against you falsely on my account. 12 Rejoice and be glad, for your reward is great in heaven, for so they persecuted the prophets who were before you.

13 "You are the salt of the earth, but if salt has lost its taste, how shall its saltiness be restored? It is no longer good for anything except to be thrown out and trampled under people's feet.

14 "You are the light of the world. A city set on a hill cannot be hidden. 15 Nor do people light a lamp and put it under a basket, but on a stand, and it gives light to all in the house. 16 In the same way, let your light shine before others, so that they may see your good works and give glory to your Father who is in heaven.

LUKE 2:1-21

In those days a decree went out from Caesar Augustus that all the world should be registered. 2 This was the first registration when Quirinius was governor of Syria. 3 And all went to be registered, each to his own town. 4 And Joseph also went up from Galilee, from the town of Nazareth, to Judea, to the city of David, which is called Bethlehem, because he was of the house and lineage of David, 5 to be registered with Mary, his betrothed, who was with child. 6 And while they were there, the time came for her to give birth. 7 And she gave birth to her firstborn son and wrapped him in swaddling cloths and laid him in a manger, because there was no place for them in the inn.

8 And in the same region there were shepherds out in the field, keeping watch over their flock by night. 9 And an angel of the Lord appeared to them, and the glory of the Lord shone around them, and they were filled with great fear. 10 And the angel said to them, "Fear not, for behold, I bring you good news of great joy that will be for all the people. 11 For unto you is born this

day in the city of David a Savior, who is Christ the Lord. 12 And this will be a sign for you: you will find a baby wrapped in swaddling cloths and lying in a manger." 13 And suddenly there was with the angel a multitude of the heavenly host praising God and saying,

14 "Glory to God in the highest,
and on earth peace among those with whom he is pleased!"

15 When the angels went away from them into heaven, the shepherds said to one another, "Let us go over to Bethlehem and see this thing that has happened, which the Lord has made known to us." 16 And they went with haste and found Mary and Joseph, and the baby lying in a manger. 17 And when they saw it, they made known the saying that had been told them concerning this child. 18 And all who heard it wondered at what the shepherds told them. 19 But Mary treasured up all these things, pondering them in her heart. 20 And the shepherds returned, glorifying and praising God for all they had heard and seen, as it had been told them.

21 And at the end of eight days, when he was circumcised, he was called Jesus, the name given by the angel before he was conceived in the womb.

JOHN 1:1-14

In the beginning was the Word, and the Word was with God, and the Word was God. 2 He was in the beginning with God. 3 All things were made through him, and without him was not any thing made that was made. 4 In him was life, and the life was the light of men. 5 The light shines in the darkness, and the darkness has not overcome it.

6 There was a man sent from God, whose name was John. 7 He came as a witness, to bear witness about the light, that all might believe through him. 8 He was not the light, but came to bear witness about the light. 9 The true light, which gives light to everyone, was coming into the world. 10 He was in the world, and the world was made through him, yet the world did not know him. 11 He came to his own, and his own people did not receive him. 12 But to all who did receive him, who believed in his name, he gave the right to become children of God, 13 who were born, not of blood nor of the will of the flesh nor of the will of man, but of God.

14 And the Word became flesh and dwelt among us, and we have seen his glory, glory as of the only Son from the Father, full of grace and truth.

JOHN 14:1-7

Let not your hearts be troubled. Believe in God; believe also in me. 2 In my Father's house are many rooms. If it were not so, would I have told you that I go to prepare a place for you? 3 And if I go and prepare a place for you, I will come again and will take you to myself, that where I am you may be also. 4 And you know the way to where I am going."5 Thomas said to him, "Lord, we do not know where you are going. How can we know the way?" 6 Jesus said to him, "I am the way, and the truth, and the life. No one comes to the Father except through me. 7 If you had known me, you would have known my Father also. From now on you do know him and have seen him."

I CORINTHIANS 13

If I speak in the tongues of men and of angels, but have not love, I am a noisy gong or a clanging cymbal. 2 And if I have prophetic powers, and understand all mysteries and all knowledge, and if I have all faith, so as to remove mountains, but have not love, I am nothing. 3 If I give away all I have, and if I deliver up my body to be burned, but have not love, I gain nothing.

4 Love is patient and kind; love does not envy or boast; it is not arrogant 5 or rude. It does not insist on its own way; it is not irritable or resentful; 6 it does not rejoice at wrongdoing, but rejoices with the truth. 7 Love bears all things, believes all things, hopes all things, endures all things. 8 Love never ends. As for prophecies, they will pass away; as for tongues, they will cease; as for knowledge, it will pass away. 9 For we know in part and we prophesy in part, 10 but when the perfect comes, the partial will pass away. 11 When I was a child, I spoke like a child, I thought like a child, I reasoned like a child. When I became a man, I gave up childish ways. 12 For now we see in a mirror dimly, but then face to face. Now I know in part; then I shall know fully, even as I have been fully known.

13 So now faith, hope, and love abide, these three; but the greatest of these is love.

CREEDS AND CATECHISMS

**THE APOSTLES'
CREED**

I believe in God, the Father almighty,
maker of heaven and earth;

And in Jesus Christ, his only Son, our Lord;
who was conceived by the Holy Ghost,
born of the Virgin Mary,
suffered under Pontius Pilate,
was crucified, dead, and buried.
He descended into hell.
The third day he rose again from the dead.
He ascended into heaven,
and sitteth on the right hand of God the Father almighty.
From thence he shall come to judge the quick and the dead.

I believe in the Holy Ghost,
the holy catholic church,
the communion of saints,
the forgiveness of sins,
the resurrection of the body,
and the life everlasting. Amen.

**THE NICENE
CREED**

We believe in one God,
the Father, the Almighty,
maker of heaven and earth,
of all that is, seen and unseen.

We believe in one Lord, Jesus Christ,
the only Son of God,
eternally begotten of the Father,
God from God, Light from Light,
true God from true God,
begotten, not made,
of one being with the Father;
through him all things were made.
For us and for our salvation
he came down from heaven:
was incarnate of the Holy Spirit and the Virgin Mary,
and became truly human.

CINDY'S ANTHOLOGY   CREEDS AND CATECHISMS

For our sake he was crucified under Pontius Pilate;
he suffered death and was buried.
On the third day he rose again
in accordance with the Scriptures;
he ascended into heaven
and is seated at the right hand of the Father.
He will come again in glory to judge the living and the dead,
and his kingdom will have no end.

We believe in the Holy Spirit, the Lord, the giver of life,
who proceeds from the Father [and the Son],
who with the Father and the Son is worshiped and glorified,
who has spoken through the prophets.
We believe in one holy catholic and apostolic Church.
We acknowledge one baptism for the forgiveness of sins.
We look for the resurrection of the dead,
and the life of the world to come. Amen.

HEIDELBERG CATECHISM: QUESTIONS 1 AND 2

What is thy only comfort in life and in death?

That I, with body and soul, both in life and in death, am not my own, but belong to my faithful Savior Jesus Christ, who with His precious blood has fully satisfied for all my sins, and redeemed me from all the power of the devil; and so preserves me, that without the will of my Father in heaven not a hair can fall from my head; yea, that all things must work together for my salvation. Wherefore, by His Holy Spirit, He also assures me of eternal life, and makes me heartily willing and ready henceforth to live unto Him.

2. How many things are necessary for thee to know, that thou in this comfort mayest live and die happily?

Three things: first, the greatness of my sin and misery. Second, how I am redeemed from all my sins and misery. Third, how I am to be thankful to God for such redemption.

PRAYER OF CONFESSION
Book of Common Prayer 1928

Almighty and most merciful Father, We have erred, and strayed from thy ways like lost sheep. We have followed too much the devices and desires of our own hearts. We have offended against thy holy laws. We have left undone those things which we ought to have done; And we have done those things which we ought not to have done; And there is no health in us. But thou, O Lord, have mercy upon us, miserable offenders. Spare thou those, O God, who confess their faults. Restore thou those who are penitent; According to thy promises declared unto mankind in Christ Jesus our Lord. And grant, O most merciful Father, for his sake; That we may hereafter live a godly, righteous, and sober life, To the glory of thy holy Name. Amen.

WEST POINT CADET PRAYER

O God, our Father, Thou Searcher of human hearts, Help us to draw near to Thee in sincerity and truth. May our religion be filled with gladness and may our worship of Thee be natural.

Strengthen and increase our admiration for honest dealing and clean thinking, and suffer not our hatred of hypocrisy and pretense ever to diminish. Encourage us in our endeavor to live above the common level of life. Make us to choose the harder right instead of the easier wrong and never to be content with a half truth when the whole can be won. Endow us with courage that is born of loyalty to all that is noble and worthy, that scorns to compromise with vice and injustice and knows no fear when truth and right are in jeopardy.

Guard us against flippancy and irreverence in the sacred things of life. Grant us new ties of friendship and new opportunities of service. Kindle our hearts in fellowship with those of a cheerful countenance, and soften our hearts with sympathy for those who sorrow and suffer.

Help us to maintain the honor of the Corps untarnished and unsullied and to show forth in our lives the ideals of West Point in doing our duty to Thee and to our Country.

All of which we ask in the name of the Great Friend and Master of All. Amen.

WESTMINSTER SHORTER CATECHISM

Q1: What is the chief end of man?

A1: Man's chief end is to glorify God, and to enjoy Him for ever.

Q2: What rule hath God given to direct us how we may glorify and enjoy Him?

A2: The Word of God, which is contained in the Scriptures of the Old and New Testaments, is the only rule to direct us how we may glorify and enjoy Him.

Q3: What do the Scriptures principally teach?

A3: The Scriptures principally teach what man is to believe concerning God, and what duty God requires of man.

Q4: What is God?

A4: God is a Spirit, infinite, eternal, and unchangeable, in his being, wisdom, power, holiness, justice, goodness, and truth.

Q5: Are there more Gods than one?

A5: There is but one only, the living and true God.

Q6: How many persons are there in the Godhead?

A6: There are three persons in the Godhead; the Father, the Son, and the Holy Ghost; and these three are one God, the same in substance, equal in power and glory.

Q7: What are the decrees of God?

A7: The decrees of God are, his eternal purpose, according to the counsel of his will, whereby, for his own glory, he hath fore-ordained whatsoever comes to pass.

Q8: How doth God execute his decrees?

A8: God executeth his decrees in the works of creation and providence.

Q9: What is the work of creation?

A9: The work of creation is, God's making all things of nothing, by the word of his power, in the space of six days, and all very good.

Q10: How did God create man?

A10: God created man male and female, after his own image, in knowledge, righteousness, and holiness, with dominion over the creatures.

Q11: What are God's works of providence?

A11: God's works of providence are, his most holy, wise, and powerful preserving and governing all his creatures, and all their actions.

Q12: What special act of providence did God exercise toward man in the estate wherein he was created?

A12: When God had created man, he entered into a covenant of life with him, upon condition of perfect obedience; forbidding him to eat of the tree of the knowledge of good and evil, upon the pain of death.

Q13: Did our first parents continue in the estate wherein they were created?

A13: Our first parents, being left to the freedom of their own will, fell from the estate wherein they were created, by sinning against God.

Q14: What is sin?

A14: Sin is any want of conformity unto, or transgression of, the law of God.

Q15: What was the sin whereby our first parents fell from the estate wherein they were created?

A15: The sin whereby our first parents fell from the estate wherein they were created, was their eating the forbidden fruit.

Q16: Did all mankind fall in Adam's first transgression?

A16: The covenant being made with Adam, not only for himself, but for his posterity; all mankind, descending from him by ordinary generation, sinned in him, and fell with him, in his first transgression.

Q17: Into what estate did the fall bring mankind?

A17: The fall brought mankind into an estate of sin and misery.

Q18: Wherein consists the sinfulness of that estate whereinto man fell?

A18: The sinfulness of that estate whereinto man fell, consists in the guilt of Adam's first sin, the want of original righteousness, and the corruption of his whole nature, which is commonly called Original Sin; together with all actual transgressions which proceed from it.

Q19: What is the misery of that estate whereinto man fell?

A19: All mankind by their fall lost communion with God, are under his wrath and curse, and so made liable to all miseries in this life, to death itself, and to the pains of hell for ever.

Q20. Did God leave all mankind to perish in the estate of sin and misery?

A20. God having, out of his mere good pleasure, from all eternity, elected some to everlasting life, did enter into a covenant of grace, to deliver them out of the estate of sin and misery, and to bring them into an estate of salvation by a Redeemer.

Q21: Who is the Redeemer of God's elect?

A21: The only Redeemer of God's elect is the Lord Jesus Christ, who, being the eternal Son of God, became man, and so was, and continueth to be, God and man in two distinct natures, and one person, for ever.

Q22: How did Christ, being the Son of God, become man?

A22: Christ, the Son of God, became man, by taking to himself a true body, and a reasonable soul, being conceived by the power of the Holy Ghost, in the womb of the Virgin Mary, and born of her yet without sin.

Q23: What offices doth Christ execute as our Redeemer?

A23: Christ, as our Redeemer, executeth the offices of a prophet, of a priest, and of a king, both in his estate of humiliation and exaltation.

Q24: How doth Christ execute the office of a prophet?

A24: Christ executeth the office of a prophet, in revealing to us, by his word and Spirit, the will of God for our salvation.

Q25: How doth Christ execute the office of a priest?

A25: Christ executeth the office of a priest, in his once offering up of himself a sacrifice to satisfy divine justice, and reconcile us to God, and in making continual intercession for us.

Q26: How doth Christ execute the office of a king?

A26: Christ executeth the office of a king, in subduing us to himself, in ruling and defending us, and in restraining and conquering all his and our enemies.

Q27: Wherein did Christ's humiliation consist?

A27: Christ's humiliation consisted in his being born, and that in a low condition, made under the law, undergoing the miseries of this life, the wrath of God, and the cursed death of the cross; in being buried, and continuing under the power of death for a time.

Q28: Wherein consisteth Christ's exaltation?

A28: Christ's exaltation consisteth in his rising again from the dead on the third day, in ascending up into heaven, in sitting at the right hand of God the Father, and in coming to judge the world at the last day.

Q29: How are we made partakers of the redemption purchased by Christ?

A29: We are made partakers of the redemption purchased by Christ, by the effectual application of it to us by his Holy Spirit.

Q30: How doth the Spirit apply to us the redemption purchased by Christ?

A30: The Spirit applieth to us the redemption purchased by Christ, by working faith in us, and thereby uniting us to Christ in our effectual calling.

Q31: What is effectual calling?

A31: Effectual calling is the work of God's Spirit, whereby convincing us of our sin and misery, enlightening our minds in the knowledge of Christ, and renewing our wills, he doth persuade and enable us to embrace Jesus Christ, freely offered to us in the gospel.

Q32: What benefits do they that are effectually called partake of in this life?

A32: They that are effectually called do in this life partake of justification, adoption, and sanctification, and the several benefits which, in this life, do either accompany or flow from them.

Q33: What is justification?

A33: Justification is an act of God's free grace, wherein He pardoneth all our sins, and accepteth us as righteous in His sight, only for the righteousness of Christ imputed to us, and received by faith alone.

Q34: What is adoption?

A34: Adoption is an act of God's free grace, whereby we are received into the number, and have a right to all the privileges of the Sons of God.

Q35: What is sanctification?

A35: Sanctification is the work of God's free grace, whereby we are renewed in the whole man after the image of God, and are enabled more and more to die unto sin, and live unto righteousness.

Q36: What are the benefits which in this life do accompany or flow from justification, adoption, and sanctification?

A36: The benefits which in this life do accompany or flow from justification, adoption, and sanc-tification, are, assurance of God's love, peace of conscience, joy in the Holy Ghost, increase of grace, and perseverance therein to the end.

Q37: What benefits do believers receive from Christ at death?

A37: The souls of believers are at their death made perfect in holiness, and do immediately pass into glory; and their bodies, being still united to Christ, do rest in their graves till the resurrection.

Q38: What benefits do believers receive from Christ at the resurrection?

A38: At the resurrection, believers being raised up in glory, shall be openly acknowledged and acquitted in the day of judgement, and made perfectly blessed in the full enjoying of God to all eternity.

Q39. What is the duty which God requireth of man?

A39. The duty which God requireth of man is obedience to His revealed will.

Q40. What did God at first reveal to man for the rule of his obedience?

A40. The rule which God at first revealed to man for his obedience, was the Moral Law.

Q41. Where is the Moral Law summarily comprehended?

A41. The Moral Law is summarily comprehended in the Ten Commandments.

Q42. What is the sum of the Ten Commandments?

A42. The sum of the Ten Commandments is, "to love the Lord our God" with all our heart, all our soul, with all our strength, and with all our mind; and our neighbor as ourselves.

Q43. What is the preface to the Ten Commandments?

A43. The preface to the Ten Commandments is in these words, "I am the Lord your God, who brought you out of the land of Egypt, out of the house of slavery."

Q44. What doth the preface to the Ten Commandments teach us?

A44. The preface to the Ten Commandments teacheth us, That because God is The Lord, and our God, and Redeemer, therefore we are bound to keep all His commandments.

Q45: Which is the First Commandment?

A45: The First Commandment is, "thou shalt have no other gods before Me."

Q46: What is required in the First Commandment?

A46: The First Commandment requireth us to know and acknowledge God to be only true God, and our God; and to worship and glorify Him accordingly.

Q47: What is forbidden in the First Commandment?

A47: The First Commandment forbiddeth the denying, or not worshipping and glorifying the true God, as God, [and our God,] and the giving of that worship and glory to any other which is due to Him alone.

Q48: What are we specially taught by these words, "before me" in the First Commandment?

A48: These words "before me" in the First Commandment, teach us, That God who seeth all things, taketh notice of, and is much displeased with, the sin of having any other God.

Q49: Which is the Second Commandment?

A49: The Second Commandment is, "thou shalt not make unto thee any graven image, or any likeness of any thing that is in heaven above, or that is in the earth beneath, or that is in the water under the earth, thou shalt not bow down thyself to them, nor serve them: for I the Lord thy God am a jealous God, visiting the iniquity of the fathers upon the children, unto the third and fourth generation of them that hate Me; and showing mercy unto thousands of them that love Me, and keep my commandments."

Q50: What is required in the Second Commandment?

A50: The Second Commandment requireth the receiving, observing, and keeping pure and entire, all such religious worship and ordinances as God hath appointed in His Word.

Q51: What is forbidden in the Second Commandment?

A51: The Second Commandment forbiddeth the worshipping of God by images, or any other way not appointed in His Word.

Q52: What are the reasons annexed to the Second Commandment?

A52: The reasoned annexed to the Second Commandment are, God's sovereignty over us, and the zeal He hath to His own worship.

Q53: Which is the Third Commandment?

A53: The Third Commandment is, "thou shalt not take the name of the Lord thy God in vain: for the Lord will not hold him guiltless that taketh His name in vain."

Q54: What is required in the Third Commandment?

A54: The Third Commandment requireth the holy and reverent use of God's names, titles, attributes, ordinances, Word, and works.

Q55: What is forbidden in the Third Commandment?

A55: The Third Commandment forbiddeth all profaning or abusing [of] anything whereby God maketh Himself known.

Q56: What is the reason annexed to the Third Commandment?

A56: The reason annexed to the Third Commandment is, That however the breakers of this commandment may escape punishment from men, yet the Lord our God will not suffer them to escape His righteous judgement.

Q57: Which is the Fourth Commandment?

A57: The Fourth Commandment is, "Remember the Sabbath-day, to keep it holy. Six days shalt thou labour, and do all thy work: But the seventh day is the sabbath of the LORD thy God: in it thou shalt not do any work, thou, nor thy son, nor thy daughter, thy manservant, nor thy maidservant, nor thy cattle, nor thy stranger that is within thy gates: For in six days the LORD made heaven and earth, the sea, and all that in them is, and rested the seventh day: wherefore the LORD blessed the sabbath day, and hallowed it."

Q58: What is required in the Fourth Commandment?

A58: The Fourth Commandment requireth the keeping holy to God such set times as He appointed in His Word; expressly one whole day in seven to be a holy Sabbath to Himself.

Q59: Which day of the seven hath God appointed to be the weekly Sabbath?

A59: From the beginning of the world to the resurrection of Christ, God appointed the seventh day of the week to be the weekly Sabbath; and the first day of the week ever since, to continue to the end of the world, which is the Christian Sabbath.

Q60: How is the Sabbath to be sanctified?

A60: The Sabbath is to be sanctified by a holy resting all that day, even from such worldly employments and recreations as are lawful on other days; and spending the whole time in the public and private exercises of God's worship, except so much as is to be taken up in the works of necessity and mercy.

Q61: What is forbidden in the Fourth Commandment?

A61: The Fourth Commandment forbiddeth the omission or careless performance of the duties required, and the profaning the day by idleness, or doing that which is in itself sinful, or by unnecessary thoughts, words, or works, about our worldly employments or recreations.

Q62: What are the reasons annexed to the Fourth Commandment?

A62: The reasons annexed to the Fourth Commandment are, God's allowing us six days of the week for our own employments, His challenging a special propriety in the seventh, His own example, and His blessing the Sabbath-day.

Q63: Which is the Fifth Commandment?

A63: The Fifth Commandment is, "honour thy father and thy mother, that thy days may be long upon the land which the Lord thy God giveth thee."

Q64: What is required in the Fifth Commandment?

A64: The Fifth Commandment requireth the preserving the honour, and performing the duties, belonging to every one in their several places and relations, as superiors, inferiors, or equals.

Q65: What is the forbidden in the Fifth Commandment?

A65: The Fifth Commandment forbiddeth the neglecting of, or doing anything against, the honour and duty which belongeth to every one in their several places and relations.

Q66: What is the reason annexed to the Fifth Commandment?

A66: The reason annexed to the Fifth Commandment is a promise of long life and prosperity (as far as it shall serve for God's glory and their own good) to all such as keep this commandment.

Q67: Which is the Sixth Commandment?

A67: The Sixth Commandment is, "thou shalt not kill."

Q68: What is required in the Sixth Commandment?

A68: The Sixth Commandment requireth all lawful endeavours to preserve our own life, and the life of others.

Q69: What is forbidden in the Sixth Commandment?

A69: The Sixth Commandment forbiddeth the taking away of our own life, or the life of our neighbour unjustly, or whatsoever tendeth thereunto.

Q70: Which is the Seventh Commandment?

A70: The Seventh Commandment is, "thou shalt not commit adultery."

Q71: What is required in the Seventh Commandment?

A71: The Seventh Commandment requireth the preservation of our own and our neighbor's chasity, in heart, speech, and behaviour.

Q72: What is forbidden in the Seventh Commandment?

A72: The Seventh Commandment forbiddeth all unchaste thoughts, words, and actions.

Q73: Which is the Eighth Commandment?

A73: The Eighth Commandment is, "thou shalt not steal."

Q74: What is required in the Eighth Commandment?

A74: The Eighth Commandment requireth the lawful procuring and furthering the wealth and outward estate of ourselves and others.

Q75: What is forbidden in the Eighth Commandment?

A75: The Eighth Commandment forbiddeth whatsoever doth or may unjustly hinder our own or our neighbour's wealth or outward estate.

Q76: What is the Ninth Commandment?

A76: The Ninth Commandment is, "thou shalt not bear false witness against thy neighbour."

Q77: What is required in the Ninth Commandment?

A77: The Ninth Commandment requireth the maintaining and promoting of truth between man and man, and of our own and our neighbour's good name, especially in witness-bearing.

Q78: What is forbidden in the Ninth Commandment?

A78: The Ninth Commandment forbiddeth whatsoever is prejudical to truth, or injurious to our own or our neighbour's good name.

Q79: Which is the Tenth Commandment?

A79: The Tenth Commandment is, "thou shalt not covet thy neighbour's house, thou shalt not covet thy neighbour's wife, nor his manservant, nor his maidservant, nor his ox, nor his ass, nor any thing that is thy neighbour's."

Q80: What is required in the Tenth Commandment?

A80: The Tenth Commandment requireth full contentment with our own condition, with a right and charitable frame of spirit toward our neighbour, and all this is his.

Q81: What is forbidden in the Tenth Commandment?

A81: The Tenth Commandment forbiddeth all discontentment with our own own estate, envying or grieving at the good of our neighbour, and all inordinate motions and affections to any thing that is his.

Q82: Is any man able perfectly to keep the commandments of God?

A82: No mere man since the fall is able in this life perfectly to keep the commandments of God, but doth daily break them in thought, word, and deed.

Q83: Are all transgression of the law equally heinous?

A83: Some sins in themselves, and by reason of several aggravations are more heinous in the sight of God than others.

Q84: What doth every sin deserve?

A84: Every sin deserveth God's wrath and curse, both in this life, and that which is to come.

Q85: What doth God require of us, that we may escape his wrath and curse due to us for sin?

A85: To escape the wrath and curse of God due to us for sin, God requireth of us faith in Jesus Christ, repentance unto life, with the diligent use of all the outward means whereby Christ communicateth to us the benefits of redemption.

Q86: What is faith in Jesus Christ?

A86: Faith in Jesus Christ is a saving grace, whereby we receive and rest upon him alone for salvation, as he is offered to us in the gospel.

Q87: What is repentance unto life?

A87: Repentance unto life is a saving grace, whereby a sinner, out of a true sense of his sin, and apprehension of the mercy of God in Christ, doth, with grief and hatred of his sin, turn from it unto God, with full purpose of, and endeavour after, new obedience.

Q88: What are the outward means whereby Christ communicateth to us the benefits of redemption?

A88: The outward and ordinary means whereby Christ communicateth to us the benefits of redemption, are his ordinances, especially the Word, sacraments, and prayer; all which are made effectual to the elect for salvation.

Q89: How is the Word made effectual to salvation?

A89: The Spirit of God maketh the reading, but especially the preaching of the Word, an effectual means of convincing and converting sinners, and of building them up in holiness and comfort, through faith, unto salvation.

Q90: How is the Word to be read and heard, that it may become effectual to salvation?

A90: The the Word may become effectual to salvation, we must attend thereunto with diligence, preparation, and prayer; receive it with faith and love, lay it up in our hearts, and practise it in our lives.

Q91: How do the sacraments become effectual means of salvation?

A91: The sacraments become effectual means of salvation, not from any virtue in them, or in him that doth administer them; but only by the blessing of Christ, and the working of his Spirit in them that by faith receive them.

Q92: What is a sacrament?

A92: A sacrament is an holy ordinance instituted by Christ, wherein, by sensible signs, Christ, and the benefits of the new covenant, are represented, sealed, and applied to believers.

Q93: Which are the sacraments of the New Testament?

A93: The sacraments of the New Testament are, Baptism, and the Lord's supper.

Q94: What is baptism?

A94: Baptism is a sacrament, wherein the washing with water in the name of the Father, and of the Son, and of the Holy Ghost, doth signify and seal our ingrafting into Christ, and partaking of the benefits of the covenant of grace, and our engagement to be the Lord's.

Q95: To whom is baptism to be administered?

A95: Baptism is not to be administered to any that are out of the visible church, till they profess their faith in Christ, and obedience to him; but the infants of such as are members of the visible church are to be baptized.

Q96: What is the Lord's supper?

A96: The Lord's Supper is a sacrament, wherein, by giving and receiving bread and wine, according to Christ's appointment, his death is showed forth; and the worth receivers are, not after a corporal and carnal manner, but by faith, made partakers of his body and blood, with all his benefits, to their spiritual nourishment, and growth in grace.

Q97: What is required to be the worthy receiving of the Lord's supper?

A97: It is required of them that would worthily partake of the Lord's super, that they examine themselves of their knowledge to discern the Lord's body, of their faith to feed upon him, of their repentance, love, and new obedience; lest, coming unworthily, they eat and drink judgement to themselves.

Q98: What is prayer?

A98: Prayer is an offering up of our desires unto God for things agreeable to his will, in the name of Christ, with confession of our sins, and thankful acknowledgement of his mercies.

Q99: What rule hath God given for our direction in prayer?

A99: The whole Word of God is of use to direct us in prayer; but the special rule of direction is that form of prayer which Christ taught his disciples, commonly called The Lord's Prayer.

Q100: What doth the preface of the Lord's prayer teach us?

A100: The preface of the Lord's prayer, which is, "Our Father which art in heaven," teacheth us to draw near to God with all holy reverence and confidence, as children to a father, able and ready to help us; and that we should pray with and for others.

Q101: What do we pray for in the first petition?

A101: In the first petition, which is, "Hallowed be thy name," we pray, That God would enable us and others to glorify him in all that whereby he maketh himself known; and that he would dispose all things to his own glory.

Q102: What do we pray for in the second petition?

A102: In the second petition, which is, "Thy kingdom come," we pray, That Satan's kingdom may be destroyed; and that the kingdom of grace may be advanced, ourselves and others brought into it, and kept in it; and the kingdom of glory may be hastened.

Q103: What do we pray for in the third petition?

A103: In the third petition, which is, "Thy will be done in earth, as it is in heaven," we pray, That God, by his grace, would make us able and willing to know, obey, and submit to his will in all things, as the angels do in heaven.

Q104: What do we pray for in the fourth petition?

A104: In the fourth petition, which is, "Give us this day our daily bread," we pray, That of God's free gift we may receive a competent portion of the good things of this life, and enjoy his blessing with them.

Q105: What do we pray for in the fifth petition?

A105: In the fifth petition, which is, "And forgive us our debts, as we forgive our debtors," we pray, That God, for Christ's sake, would freely pardon all our sins; which we are able to be rather encouraged to ask, because by his grace we are enabled from the heart to forgive others.

Q106: What do we pray for in the sixth petition?

A106: In the sixth petition, which is, "And lead us not into temptation, but deliver us from evil," we pray, That God would either keep us from being tempted to sin, or support and deliver us when we are tempted.

Q107: What doth the conclusion the Lord's prayer teach us?

A107: The conclusion of the Lord's prayer, which is, "For thine is the kingdom, and the power, and the glory, for ever, Amen." teacheth us, to take our encouragement in prayer from God only, and in our prayers to praise him, ascribing kingdom, power and glory to him.

And, in testimony of our desire, and assurance to be heard, we say,
Amen.

POETRY: TEN FAVORITES FOR YOUNGER CHILDREN

THE CREATION
Cecil Frances Alexander
(1818-1895)

All things bright and beautiful,
    All creatures, great and small,
All things wise and wonderful,
    The Lord God made them all.

Each little flower that opens,
    Each little bird that sings,
He made their glowing colours,
    He made their tiny wings;

The rich man in his castle,
    The poor man at his gate,
God made them, high and lowly,
    And ordered their estate.

The purple-headed mountain,
    The river running by,
The sunset and the morning,
    That brightens up the sky;

The cold wind in the winter,
    The pleasant summer sun,
The ripe fruits in the garden—
    He made them every one.

The tall trees in the greenwood,
    The meadows where we play,
The rushes by the water
    We gather every day,—

He gave us eyes to see them,
    And lips that we might tell,
How great is God Almighty,
    Who has made all things well!

THE PILGRIM
John Bunyan
(1628-1688)

Who would true valour see
        Let him come hither;
One here will constant be,
        Come wind, come Weather.
There's no discouragement,
Shall make him once relent,
His first avow'd intent,
        To be a pilgrim,

Who so beset him round,
        With dismal stories,
Do but themselves confound;
        His strength the more is.
No Lion can him fright,
He'l with a giant fight,
But he will have a right,
        To be a pilgrim.

Hobgoblin, nor foul fiend,
        Can daunt his spirit;
He knows, he at the end,
        Shall life inherit.
Then fancies fly away,
He'l fear not what men say,
He'l labour night and day
        To be a Pilgrim.

LITTLE THINGS
Julia Abigail Fletcher
Carney (1823-1908)

Little drops of water,
        Little grains of sand,
Make the mighty ocean
        And the pleasant land.

So the little moments,
        Humble though they be,
Make the mighty ages
        Of Eternity.

So the little errors
        Lead the soul away
From the paths of virtue
        Far in sin to stray.

Little deeds of kindness,
  Little words of love,
Make our earth an Eden,
  Like the Heaven above.

DUTCH LULLABY
Eugene Field
(1850-1895)

Wynken, Blynken, and Nod one night
  Sailed off in a wooden shoe—
Sailed on a river of crystal light,
  Into a sea of dew.
  "Where are you going, and what do you wish?"
  The old moon asked of the three.
  "We have come to fish for the herring fish
  That live in this beautiful sea;
  Nets of silver and gold have we!"
      Said Wynken,
      Blynken,
      And Nod.

The old moon laughed and sang a song,
  As they rocked in the wooden shoe,
And the wind that sped them all night long
  Ruffled the waves of dew.
  The little stars were the herring fish
  That lived in that beautiful sea—
  "Now cast your nets wherever you wish—
  Never afeard are we!"
  So cried the stars to the fishermen three:
      Wynken,
      Blynken,
      And Nod.

All night long their nets they threw
  To the stars in the twinkling foam—
Then down from the skies came the wooden shoe,
  Bringing the fishermen home;
'T was all so pretty a sail it seemed
  As if it could not be,
And some folks thought 't was a dream they'd dreamed

Of sailing that beautiful sea—
But I shall name you the fishermen three:
    Wynken,
    Blynken,
    And Nod.

Wynken and Blynken are two little eyes,
    And Nod is a little head,
And the wooden shoe that sailed the skies
    Is a wee one's trundle-bed.
So shut your eyes while mother sings
    Of wonderful sights that be,
And you shall see the beautiful things
    As you rock in the misty sea,
    Where the old shoe rocked the fishermen three:
    Wynken,
    Blynken,
    And Nod.

THE PASTURE
Robert Frost
(1874-1963)

I'm going out to clean the pasture spring;
I'll only stop to rake the leaves away
(And wait to watch the water clear, I may):
I sha'n't be gone long.—You come too.

I'm going out to fetch the little calf
That's standing by the mother. It's so young,
It totters when she licks it with her tongue.
I sha'n't be gone long.—You come too.

CLOUDS
Christina Rossetti
(1830-1894)

White sheep, white sheep,
    On a blue hill,
When the wind stops,
You all stand still.
When the wind blows,
You walk away slow.
White sheep, white sheep,
Where do you go?

WHO HAS SEEN THE WIND?

Christina Rossetti
(1830-1894)

Who has seen the wind?
　Neither I nor you:
But when the leaves hang trembling,
　The wind is passing through.

Who has seen the wind?
　Neither you nor I:
But when the trees bow down their heads,
　The wind is passing by.

LULLABY OF AN INFANT CHIEF

Sir Walter Scott
(1771-1832)

O, hush thee, my babie, thy sire was a knight,
　Thy mother a lady, both lovely and bright;
The woods and the glens, from the towers which we see,
They are all belonging, dear babie, to thee.
　　　O ho ro, i ri ri, cadul gu lo.

O, fear not the bugle, though loudly it blows,
It calls but the warders that guard thy repose;
Their bows would be bended, their blades would be red,
Ere the step of a foeman draws near to thy bed.
　　　O ho ro, i ri ri, cadul gu lo.

O, hush thee, my babie, the time soon will come,
When thy sleep shall be broken by trumpet and drum;
Then hush thee, my darling, take rest while you may,
For strife comes with manhood, and waking with day.
　　　O ho ro, i ri ri, cadul gu lo.

BED IN SUMMER

Robert Louis Stevenson
(1850-1894)

In winter I get up at night
And dress by yellow candle-light.
In summer, quite the other way,
I have to go to bed by day.

I have to go to bed and see
The birds still hopping on the tree,
Or hear the grown-up people's feet
Still going past me in the street.

And does it not seem hard to you,
When all the sky is clear and blue,
And I should like so much to play,
To have to go to bed by day?

WHETHER THE WEATHER

Anonymous

Whether the weather be fine
Or whether the weather be not,
Whether the weather be cold
Or whether the weather be hot,
We'll weather the weather
Whatever the weather,
Whether we like it or not.

POETRY: FAVORITES FOR MIDDLE SCHOOL AND UP

BE STRONG

Maltbie D. Babcock

(1858-1901)

Be strong!
We are not here to play, to dream, to drift;
We have hard work to do and loads to lift;
Shun not the struggle, face it, 'tis God's gift.

Be strong!
Say not the days are evil—who's to blame?
And fold the hands and acquiesce—O shame!
Stand up, speak out, and bravely, in God's Name.

Be strong!
It matters not how deep intrenched the wrong,
How hard the battle goes, the day, how long;
Faint not, fight on! Tomorrow comes the song. Amen.

THE TYGER

William Blake

(1757-1827)

Tyger Tyger, burning bright,
In the forests of the night;
What immortal hand or eye,
Could frame thy fearful symmetry?

In what distant deeps or skies.
Burnt the fire of thine eyes?
On what wings dare he aspire?
What the hand, dare seize the fire?

And what shoulder, & what art,
Could twist the sinews of thy heart?
And when thy heart began to beat,
What dread hand? & what dread feet?

What the hammer? what the chain,
In what furnace was thy brain?
What the anvil? what dread grasp,
Dare its deadly terrors clasp!

When the stars threw down their spears
And water'd heaven with their tears:
Did he smile his work to see?
Did he who made the Lamb make thee?

Tyger Tyger burning bright,
In the forests of the night:
What immortal hand or eye,
Dare frame thy fearful symmetry?

THE LAMB
William Blake
(1757-1827)

Little Lamb who made thee
    Dost thou know who made thee
Gave thee life & bid thee feed.
By the stream & o'er the mead;
Gave thee clothing of delight,
Softest clothing wooly bright;
Gave thee such a tender voice,
Making all the vales rejoice!
    Little Lamb who made thee
    Dost thou know who made thee

    Little Lamb I'll tell thee,
    Little Lamb I'll tell thee!
He is called by thy name,
For he calls himself a Lamb:
He is meek & he is mild,
He became a little child:
I a child & thou a lamb,
We are called by his name.
    Little Lamb God bless thee.
    Little Lamb God bless thee.

SONNET 43, "HOW DO I LOVE THEE?"

Elizabeth Barrett Browning (1806-1861)

How do I love thee? Let me count the ways.
I love thee to the depth and breadth and height
My soul can reach, when feeling out of sight
For the ends of being and ideal grace.
I love thee to the level of every day's
Most quiet need, by sun and candle-light.
I love thee freely, as men strive for right;
I love thee purely, as they turn from praise.
I love thee with the passion put to use
In my old griefs, and with my childhood's faith.
I love thee with a love I seemed to lose
With my lost saints. I love thee with the breath,
Smiles, tears, of all my life; and, if God choose,
I shall but love thee better after death.

OUT IN THE FIELDS WITH GOD

Louise Imogen Guiney (1861-1920)

The little cares which fretted me,
I lost them yesterday
Among the fields, above the sea,
Among the winds at play;
Among the lowing of the herds,
The rustling of the trees,
Among the singing of the birds,
The humming of the bees.

The foolish fears of what may come,
I cast them all away
Among the clover-scented grass,
Among the new-mown hay;
Among the hushing of the corn,
Where drowsing poppies nod.
Ill thoughts can die, and good be born,
Out in the fields of God.

TO A MOUSE

Robert Burns
(1759-1796)

Wee, sleeket, cowran, tim'rous beastie,
O, what a panic's in thy breastie!
Thou need na start awa sae hasty,
Wi' bickerin brattle!
I wad be laith to rin an' chase thee
Wi' murd'ring pattle!

I'm truly sorry Man's dominion
Has broken Nature's social union,
An' justifies that ill opinion,
Which makes thee startle,
At me, thy poor, earth-born companion,
An' fellow-mortal!

I doubt na, whyles, but thou may thieve;
What then? poor beastie, thou maun live!
A daimen-icker in a thrave
'S a sma' request:
I'll get a blessin wi' the lave,
An' never miss 't!

Thy wee-bit housie, too, in ruin!
It's silly wa's the win's are strewin!
An' naething, now, to big a new ane,
O' foggage green!
An' bleak December's winds ensuin,
Baith snell an' keen!

Thou saw the fields laid bare an' waste,
An' weary Winter comin fast,
An' cozie here, beneath the blast,
Thou thought to dwell,
Till crash! the cruel coulter past
Out thro' thy cell.

That wee-bit heap o' leaves an' stibble
Has cost thee monie a weary nibble!
Now thou's turn'd out, for a' thy trouble,
But house or hald,
To thole the Winter's sleety dribble,
An' cranreuch cauld!

But Mousie, thou art no thy-lane,
In proving foresight may be vain:
The best laid schemes o' Mice an' Men
    Gang aft agley,
An' lea'e us nought but grief an' pain,
    For promis'd joy!

Still, thou art blest, compar'd wi' me!
The present only toucheth thee:
But Och! I backward cast my e'e,
    On prospects drear!
An' forward tho' I canna see,
    I guess an' fear!

A RED, RED ROSE

Robert Burns
(1759–1796)

O my Luve is like a red, red rose
    That's newly sprung in June;
O my Luve is like the melody
    That's sweetly played in tune.

So fair art thou, my bonnie lass,
    So deep in luve am I;
And I will luve thee still, my dear,
    Till a' the seas gang dry.

Till a' the seas gang dry, my dear,
    And the rocks melt wi' the sun;
I will love thee still, my dear,
    While the sands o' life shall run.

And fare thee weel, my only luve!
    And fare thee weel awhile!
And I will come again, my luve,
    Though it were ten thousand mile.

THE DESTRUCTION OF SENNACHERIB

George Gordon, Lord Byron, (1788-1824)

The Assyrian came down like the wolf on the fold,
And his cohorts were gleaming in purple and gold;
And the sheen of their spears was like stars on the sea,
When the blue wave rolls nightly on deep Galilee.

Like the leaves of the forest when Summer is green,
That host with their banners at sunset were seen:
Like the leaves of the forest when Autumn hath blown,
That host on the morrow lay withered and strown.

For the Angel of Death spread his wings on the blast,
And breathed in the face of the foe as he passed;
And the eyes of the sleepers waxed deadly and chill,
And their hearts but once heaved, and for ever grew still!

And there lay the steed with his nostril all wide,
But through it there rolled not the breath of his pride;
And the foam of his gasping lay white on the turf,
And cold as the spray of the rock-beating surf.

And there lay the rider distorted and pale,
With the dew on his brow, and the rust on his mail:
And the tents were all silent, the banners alone,
The lances unlifted, the trumpet unblown.

And the widows of Ashur are loud in their wail,
And the idols are broke in the temple of Baal;
And the might of the Gentile, unsmote by the sword,
Hath melted like snow in the glance of the Lord!

JABBERWOCKY

Lewis Carroll
(1832–1898)

'Twas brillig, and the slithy toves
Did gyre and gimble in the wabe:
All mimsy were the borogoves,
And the mome raths outgrabe.

"Beware the Jabberwock, my son!
The jaws that bite, the claws that catch!
Beware the Jubjub bird, and shun
The frumious Bandersnatch!"

He took his vorpal sword in hand;
    Long time the manxome foe he sought—
So rested he by the Tumtum tree
    And stood awhile in thought.

And, as in uffish thought he stood,
    The Jabberwock, with eyes of flame,
Came whiffling through the tulgey wood,
    And burbled as it came!

One, two! One, two! And through and through
    The vorpal blade went snicker-snack!
He left it dead, and with its head
    He went galumphing back.

"And hast thou slain the Jabberwock?
    Come to my arms, my beamish boy!
O frabjous day! Callooh! Callay!"
    He chortled in his joy.

'Twas brillig, and the slithy toves
    Did gyre and gimble in the wabe:
All mimsy were the borogoves,
    And the mome raths outgrabe.

NOBILITY

Alice Cary
(1820–1871)

True worth is in *being*, not seeming,—
    In doing, each day that goes by,
Some little good—not in dreaming
    Of great things to do by and by.
For whatever men say in their blindness,
    And spite of the fancies of youth,
There's nothing so kingly as kindness,
    And nothing so royal as truth.

We get back our mete as we measure—
    We cannot do wrong and feel right,
Nor can we give pain and gain pleasure,
    For justice avenges each slight.
The air for the wing of the sparrow,
    The bush for the robin and wren,
But always the path that is narrow
    And straight, for the children of men.

'Tis not in the pages of story
    The heart of its ills to beguile,
Though he who makes courtship to glory
    Gives all that he hath for her smile.
For when from her heights he has won her,
    Alas! it is only to prove
That nothing's so sacred as honor,
    And nothing so loyal as love!

We cannot make bargains for blisses,
    Nor catch them like fishes in nets;
And sometimes the thing our life misses
    Helps more than the thing which it gets.
For good lieth not in pursuing,
    Nor gaining of great nor of small,
But just in the doing, and doing
    As we would be done by, is all.

Through envy, through malice, through hating,
    Against the world, early and late,
No jot of our courage abating—
    Our part is to work and to wait
And slight is the sting of his trouble
    Whose winnings are less than his worth.
For he who is honest is noble
    Whatever his fortunes or birth.

THE NEW-ENGLAND BOY'S SONG ABOUT THANKSGIVING DAY

Lydia Maria Child
(1802-1880)

Over the river, and through the wood,
    To grandfather's house we go;
      The horse knows the way,
      To carry the sleigh,
    Through the white and drifted snow.

Over the river, and through the wood,
    To grandfather's house away!
      We would not stop
      For doll or top,
    For 't is Thanksgiving day.

Over the river, and through the wood,
Oh, how the wind does blow!
It stings the toes,
And bites the nose,
As over the ground we go.

Over the river, and through the wood,
With a clear blue winter sky,
The dogs do bark,
And children hark,
As we go jingling by.

Over the river, and through the wood,
To have a first-rate play—
Hear the bells ring
Ting a ling ding,
Hurra for Thanksgiving day!

Over the river, and through the wood—
No matter for winds that blow;
Or if we get
The sleigh upset,
Into a bank of snow.

Over the river, and through the wood,
To see little John and Ann;
We will kiss them all,
And play snow-ball,
And stay as long as we can.

Over the river, and through the wood,
Trot fast, my dapple grey!
Spring over the ground,
Like a hunting hound,
For 't is Thanksgiving day!

Over the river, and through the wood,
And straight through the barn-yard gate;
We seem to go
Extremely slow,
It is so hard to wait.

Over the river, and through the wood,
 Old Jowler hears our bells;
  He shakes his pow,
  With a loud bow wow,
 And thus the news he tells.

Over the river, and through the wood—
 When grandmother sees us come,
  She will say, Oh dear,
  The children are here,
 Bring a pie for every one.

Over the river, and through the wood—
 Now grandmother's cap I spy!
  Hurra for the fun!
  Is the pudding done?
 Hurra for the pumpkin pie!

KUBLA KHAN

Samuel Taylor
Coleridge (1772–1834)
Or, a vision in a dream.
A Fragment.

In Xanadu did Kubla Khan
 A stately pleasure-dome decree:
  Where Alph, the sacred river, ran
  Through caverns measureless to man
   Down to a sunless sea.
  So twice five miles of fertile ground
  With walls and towers were girdled round;
And there were gardens bright with sinuous rills,
Where blossomed many an incense-bearing tree;
And here were forests ancient as the hills,
Enfolding sunny spots of greenery.

But oh! that deep romantic chasm which slanted
Down the green hill athwart a cedarn cover!
A savage place! as holy and enchanted
As e'er beneath a waning moon was haunted
By woman wailing for her demon-lover!
And from this chasm, with ceaseless turmoil seething,
As if this earth in fast thick pants were breathing,
A mighty fountain momently was forced:
Amid whose swift half-intermitted burst
Huge fragments vaulted like rebounding hail,

Or chaffy grain beneath the thresher's flail:
And mid these dancing rocks at once and ever
It flung up momently the sacred river.
Five miles meandering with a mazy motion
Through wood and dale the sacred river ran,
Then reached the caverns measureless to man,
And sank in tumult to a lifeless ocean;
And 'mid this tumult Kubla heard from far
Ancestral voices prophesying war!
   The shadow of the dome of pleasure
      Floated midway on the waves;
   Where was heard the mingled measure
      From the fountain and the caves.
It was a miracle of rare device,
A sunny pleasure-dome with caves of ice!

   A damsel with a dulcimer
      In a vision once I saw:
   It was an Abyssinian maid
      And on her dulcimer she played,
   Singing of Mount Abora.
   Could I revive within me
      Her symphony and song,
To such a deep delight 'twould win me,
That with music loud and long,
I would build that dome in air,
That sunny dome! those caves of ice!
And all who heard should see them there,
And all should cry, Beware! Beware!
His flashing eyes, his floating hair!
Weave a circle round him thrice,
   And close your eyes with holy dread
   For he on honey-dew hath fed,
And drunk the milk of Paradise.

HOW DID YOU DIE?

Edmund Vance Cooke
(1866-1932)

Did you tackle that trouble that came your way
    With a resolute heart and cheerful?
Or hide your face from the light of day
    With a craven soul and fearful?
Oh, a trouble's a ton, or a trouble's an ounce,
    Or a trouble is what you make it,
And it isn't the fact that you're hurt that counts,
    But only how did you take it?

You are beaten to earth? Well, well, what's that?
    Come up with a smiling face.
It's nothing against you to fall down flat,
    But to lie there—that's disgrace.
The harder you're thrown, why the higher you bounce;
    Be proud of your blackened eye!
It isn't the fact that you're licked that counts,
    It's how did you fight—and why?

And though you be done to the death, what then?
    If you battled the best you could,
If you played your part in the world of men,
    Why, the Critic will call it good.
Death comes with a crawl, or comes with a pounce,
    And whether he's slow or spry,
It isn't the fact that you're dead that counts,
    But only how did you die?

THE LISTENERS

Walter de la Mare
(1873–1956)

'Is there anybody there?' said the Traveller,
    Knocking on the moonlit door;
And his horse in the silence champed the grasses
    Of the forest's ferny floor:
And a bird flew up out of the turret,
    Above the Traveller's head:
And he smote upon the door again a second time;
    'Is there anybody there?' he said.
But no one descended to the Traveller;
    No head from the leaf-fringed sill
Leaned over and looked into his grey eyes,
    Where he stood perplexed and still.

But only a host of phantom listeners
    That dwelt in the lone house then
Stood listening in the quiet of the moonlight
    To that voice from the world of men:
Stood thronging the faint moonbeams on the dark stair,
    That goes down to the empty hall,
Hearkening in an air stirred and shaken
    By the lonely Traveller's call.
And he felt in his heart their strangeness,
    Their stillness answering his cry,
While his horse moved, cropping the dark turf,
    'Neath the starred and leafy sky;
For he suddenly smote on the door, even
    Louder, and lifted his head:—
'Tell them I came, and no one answered,
    That I kept my word,' he said.
Never the least stir made the listeners,
    Though every word he spake
Fell echoing through the shadowiness of the still house
    From the one man left awake:
Ay, they heard his foot upon the stirrup,
    And the sound of iron on stone,
And how the silence surged softly backward,
    When the plunging hoofs were gone.

THERE IS NO FRIGATE LIKE A BOOK

Emily Dickinson
(1830–1886)

There is no frigate like a book
    To take us lands away,
Nor any coursers like a page
    Of prancing poetry.

This traverse may the poorest take
    Without oppress of toll;
How frugal is the chariot
    That bears a human soul!

"HOPE" IS THE THING WITH FEATHERS

Emily Dickinson
(1830–1886)

"Hope" is the thing with feathers
That perches in the soul,
And sings the tune without the words,
And never stops at all,

And sweetest in the gale is heard;
And sore must be the storm
That could abash the little bird
That kept so many warm.

I've heard it in the chillest land,
And on the strangest sea;
Yet, never, in extremity,
It asked a crumb of me.

SONNET X, "DEATH, BE NOT PROUD"

John Donne
(1572–1631)

Death, be not proud, though some have called thee
Mighty and dreadful, for thou art not so:
For those whom thou think'st thou dost overthrow
Die not, poor Death, nor yet canst thou kill me.
From rest and sleep, which but thy pictures be,
Much pleasure; then from thee much more must flow;
And soonest our best men with thee do go—
Rest of their bones, and soul's delivery!
Thou art slave to fate, chance, kings, and desperate men,
And dost with poison, war, and sickness dwell;
And poppy or charms can make us sleep as well
And better than thy stroke; why swell'st thou then?
One short sleep past, we wake eternally,
And death shall be no more; Death, thou shalt die.

MENDING WALL

Robert Frost
(1874-1963)

Something there is that doesn't love a wall,
That sends the frozen-ground-swell under it,
And spills the upper boulders in the sun;
And makes gaps even two can pass abreast.
The work of hunters is another thing:
I have come after them and made repair
Where they have left not one stone on a stone,
But they would have the rabbit out of hiding,
To please the yelping dogs. The gaps I mean,
No one has seen them made or heard them made,

But at spring mending-time we find them there.
I let my neighbour know beyond the hill;
And on a day we meet to walk the line
And set the wall between us once again.
We keep the wall between us as we go.
To each the boulders that have fallen to each.
And some are loaves and some so nearly balls
We have to use a spell to make them balance:
"Stay where you are until our backs are turned!"
We wear our fingers rough with handling them.
Oh, just another kind of out-door game,
One on a side. It comes to little more:
There where it is we do not need the wall:
He is all pine and I am apple orchard.
My apple trees will never get across
And eat the cones under his pines, I tell him.
He only says, "Good fences make good neighbours."
Spring is the mischief in me, and I wonder
If I could put a notion in his head:
"Why do they make good neighbours? Isn't it
Where there are cows? But here there are no cows.
Before I built a wall I'd ask to know
What I was walling in or walling out,
And to whom I was like to give offense.
Something there is that doesn't love a wall,
That wants it down." I could say "Elves" to him,
But it's not elves exactly, and I'd rather
He said it for himself. I see him there
Bringing a stone grasped firmly by the top
In each hand, like an old-stone savage armed.
He moves in darkness as it seems to me,
Not of woods only and the shade of trees.
He will not go behind his father's saying,
And he likes having thought of it so well
He says again, "Good fences make good neighbours."

THE ROAD NOT TAKEN

Robert Frost
(1874-1963)

Two roads diverged in a yellow wood,
And sorry I could not travel both
And be one traveler, long I stood
And looked down one as far as I could
To where it bent in the undergrowth;

Then took the other, as just as fair,
And having perhaps the better claim,
Because it was grassy and wanted wear;
Though as for that the passing there
Had worn them really about the same,

And both that morning equally lay
In leaves no step had trodden black.
Oh, I kept the first for another day!
Yet knowing how way leads on to way,
I doubted if I should ever come back.

I shall be telling this with a sigh
Somewhere ages and ages hence:
Two roads diverged in a wood, and I—
I took the one less traveled by,
And that has made all the difference.

STOPPING BY WOODS ON A SNOWY EVENING

Robert Frost
(1874-1963)

Whose woods these are I think I know.
His house is in the village though;
He will not see me stopping here
To watch his woods fill up with snow.

My little horse must think it queer
To stop without a farmhouse near
Between the woods and frozen lake
The darkest evening of the year.

He gives his harness bells a shake
To ask if there is some mistake.
The only other sound's the sweep
Of easy wind and downy flake.

The woods are lovely, dark and deep,
But I have promises to keep,
And miles to go before I sleep,
And miles to go before I sleep.

MODERN MAJOR-GENERAL'S SONG

W. S. Gilbert
(1836-1911)
From *The Pirates of Penzance* an 1879 musical by Gilbert (lyrics) and Sullivan (music)

I am the very model of a modern Major-General,
I've information vegetable, animal, and mineral,
I know the kings of England, and I quote the fights historical
From Marathon to Waterloo, in order categorical;
I'm very well acquainted, too, with matters mathematical,
I understand equations, both the simple and quadratical,
About binomial theorem I'm teeming with a lot o' news,
With many cheerful facts about the square of the hypotenuse!

I'm very good at integral and differential calculus;
I know the scientific names of beings animalculous:
In short, in matters vegetable, animal, and mineral,
I am the very model of a modern Major-General!

I know our mythic history, King Arthur's and Sir Caradoc's;
I answer hard acrostics, I've a pretty taste for paradox,
I quote in elegiacs all the crimes of Heliogabalus,
In conics I can floor peculiarities parabolous;
I can tell undoubted Raphaels from Gerard Dows and Zoffanies,
I know the croaking chorus from "The Frogs" of Aristophanes!
Then I can hum a fugue of which I've heard the music's din afore,
And whistle all the airs from that infernal nonsense *Pinafore*.

Then I can write a washing bill in Babylonic cuneiform,
And tell you ev'ry detail of Caractacus's uniform:
In short, in matters vegetable, animal, and mineral,
I am the very model of a modern Major-General!

In fact, when I know what is meant by "mamelon" and "ravelin",
When I can tell at sight a Mauser rifle from a javelin,
When such affairs as sorties and surprises I'm more wary at,
And when I know precisely what is meant by "commissariat",
When I have learnt what progress has been made in modern gunnery,
When I know more of tactics than a novice in a nunnery—
In short, when I've a smattering of elemental strategy—
You'll say a better Major-General has never *sat agee*.

For my military knowledge, though I'm plucky and adventury,
Has only been brought down to the beginning of the century;
But still, in matters vegetable, animal, and mineral,
I am the very model of a modern Major-General.

WEATHERS

Thomas Hardy
(1840-1948)

This is the weather the cuckoo likes,
  And so do I;
When showers betumble the chestnut spikes,
  And nestlings fly;
And the little brown nightingale bills his best,
And they sit outside at "The Travellers' Rest,"
And maids come forth sprig-muslin drest,
And citizens dream of the south and west,
  And so do I.

II
This is the weather the shepherd shuns,
  And so do I;
When beeches drip in browns and duns,
  And thresh, and ply;
And hill-hid tides throb, throe on throe,
And meadow rivulets overflow,
And drops on gate-bars hang in a row,
And rooks in families homeward go,
  And so do I.

EASTER WINGS
George Herbert
(1593–1633)

Lord, who createdst man in wealth and store,
  Though foolishly he lost the same,
    Decaying more and more,
      Till he became
        Most poore:
        With thee
      O let me rise
    As larks, harmoniously,
  And sing this day thy victories:
Then shall the fall further the flight in me.

My tender age in sorrow did beginne
  And still with sicknesses and shame.
    Thou didst so punish sinne,
      That I became
        Most thinne.
        With thee
      Let me combine,
    And feel thy victorie:
  For, if I imp my wing on thine,
Affliction shall advance the flight in me.

EASTER
Gerard Manley Hopkins
(1844–1889)

Break the box and shed the nard;
  Stop not now to count the cost;
Hither bring pearl, opal, sard;
  Reck not what the poor have lost;
Upon Christ throw all away:
  Know ye, this is Easter Day.

  Build His church and deck His shrine,
Empty though it be on earth;
  Ye have kept your choicest wine—
Let it flow for heavenly mirth;
  Pluck the harp and breathe the horn:
Know ye not 'tis Easter morn?

  Gather gladness from the skies;
Take a lesson from the ground;
  Flowers do ope their heavenward eyes
And a Spring-time joy have found;
  Earth throws Winter's robes away,
Decks herself for Easter Day.

Beauty now for ashes wear,
Perfumes for the garb of woe,
Chaplets for dishevelled hair,
Dances for sad footsteps slow;
Open wide your hearts that they
Let in joy this Easter Day.

    Seek God's house in happy throng;
Crowded let His table be;
Mingle praises, prayer, and song,
Singing to the Trinity.
Henceforth let your souls always
Make each morn an Easter Day.

GOD'S GRANDEUR
Gerard Manley Hopkins
(1844–1889)

The world is charged with the grandeur of God.
  It will flame out, like shining from shook foil;
  It gathers to a greatness, like the ooze of oil
Crushed. Why do men then now not reck his rod?
Generations have trod, have trod, have trod;
  And all is seared with trade; bleared, smeared with toil;
  And wears man's smudge and shares man's smell: the soil
Is bare now, nor can foot feel, being shod.

And for all this, nature is never spent;
  There lives the dearest freshness deep down things;
And though the last lights off the black West went
  Oh, morning, at the brown brink eastward, springs —
Because the Holy Ghost over the bent
  World broods with warm breast and with ah! bright wings.

PIED BEAUTY
Gerard Manley Hopkins
(1844–1889)

Glory be to God for dappled things—
  For skies of couple-colour as a brinded cow;
    For rose-moles all in stipple upon trout that swim;
Fresh-firecoal chestnut-falls; finches' wings;
    Landscape plotted and pieced—fold, fallow, and plough;
    And áll trádes, their gear and tackle and trim.

All things counter, original, spare, strange;
  Whatever is fickle, freckled (who knows how?)
    With swift, slow; sweet, sour; adazzle, dim;
He fathers-forth whose beauty is past change:
    Praise him.

TREES
Joyce Kilmer
(1886-1894)

I think that I shall never see
A poem lovely as a tree.

A tree whose hungry mouth is prest
Against the earth's sweet flowing breast;

A tree that looks at God all day,
And lifts her leafy arms to pray;

A tree that may in Summer wear
A nest of robins in her hair;

Upon whose bosom snow has lain;
Who intimately lives with rain.

Poems are made by fools like me,
But only God can make a tree.

IF—
Rudyard Kipling
(1865-1936)

If you can keep your head when all about you
   Are losing theirs and blaming it on you,
If you can trust yourself when all men doubt you,
   But make allowance for their doubting too;
If you can wait and not be tired by waiting,
   Or being lied about, don't deal in lies,
Or being hated, don't give way to hating,
   And yet don't look too good, nor talk too wise:

If you can dream—and not make dreams your master;
   If you can think—and not make thoughts your aim;
If you can meet with Triumph and Disaster
   And treat those two impostors just the same;
If you can bear to hear the truth you've spoken
   Twisted by knaves to make a trap for fools,
Or watch the things you gave your life to, broken,
   And stoop and build 'em up with worn-out tools:

If you can make one heap of all your winnings
   And risk it on one turn of pitch-and-toss,
And lose, and start again at your beginnings
   And never breathe a word about your loss;
If you can force your heart and nerve and sinew
   To serve your turn long after they are gone,
And so hold on when there is nothing in you
   Except the Will which says to them: 'Hold on!'

If you can talk with crowds and keep your virtue,
　　Or walk with Kings—nor lose the common touch,
If neither foes nor loving friends can hurt you,
　　If all men count with you, but none too much;
If you can fill the unforgiving minute
　　With sixty seconds' worth of distance run,
Yours is the Earth and everything that's in it,
　　And—which is more—you'll be a Man, my son!

RECESSIONAL

Rudyard Kipling
(1865-1936)

God of our fathers, known of old,
　　Lord of our far-flung battle-line,
Beneath whose awful Hand we hold
　　Dominion over palm and pine—
Lord God of Hosts, be with us yet,
Lest we forget—lest we forget!

The tumult and the shouting dies;
　　The Captains and the Kings depart:
Still stands Thine ancient sacrifice,
　　An humble and a contrite heart.
Lord God of Hosts, be with us yet,
Lest we forget—lest we forget!

Far-called, our navies melt away;
　　On dune and headland sinks the fire:
Lo, all our pomp of yesterday
　　Is one with Nineveh and Tyre!
Judge of the Nations, spare us yet,
Lest we forget—lest we forget!

If, drunk with sight of power, we loose
　　Wild tongues that have not Thee in awe,
Such boastings as the Gentiles use,
　　Or lesser breeds without the Law—
Lord God of Hosts, be with us yet,
Lest we forget—lest we forget!

For heathen heart that puts her trust
   In reeking tube and iron shard,
All valiant dust that builds on dust,
   And guarding, calls not Thee to guard,
For frantic boast and foolish word—
Thy mercy on Thy People, Lord!

THE NEW COLOSSUS
Emma Lazarus
(1849-1887)

Not like the brazen giant of Greek fame,
   With conquering limbs astride from land to land,
   Here at our sea-washed, sunset gates shall stand
A mighty woman with a torch, whose flame
Is the imprisoned lightning, and her name
   Mother of Exiles. From her beacon-hand
   Glows world-wide welcome; her mild eyes command
The air-bridged harbor that twin cities frame.

"Keep, ancient lands, your storied pomp!" cries she
   With silent lips. "Give me your tired, your poor,
Your huddled masses yearning to breathe free,
   The wretched refuse of your teeming shore.
Send these, the homeless, tempest-tost to me,
   I lift my lamp beside the golden door!"

THE ARROW AND THE SONG
Henry Wadsworth
Longfellow (1807-1882)

I shot an arrow into the air,
   It fell to earth, I knew not where;
For, so swiftly it flew, the sight
Could not follow it in its flight.

I breathed a song into the air,
It fell to earth, I knew not where;
For who has sight so keen and strong,
That it can follow the flight of song?

Long, long afterward, in an oak
I found the arrow, still unbroke;
And the song, from beginning to end,
I found again in the heart of a friend.

PAUL REVERE'S RIDE

Henry Wadsworth
Longfellow (1807-1882)

Listen, my children, and you shall hear
Of the midnight ride of Paul Revere,
On the eighteenth of April, in Seventy-five;
Hardly a man is now alive
Who remembers that famous day and year.

He said to his friend, "If the British march
    By land or sea from the town to-night,
Hang a lantern aloft in the belfry arch
    Of the North Church tower as a signal light,—
One, if by land, and two, if by sea;
And I on the opposite shore will be,
Ready to ride and spread the alarm
Through every Middlesex village and farm,
For the country folk to be up and to arm."

Then he said, "Good night!" and with muffled oar
Silently rowed to the Charlestown shore,
Just as the moon rose over the bay,
Where swinging wide at her moorings lay
The Somerset, British man-of-war;
A phantom ship, with each mast and spar
Across the moon like a prison bar,
And a huge black hulk, that was magnified
By its own reflection in the tide.

Meanwhile, his friend, through alley and street,
    Wanders and watches with eager ears,
    Till in the silence around him he hears
        The muster of men at the barrack door,
The sound of arms, and the tramp of feet,
    And the measured tread of the grenadiers,
        Marching down to their boats on the shore.

Then he climbed the tower of the Old North Church,
    By the wooden stairs, with stealthy tread,
    To the belfry-chamber overhead,
And startled the pigeons from their perch
On the sombre rafters, that round him made
Masses and moving shapes of shade,—
By the trembling ladder, steep and tall,
To the highest window in the wall,

Where he paused to listen and look down
A moment on the roofs of the town,
And the moonlight flowing over all.

Beneath, in the churchyard, lay the dead,
  In their night-encampment on the hill,
  Wrapped in silence so deep and still
That he could hear, like a sentinel's tread,
The watchful night-wind, as it went
Creeping along from tent to tent,
  And seeming to whisper, "All is well!"
  A moment only he feels the spell
Of the place and the hour, and the secret dread
Of the lonely belfry and the dead;
For suddenly all his thoughts are bent
On a shadowy something far away,
Where the river widens to meet the bay,—
A line of black that bends and floats
On the rising tide, like a bridge of boats.

Meanwhile, impatient to mount and ride,
Booted and spurred, with a heavy stride
  On the opposite shore walked Paul Revere.
Now he patted his horse's side,
  Now gazed at the landscape far and near,
Then, impetuous, stamped the earth,
And turned and tightened his saddle girth;
But mostly he watched with eager search
The belfry-tower of the Old North Church,
As it rose above the graves on the hill,
Lonely and spectral and sombre and still.
And lo! as he looks, on the belfry's height
A glimmer, and then a gleam of light!
He springs to the saddle, the bridle he turns,
But lingers and gazes, till full on his sight
A second lamp in the belfry burns.

A hurry of hoofs in a village street,
  A shape in the moonlight, a bulk in the dark,
  And beneath, from the pebbles, in passing, a spark
Struck out by a steed flying fearless and fleet:
  That was all! And yet, through the gloom and the light,

The fate of a nation was riding that night;
And the spark struck out by that steed, in his flight,
Kindled the land into flame with its heat.
He has left the village and mounted the steep,
And beneath him, tranquil and broad and deep,
Is the Mystic, meeting the ocean tides;
And under the alders, that skirt its edge,
Now soft on the sand, now loud on the ledge,
Is heard the tramp of his steed as he rides.

It was twelve by the village clock,
When he crossed the bridge into Medford town.
He heard the crowing of the cock,
And the barking of the farmer's dog,
And felt the damp of the river fog,
That rises after the sun goes down.

It was one by the village clock,
When he galloped into Lexington.
He saw the gilded weathercock
Swim in the moonlight as he passed,
And the meeting-house windows, blank and bare,
Gaze at him with a spectral glare,
As if they already stood aghast
At the bloody work they would look upon.

It was two by the village clock,
When he came to the bridge in Concord town.
He heard the bleating of the flock,
And the twitter of birds among the trees,
And felt the breath of the morning breeze
Blowing over the meadows brown.
And one was safe and asleep in his bed
Who at the bridge would be first to fall,
Who that day would be lying dead,
Pierced by a British musket-ball.

You know the rest. In the books you have read,
How the British Regulars fired and fled,—
How the farmers gave them ball for ball,
From behind each fence and farm-yard wall,

Chasing the red-coats down the lane,
Then crossing the fields to emerge again
Under the trees at the turn of the road,
And only pausing to fire and load.

So through the night rode Paul Revere;
    And so through the night went his cry of alarm
To every Middlesex village and farm,—
A cry of defiance and not of fear,
A voice in the darkness, a knock at the door,
And a word that shall echo forevermore!
For, borne on the night-wind of the Past,
Through all our history, to the last,
In the hour of darkness and peril and need,
    The people will waken and listen to hear
The hurrying hoof-beats of that steed,
    And the midnight message of Paul Revere.

THE VILLAGE BLACKSMITH

Henry Wadsworth
Longfellow (1807-1882)

Under a spreading chestnut tree
    The village smithy stands;
The smith, a mighty man is he,
    With large and sinewy hands;
And the muscles of his brawny arms
    Are strong as iron bands.

His hair is crisp, and black, and long,
    His face is like the tan;
His brow is wet with honest sweat,
    He earns whate'er he can,
And looks the whole world in the face,
    For he owes not any man.

Week in, week out, from morn till night,
    You can hear his bellows blow;
You can hear him swing his heavy sledge
    With measured beat and slow,
Like a sexton ringing the village bell,
    When the evening sun is low.

And children coming home from school
    Look in at the open door;
They love to see the flaming forge,
    And hear the bellows roar,
And watch the burning sparks that fly
    Like chaff from a threshing-floor.

He goes on Sunday to the church,
    And sits among his boys;
He hears the parson pray and preach,
    He hears his daughter's voice,
Singing in the village choir,
    And it makes his heart rejoice.

It sounds to him like her mother's voice,
    Singing in Paradise!
He needs must think of her once more,
    How in the grave she lies;
And with his hard, rough hand he wipes
    A tear out of his eyes.

Toiling,—rejoicing,—sorrowing,
    Onward through life he goes;
Each morning sees some task begin,
    Each evening sees it close;
Something attempted, something done,
    Has earned a night's repose.

Thanks, thanks to thee, my worthy friend,
    For the lesson thou hast taught!
Thus at the flaming forge of life
    Our fortunes must be wrought;
Thus on its sounding anvil shaped
    Each burning deed and thought!

HORATIUS AT THE BRIDGE

Thomas Babington,
Lord Macaulay
(1800-1859)

Lars Porsena of Clusium,
  By the Nine Gods he swore
That the great house of Tarquin
    Should suffer wrong no more.
By the Nine Gods he swore it,
    And named a trysting-day,
And bade his messengers ride forth,
    East and west and south and north,
To summon his array.

East and west and south and north
    The messengers ride fast,
And tower and town and cottage
    Have heard the trumpet's blast.
Shame on the false Etruscan
    Who lingers in his home,
When Porsena of Clusium
    Is on the march for Rome!

The horsemen and the footmen
    Are pouring in amain
From many a stately market-place,
    From many a fruitful plain,
From many a lonely hamlet,
    Which, hid by beech and pine,
Like an eagle's nest hangs on the crest
    Of purple Apennine:

From lordly Volaterræ,
    Where scowls the far-famed hold
Piled by the hands of giants
    For godlike kings of old;
From sea-girt Populonia,
    Whose sentinels descry
Sardinia's snowy mountain-tops
    Fringing the southern sky;

From the proud mart of Pisæ,
    Queen of the western waves,
Where ride Massilia's triremes,
    Heavy with fair-haired slaves;

From where sweet Clanis wanders
    Through corn and vines and flowers,
From where Cortona lifts to heaven
    Her diadem of towers.

Tall are the oaks whose acorns
    Drop in dark Auser's rill;
Fat are the stags that champ the boughs
    Of the Ciminian hill;
Beyond all streams, Clitumnus
    Is to the herdsman dear;
Best of all pools the fowler loves
    The great Volsinian mere.

But now no stroke of woodman
    Is heard by Auser's rill;
No hunter tracks the stag's green path
    Up the Ciminian hill;
Unwatched along Clitumnus
    Grazes the milk-white steer;
Unharmed the water-fowl may dip
    In the Volsinian mere.

The harvests of Arretium,
    This year, old men shall reap;
This year, young boys in Umbro
    Shall plunge the struggling sheep;
And in the vats of Luna,
    This year, the must shall foam
Round the white feet of laughing girls
    Whose sires have marched to Rome.

There be thirty chosen prophets,
    The wisest of the land,
Who always by Lars Porsena
    Both morn and evening stand.
Evening and morn the Thirty
    Have turned the verses o'er,
Traced from the right on linen white
    By mighty seers of yore;

MORNING TIME: A LITURGY OF LOVE

And with one voice the Thirty
    Have their glad answer given:
"Go forth, go forth, Lars Porsena,—
    Go forth, beloved of Heaven!
Go, and return in glory
    To Clusium's royal dome,
And hang round Nurscia's altars
    The golden shields of Rome!"

And now hath every city
    Sent up her tale of men;
The foot are fourscore thousand,
    The horse are thousands ten.
Before the gates of Sutrium
    Is met the great array;
A proud man was Lars Porsena
    Upon the trysting-day.

For all the Etruscan armies
    Were ranged beneath his eye,
And many a banished Roman,
    And many a stout ally;
And with a mighty following,
    To join the muster, came
The Tusculan Mamilius,
    Prince of the Latian name.

But by the yellow Tiber
    Was tumult and affright;
From all the spacious champaign
    To Rome men took their flight.
A mile around the city
    The throng stopped up the ways;
A fearful sight it was to see
    Through two long nights and days.

For aged folk on crutches,
    And women great with child,
And mothers, sobbing over babes
    That clung to them and smiled,
And sick men borne in litters

High on the necks of slaves,
  And troops of sunburned husbandmen
With reaping-hooks and staves,

And droves of mules and asses
  Laden with skins of wine,
And endless flocks of goats and sheep,
  And endless herds of kine,
And endless trains of wagons,
  That creaked beneath the weight
Of corn-sacks and of household goods,
  Choked every roaring gate.

Now, from the rock Tarpeian,
  Could the wan burghers spy
The line of blazing villages
  Red in the midnight sky.
The Fathers of the City,
  They sat all night and day,
For every hour some horseman came
  With tidings of dismay.

To eastward and to westward
  Have spread the Tuscan bands,
Nor house, nor fence, nor dovecote
  In Crustumerium stands.
Verbenna down to Ostia
  Hath wasted all the plain;
Astur hath stormed Janiculum,
  And the stout guards are slain.

I wis, in all the Senate
  There was no heart so bold
But sore it ached, and fast it beat,
  When that ill news was told.
Forthwith up rose the Consul,
  Up rose the Fathers all;
In haste they girded up their gowns,
  And hied them to the wall.

They held a council, standing
    Before the River-gate;
Short time was there, ye well may guess,
    For musing or debate.
Out spake the Consul roundly:
    "The bridge must straight go down;
For, since Janiculum is lost,
    Naught else can save the town."

Just then a scout came flying,
    All wild with haste and fear:
"To arms! to arms! Sir Consul,—
    Lars Porsena is here."
On the low hills to westward
    The Consul fixed his eye,
And saw the swarthy storm of dust
    Rise fast along the sky.

And nearer fast and nearer
    Doth the red whirlwind come;
And louder still, and still more loud,
    From underneath that rolling cloud,
Is heard the trumpets' war-note proud,
    The trampling and the hum.
And plainly and more plainly
    Now through the gloom appears,
Far to left and far to right,
    In broken gleams of dark-blue light,
The long array of helmets bright,
    The long array of spears.

And plainly and more plainly,
    Above that glimmering line,
Now might ye see the banners
    Of twelve fair cities shine;
But the banner of proud Clusium
    Was highest of them all,—
The terror of the Umbrian,
    The terror of the Gaul.

And plainly and more plainly
 Now might the burghers know,
By port and vest, by horse and crest,
 Each warlike Lucumo:
There Cilnius of Arretium
 On his fleet roan was seen;
And Astur of the fourfold shield,
 Girt with the brand none else may wield;
Tolumnius with the belt of gold,
 And dark Verbenna from the hold
By reedy Thrasymene.

Fast by the royal standard,
 O'erlooking all the war,
Lars Porsena of Clusium
 Sat in his ivory car.
By the right wheel rode Mamilius,
 Prince of the Latian name;
And by the left false Sextus,
 That wrought the deed of shame.

But when the face of Sextus
 Was seen among the foes,
A yell that rent the firmament
 From all the town arose.
On the house-tops was no woman
 But spat towards him and hissed,
No child but screamed out curses,
 And shook its little fist.

But the Consul's brow was sad,
 And the Consul's speech was low,
And darkly looked he at the wall,
 And darkly at the foe;
"Their van will be upon us
 Before the bridge goes down;
And if they once may win the bridge,
 What hope to save the town?"

Then out spake brave Horatius,
 The Captain of the gate:

"To every man upon this earth
  Death cometh soon or late.
And how can man die better
  Than facing fearful odds
For the ashes of his fathers
  And the temples of his gods,

"And for the tender mother
  Who dandled him to rest,
And for the wife who nurses
  His baby at her breast,
And for the holy maidens
  Who feed the eternal flame,—
To save them from false Sextus
  That wrought the deed of shame?

"Hew down the bridge, Sir Consul,
  With all the speed ye may;
I, with two more to help me,
  Will hold the foe in play.
In yon strait path a thousand
  May well be stopped by three:
Now who will stand on either hand,
  And keep the bridge with me?"

Then out spake Spurius Lartius,—
  A Ramnian proud was he:
"Lo, I will stand at thy right hand,
  And keep the bridge with thee."
And out spake strong Herminius,—
  Of Titian blood was he:
"I will abide on thy left side,
  And keep the bridge with thee."

"Horatius," quoth the Consul,
  "As thou sayest so let it be,"
And straight against that great array
  Went forth the dauntless three.
For Romans in Rome's quarrel
  Spared neither land nor gold,
Nor son nor wife, nor limb nor life,
  In the brave days of old.

Then none was for a party—
   Then all were for the state;
Then the great man helped the poor,
And the poor man loved the great;
   Then lands were fairly portioned!
Then spoils were fairly sold:
   The Romans were like brothers
In the brave days of old.

Now Roman is to Roman
   More hateful than a foe,
And the tribunes beard the high,
   And the fathers grind the low.
As we wax hot in faction,
   In battle we wax cold;
Wherefore men fight not as they fought
   In the brave days of old.

Now while the three were tightening
   Their harness on their backs,
The Consul was the foremost man
   To take in hand an axe;
And fathers, mixed with commons,
   Seized hatchet, bar, and crow,
And smote upon the planks above,
   And loosed the props below.

Meanwhile the Tuscan army,
   Right glorious to behold,
Came flashing back the noonday light,
   Rank behind rank, like surges bright
Of a broad sea of gold.
   Four hundred trumpets sounded
A peal of warlike glee,
   As that great host with measured tread,
And spears advanced, and ensigns spread,
   Rolled slowly toward the bridge's head,
Where stood the dauntless three.

The three stood calm and silent,
   And looked upon the foes,

And a great shout of laughter
    From all the vanguard rose;
And forth three chiefs came spurring
    Before that deep array;
To earth they sprang, their swords they drew,
    And lifted high their shields, and flew
To win the narrow way.

Aunus, from green Tifernum,
    Lord of the Hill of Vines;
And Seius, whose eight hundred slaves
    Sicken in Ilva's mines;
And Picus, long to Clusium
    Vassal in peace and war,
Who led to fight his Umbrian powers
    From that gray crag where, girt with towers,
The fortress of Nequinum lowers
    O'er the pale waves of Nar.

Stout Lartius hurled down Aunus
    Into the stream beneath;
Herminius struck at Seius,
    And clove him to the teeth;
At Picus brave Horatius
    Darted one fiery thrust,
And the proud Umbrian's gilded arms
    Clashed in the bloody dust.

Then Ocnus of Falerii
    Rushed on the Roman three;
And Lausulus of Urgo,
    The rover of the sea;
And Aruns of Volsinium,
    Who slew the great wild boar,—
The great wild boar that had his den
    Amidst the reeds of Cosa's fen,
And wasted fields, and slaughtered men,
    Along Albinia's shore.

Herminius smote down Aruns;
    Lartius laid Ocnus low;

Right to the heart of Lausulus
    Horatius sent a blow:
"Lie there," he cried, "fell pirate!
    No more, aghast and pale,
From Ostia's walls the crowd shall mark
    The track of thy destroying bark;
No more Campania's hinds shall fly
    To woods and caverns, when they spy
Thy thrice-accursèd sail!"

But now no sound of laughter
    Was heard among the foes;
A wild and wrathful clamor
    From all the vanguard rose.
Six spears' length from the entrance,
    Halted that mighty mass,
And for a space no man came forth
    To win the narrow pass.

But, hark! the cry is Astur:
    And lo! the ranks divide;
And the great lord of Luna
    Comes with his stately stride.
Upon his ample shoulders
    Clangs loud the fourfold shield,
And in his hand he shakes the brand
    Which none but he can wield.

He smiled on those bold Romans,
    A smile serene and high;
He eyed the flinching Tuscans,
    And scorn was in his eye.
Quoth he, "The she-wolf's litter
    Stand savagely at bay;
But will ye dare to follow,
    If Astur clears the way?"

Then, whirling up his broadsword
    With both hands to the height,
He rushed against Horatius,
    And smote with all his might.

With shield and blade Horatius
   Right deftly turned the blow.
The blow, though turned, came yet too nigh;
   It missed his helm, but gashed his thigh.
The Tuscans raised a joyful cry
   To see the red blood flow.

He reeled, and on Herminius
   He leaned one breathing-space,
Then, like a wild-cat mad with wounds,
   Sprang right at Astur's face.
Through teeth and skull and helmet
   So fierce a thrust he sped,
The good sword stood a handbreadth out
   Behind the Tuscan's head.

And the great lord of Luna
   Fell at that deadly stroke,
As falls on Mount Avernus
   A thunder-smitten oak.
Far o'er the crashing forest
   The giant arms lie spread;
And the pale augurs, muttering low
   Gaze on the blasted head.

On Astur's throat Horatius
   Right firmly pressed his heel,
And thrice and four times tugged amain,
   Ere he wrenched out the steel.
And "See," he cried, "the welcome,
   Fair guests, that waits you here!
What noble Lucumo comes next
   To taste our Roman cheer?"

But at his haughty challenge
   A sullen murmur ran,
Mingled with wrath and shame and dread,
   Along that glittering van.
There lacked not men of prowess,
   Nor men of lordly race,
For all Etruria's noblest
   Were round the fatal place.

But all Etruria's noblest
    Felt their hearts sink to see
On the earth the bloody corpses,
    In the path the dauntless three;
And from the ghastly entrance,
    Where those bold Romans stood,
All shrank,—like boys who, unaware,
    Ranging the woods to start a hare,
Come to the mouth of the dark lair
    Where, growling low, a fierce old bear
Lies amidst bones and blood.

Was none who would be foremost
    To lead such dire attack;
But those behind cried "Forward!"
    And those before cried "Back!"
And backward now and forward
    Wavers the deep array;
And on the tossing sea of steel
    To and fro the standards reel,
And the victorious trumpet-peal
    Dies fitfully away.

Yet one man for one moment
    Strode out before the crowd;
Well known was he to all the three,
    And they gave him greeting loud:
"Now welcome, welcome, Sextus!
    Now welcome to thy home!
Why dost thou stay, and turn away?
    Here lies the road to Rome."

Thrice looked he at the city;
    Thrice looked he at the dead:
And thrice came on in fury,
    And thrice turned back in dread;
And, white with fear and hatred,
   Scowled at the narrow way
    Where, wallowing in a pool of blood,
The bravest Tuscans lay.

But meanwhile axe and lever
    Have manfully been plied:
And now the bridge hangs tottering
    Above the boiling tide.
"Come back, come back, Horatius!"
    Loud cried the Fathers all,—
"Back, Lartius! back, Herminius!
    Back, ere the ruin fall!"

Back darted Spurius Lartius,—
    Herminius darted back;
And, as they passed, beneath their feet
    They felt the timbers crack.
But when they turned their faces,
    And on the farther shore
Saw brave Horatius stand alone,
    They would have crossed once more;

But with a crash like thunder
    Fell every loosened beam,
And, like a dam, the mighty wreck
    Lay right athwart the stream;
And a long shout of triumph
    Rose from the walls of Rome,
As to the highest turret-tops
    Was splashed the yellow foam.

And like a horse unbroken,
    When first he feels the rein,
The furious river struggled hard,
    And tossed his tawny mane,
And burst the curb, and bounded,
    Rejoicing to be free;
And whirling down, in fierce career,
    Battlement and plank and pier,
Rushed headlong to the sea.

Alone stood brave Horatius,
    But constant still in mind,—
Thrice thirty thousand foes before,
    And the broad flood behind.

"Down with him!" cried false Sextus,
    With a smile on his pale face;
"Now yield thee," cried Lars Porsena,
    "Now yield thee to our grace!"

Round turned he, as not deigning
    Those craven ranks to see;
Naught spake he to Lars Porsena,
    To Sextus naught spake he;
But he saw on Palatinus
    The white porch of his home;
And he spake to the noble river
    That rolls by the towers of Rome:

"O Tiber! Father Tiber!
    To whom the Romans pray,
A Roman's life, a Roman's arms,
    Take thou in charge this day!"
So he spake, and, speaking, sheathed
    The good sword by his side,
And, with his harness on his back,
    Plunged headlong in the tide.

No sound of joy or sorrow
    Was heard from either bank,
But friends and foes in dumb surprise,
    With parted lips and straining eyes,
Stood gazing where he sank;
    And when above the surges
They saw his crest appear,
    All Rome sent forth a rapturous cry,
And even the ranks of Tuscany
    Could scarce forbear to cheer.

But fiercely ran the current,
    Swollen high by months of rain;
And fast his blood was flowing,
    And he was sore in pain,
And heavy with his armor,
    And spent with changing blows;
And oft they thought him sinking,
    But still again he rose.

Never, I ween, did swimmer.
  In such an evil case,
Struggle through such a raging flood
  Safe to the landing-place;
But his limbs were borne up bravely
  By the brave heart within,
And our good Father Tiber
  Bare bravely up his chin.

"Curse on him!" quoth false Sextus,—
  "Will not the villain drown?
But for this stay, ere close of day
  We should have sacked the town!"
"Heaven help him!" quoth Lars Porsena,
  "And bring him safe to shore;
For such a gallant feat of arms
  Was never seen before."

And now he feels the bottom;
  Now on dry earth he stands;
Now round him throng the Fathers
  To press his gory hands;
And now, with shouts and clapping,
  And noise of weeping loud,
He enters through the River-gate,
  Borne by the joyous crowd.

They gave him of the corn-land,
  That was of public right,
As much as two strong oxen
  Could plough from morn till night;
And they made a molten image,
  And set it up on high,—
And there it stands unto this day
  To witness if I lie.

It stands in the Comitium,
  Plain for all folk to see,—
Horatius in his harness,
  Halting upon one knee;
And underneath is written,

In letters all of gold,
How valiantly he kept the bridge
   In the brave days of old.

And still his name sounds stirring
   Unto the men of Rome,
As the trumpet-blast that cries to them
   To charge the Volscian home;
And wives still pray to Juno
   For boys with hearts as bold
As his who kept the bridge so well
   In the brave days of old.

And in the nights of winter,
   When the cold north-winds blow,
And the long howling of the wolves
   Is heard amidst the snow;
When round the lonely cottage
   Roars loud the tempest's din,
And the good logs of Algidus
   Roar louder yet within;

When the oldest cask is opened,
   And the largest lamp is lit;
When the chestnuts glow in the embers,
   And the kid turns on the spit;
When young and old in circle
   Around the firebrands close;
When the girls are weaving baskets,
   And the lads are shaping bows;

When the goodman mends his armor,
   And trims his helmet's plume;
When the goodwife's shuttle merrily
   Goes flashing through the loom;
With weeping and with laughter
   Still is the story told,
How well Horatius kept the bridge
   In the brave days of old.

SEA FEVER
John Masefield
(1878-1967)

I must down to the seas again, to the lonely sea and the sky,
And all I ask is a tall ship and a star to steer her by;
And the wheel's kick and the wind's song and the white sail's shaking,
And a grey mist on the sea's face, and a grey dawn breaking.

I must down to the seas again, for the call of the running tide
Is a wild call and a clear call that may not be denied;
And all I ask is a windy day with the white clouds flying,
And the flung spray and the blown spume, and the sea-gulls crying.

I must down to the seas again, to the vagrant gypsy life,
To the gull's way and the whale's way where the wind's like a whetted knife;
And all I ask is a merry yarn from a laughing fellow-rover,
And quiet sleep and a sweet dream when the long trick's over.

IN FLANDERS FIELDS
John McCrae
(1872-1918)

In Flanders fields the poppies blow
Between the crosses, row on row,
That mark our place; and in the sky
The larks, still bravely singing, fly
Scarce heard amid the guns below.

We are the Dead. Short days ago
We lived, felt dawn, saw sunset glow,
Loved and were loved, and now we lie,
        In Flanders fields.

Take up our quarrel with the foe:
To you from failing hands we throw
The torch; be yours to hold it high.
If ye break faith with us who die
We shall not sleep, though poppies grow
        In Flanders fields.

COLUMBUS
Joaquin Miller
(1837-1913)

Behind him lay the gray Azores,
    Behind the Gates of Hercules;
Before him not the ghost of shores,
    Before him only shoreless seas.
The good mate said: "Now must we pray,
    For lo! the very stars are gone.
Brave Admiral, speak, what shall I say?"
    "Why, say, 'Sail on! sail on! and on!'"

"My men grow mutinous day by day;
    My men grow ghastly wan and weak."
The stout mate thought of home; a spray
    Of salt wave washed his swarthy cheek.
"What shall I say, brave Admiral, say,
    If we sight naught but seas at dawn?"
"Why, you shall say at break of day,
    'Sail on! sail on! sail on! and on!'"

They sailed and sailed, as winds might blow,
    Until at last the blanched mate said:
"Why, now not even God would know
    Should I and all my men fall dead.
These very winds forget their way,
    For God from these dread seas is gone.
Now speak, brave Admiral, speak and say"—
    He said: "Sail on! sail on! and on!"

They sailed. They sailed. Then spake the mate:
    "This mad sea shows his teeth to-night.
He curls his lip, he lies in wait,
    With lifted teeth, as if to bite!
Brave Admiral, say but one good word:
    What shall we do when hope is gone?"
The words leapt like a leaping sword:
    "Sail on! sail on! sail on! and on!"

Then, pale and worn, he kept his deck,
    And peered through darkness. Ah, that night
Of all dark nights! And then a speck—
    A light! A light! A light! A light!
It grew, a starlit flag unfurled!
    It grew to be Time's burst of dawn.
He gained a world; he gave that world
    Its grandest lesson: "On! sail on!"

SONNET ON HIS BLINDNESS

John Milton
(1608-1674)

When I consider how my light is spent
Ere half my days in this dark world and wide,
And that one talent which is death to hide
Lodg'd with me useless, though my soul more bent
To serve therewith my Maker, and present
My true account, lest he returning chide,
"Doth God exact day-labour, light denied?"
I fondly ask. But Patience, to prevent
That murmur, soon replies: "God doth not need
Either man's work or his own gifts: who best
Bear his mild yoke, they serve him best. His state
Is kingly; thousands at his bidding speed
And post o'er land and ocean without rest:
They also serve who only stand and wait."

INVOCATION TO LIGHT

John Milton
(1608-1674)
From *Paradise Lost*,
Book III

Hail holy light, ofspring of Heav'n first-born,
Or of th' Eternal Coeternal beam
May I express thee unblam'd? since God is light,
And never but in unapproachèd light
Dwelt from Eternitie, dwelt then in thee,
Bright effluence of bright essence increate.
Or hear'st thou rather pure Ethereal stream,
Whose Fountain who shall tell? before the Sun,
Before the Heavens thou wert, and at the voice
Of God, as with a Mantle didst invest
The rising world of waters dark and deep,
Won from the void and formless infinite.
Thee I re-visit now with bolder wing,
Escap't the Stygian Pool, though long detain'd
In that obscure sojourn, while in my flight
Through utter and through middle darkness borne
With other notes then to th' Orphean Lyre
I sung of Chaos and Eternal Night,
Taught by the heav'nly Muse to venture down
The dark descent, and up to reascend,
Though hard and rare: thee I revisit safe,
And feel thy sovran vital Lamp; but thou
Revisit'st not these eyes, that rowle in vain
To find thy piercing ray, and find no dawn;
So thick a drop serene hath quencht thir Orbs,

Or dim suffusion veild. Yet not the more
Cease I to wander where the Muses haunt
Cleer Spring, or shadie Grove, or Sunnie Hill,
Smit with the love of sacred song; but chief
Thee Sion and the flowrie Brooks beneath
That wash thy hallowd feet, and warbling flow,
Nightly I visit: nor somtimes forget
Those other two equal'd with me in Fate,
So were I equal'd with them in renown.
Blind Thamyris and blind Mæonides,
And Tiresias and Phineus Prophets old.
Then feed on thoughts, that voluntarie move
Harmonious numbers; as the wakeful Bird
Sings darkling, and in shadiest Covert hid
Tunes her nocturnal Note. Thus with the Year
Seasons return, but not to me returns
Day, or the sweet approach of Ev'n or Morn,
Or sight of vernal bloom, or Summers Rose,
Or flocks, or herds, or human face divine;
But cloud in stead, and ever-during dark
Surrounds me, from the chearful waies of men
Cut off, and for the Book of knowledg fair
Presented with a Universal blanc
Of Natures works to mee expung'd and ras'd,
And wisdome at one entrance quite shut out.
So much the rather thou Celestial light
Shine inward, and the mind through all her powers
Irradiate, there plant eyes, all mist from thence
Purge and disperse, that I may see and tell
Of things invisible to mortal sight.

IN THE BLEAK MIDWINTER

Christina Rossetti
(1830-1894)

In the bleak midwinter,
    Frosty wind made moan,
Earth stood hard as iron,
    Water like a stone;
Snow had fallen, snow on snow,
    Snow on snow,
In the bleak midwinter,
    Long ago.

Our God, Heaven cannot hold Him,
    Nor earth sustain;
Heaven and earth shall flee away
    When He comes to reign.
In the bleak midwinter
    A stable place sufficed
The Lord God Almighty,
    Jesus Christ.

Enough for Him, whom cherubim,
    Worship night and day,
Breastful of milk
    And a mangerful of hay;
Enough for Him, whom angels
    Fall down before,
The ox and ass and camel
    Which adore.

Angels and archangels
    May have gathered there,
Cherubim and seraphim
    Thronged the air;
But His mother only,
    In her maiden bliss,
Worshipped the Beloved
    With a kiss.

What can I give Him,
    Poor as I am?
If I were a shepherd,
    I would bring a lamb;
If I were a Wise Man,
    I would do my part;
Yet what I can I give Him:
    give my heart.

OZYMANDIAS
Percy Bysshe Shelley
(1792-1822)

I met a traveller from an antique land,
Who said—"Two vast and trunkless legs of stone
Stand in the desert. Near them, on the sand,
Half sunk a shattered visage lies, whose frown,

CINDY'S ANTHOLOGY   POETRY: FAVORITES FOR MIDDLE SCHOOL AND UP

And wrinkled lip, and sneer of cold command,
Tell that its sculptor well those passions read
Which yet survive, stamped on these lifeless things,
The hand that mocked them, and the heart that fed;
And on the pedestal, these words appear:
My name is Ozymandias, King of Kings;
Look on my Works, ye Mighty, and despair!
Nothing beside remains. Round the decay
Of that colossal Wreck, boundless and bare
The lone and level sands stretch far away."

THE FOOL'S PRAYER

Edward Rowland Sill
(1841-1887)

The royal feast was done; the King
    Sought some new sport to banish care,
  And to his jester cried: "Sir Fool,
Kneel now, and make for us a prayer!"

The jester doffed his cap and bells,
    And stood the mocking court before;
They could not see the bitter smile
    Behind the painted grin he wore.

He bowed his head, and bent his knee
    Upon the monarch's silken stool;
His pleading voice arose: "O Lord,
    Be merciful to me, a fool!

"No pity, Lord, could change the heart
    From red with wrong to white as wool;
The rod must heal the sin: but, Lord,
    Be merciful to me, a fool!

"'T is not by guilt the onward sweep
    Of truth and right, O Lord, we stay;
'T is by our follies that so long
    We hold the earth from heaven away.

"These clumsy feet, still in the mire,
    Go crushing blossoms without end;
These hard, well-meaning hands we thrust
    Among the heart-strings of a friend.

"The ill-timed truth we might have kept—
    Who knows how sharp it pierced and stung?
The word we had not sense to say—
    Who knows how grandly it had rung?

"Our faults no tenderness should ask,
    The chastening stripes must cleanse them all;
But for our blunders—oh, in shame
    Before the eyes of heaven we fall.

"Earth bears no balsam for mistakes;
    Men crown the knave, and scourge the tool
That did his will; but Thou, O Lord,
    Be merciful to me, a fool!"

The room was hushed; in silence rose
    The King, and sought his gardens cool,
And walked apart, and murmured low,
    "Be merciful to me, a fool!"

OPPORTUNITY
Edward Rowland Sill
(1841-1887)

This I beheld, or dreamed it in a dream:—
    There spread a cloud of dust along a plain;
And underneath the cloud, or in it, raged
A furious battle, and men yelled, and swords
    Shocked upon swords and shields. A prince's banner
Wavered, then staggered backward, hemmed by foes.
A craven hung along the battle's edge,
And thought, "Had I a sword of keener steel—
That blue blade that the king's son bears,—but this
Blunt thing—!" He snapped and flung it from his hand,
And lowering crept away and left the field.

Then came the king's son, wounded sore bested,
And weaponless, and saw the broken sword
    Hilt-buried in the dry and trodden sand,
And ran and snatched it, and with battle shout
Lifted afresh he hewed his enemy down
And saved a great cause that heroic day.

KEEP A-GOIN'!
Frank Lebby Stanton
(1857-1927)

Ef you strike a thorn or rose,
    Keep a-goin'!
Ef it hails, or ef it snows,
    Keep a-goin'!
'Taint no use to sit an' whine,
When the fish ain't on yer line;
Bait yer hook an' keep a-tryin'—
    Keep a-goin'!

When the weather kills yer crop,
    Keep a-goin'!
When you tumble from the top,
    Keep a-goin'!
S'pose you're out of every dime,
Bein' so ain't any crime;
Tell the world you're feelin' prime—
    Keep a-goin'!

When it looks like all is up,
    Keep a-goin'!
Drain the sweetness from the cup,
    Keep a-goin'!
See the wild birds on the wing,
Hear the bells that sweetly ring,
When you feel like sighin' sing—
    Keep a-goin'!

AUTUMN FIRES
Robert Louis Stevenson
(1850-1894)

In the other gardens
    And all up the vale,
From the autumn bonfires
    See the smoke trail!

Pleasant summer over
    And all the summer flowers,
The red fire blazes,
    The grey smoke towers.

Sing a song of seasons!
    Something bright in all!
Flowers in the summer,
    Fires in the fall!

REQUIEM
Robert Louis Stevenson
(1850-1894)

Under the wide and starry sky,
    Dig the grave and let me lie.
Glad did I live and gladly die,
    And I laid me down with a will.

This be the verse you grave for me:
Here he lies where he longed to be;
Home is the sailor, home from sea,
    And the hunter home from the hill.

**WHERE GO THE
BOATS**
Robert Louis Stevenson
(1850-1894)

Dark brown is the river.
    Golden is the sand.
It flows along for ever,
    With trees on either hand.

Green leaves a-floating,
    Castles of the foam,
Boats of mine a-boating—
    Where will all come home?

On goes the river
    And out past the mill,
Away down the valley,
    Away down the hill.

Away down the river,
    A hundred miles or more,
Other little children
    Shall bring my boats ashore.

**WHOLE DUTY
OF CHILDREN**
Robert Louis Stevenson
(1850-1894)

A child should always say what's true
    And speak when he is spoken to,
And behave mannerly at table;
At least as far as he is able.

WINDY NIGHTS

Robert Louis Stevenson
(1850-1894)

Whenever the moon and stars are set,
   Whenever the wind is high,
All night long in the dark and wet,
   A man goes riding by.
Late in the night when the fires are out,
Why does he gallop and gallop about?

Whenever the trees are crying aloud,
   And ships are tossed at sea,
By, on the highway, low and loud,
   By at the gallop goes he.
By at the gallop he goes, and then
By he comes back at the gallop again.

THE CHARGE OF THE LIGHT BRIGADE

Alfred, Lord Tennyson
(1809-1892)

Half a league, half a league,
   Half a league onward,
All in the valley of Death
   Rode the six hundred.
"Forward, the Light Brigade!
Charge for the guns!" he said.
Into the valley of Death
   Rode the six hundred.

II
"Forward, the Light Brigade!"
Was there a man dismayed?
Not though the soldier knew
   Someone had blundered.
Theirs not to make reply,
Theirs not to reason why,
Theirs but to do and die.
Into the valley of Death
   Rode the six hundred.

III
Cannon to right of them,
Cannon to left of them,
Cannon in front of them
   Volleyed and thundered;
Stormed at with shot and shell,

Boldly they rode and well,
Into the jaws of Death,
Into the mouth of hell
   Rode the six hundred.

IV
Flashed all their sabres bare,
Flashed as they turned in air
Sabring the gunners there,
Charging an army, while
   All the world wondered.
Plunged in the battery-smoke
Right through the line they broke;
Cossack and Russian
Reeled from the sabre stroke
   Shattered and sundered.
Then they rode back, but not
 Not the six hundred.

V
Cannon to right of them,
Cannon to left of them,
Cannon behind them
   Volleyed and thundered;
Stormed at with shot and shell,
While horse and hero fell.
They that had fought so well
Came through the jaws of Death,
Back from the mouth of hell,
All that was left of them,
   Left of six hundred.

VI
When can their glory fade?
O the wild charge they made!
   All the world wondered.
Honour the charge they made!
Honour the Light Brigade,
   Noble six hundred!

CROSSING THE BAR

Alfred, Lord Tennyson
(1809-1892)

Sunset and evening star,
And one clear call for me!
And may there be no moaning of the bar,
When I put out to sea,

But such a tide as moving seems asleep,
Too full for sound and foam,
When that which drew from out the boundless deep
Turns again home.

Twilight and evening bell,
And after that the dark!
And may there be no sadness of farewell,
When I embark;

For tho' from out our bourne of Time and Place
The flood may bear me far,
I hope to see my Pilot face to face
When I have crost the bar.

ENGLISH WAR SONG

Alfred, Lord Tennyson
(1809-1892)

Who fears to die? Who fears to die?
Is there any here who fears to die
He shall find what he fears, and none shall grieve
For the man who fears to die:
But the withering scorn of the many shall cleave
To the man who fears to die.

Chorus
Shout for England!
Ho! for England!
George for England!
Merry England!
England for aye!

The hollow at heart shall crouch forlorn,
He shall eat the bread of common scorn;
It shall be steeped in the salt, salt tear,
Shall be steeped in his own salt tear:
Far better, far better he never were born
Than to shame merry England here.
[Chorus]

There standeth our ancient enemy;
  Hark! he shouteth—the ancient enemy!
On the ridge of the hill his banners rise;
  They stream like fire in the skies;
Hold up the Lion of England on high
  Till it dazzle and blind his eyes.
[Chorus]

  Come along! we alone of the earth are free;
  The child in our cradles is bolder than he;
For where is the heart and strength of slaves?
  Oh! where is the strength of slaves?
He is weak! we are strong; he a slave, we are free;
  Come along! we will dig their graves.
[Chorus]

  There standeth our ancient enemy;
  Will he dare to battle with the free?
Spur along! spur amain! charge to the fight:
  Charge! charge to the fight!
Hold up the Lion of England on high!
  Shout for God and our right!
[Chorus]

CASEY AT THE BAT

Ernest Lawrence Thayer (1863-1940)
A Ballad of the Republic, Sung in the Year 1888

It looked extremely rocky for the Mudville nine that day;
The score stood four to six, with but an inning left to play.
And so, when Cooney died at first, and Barrows did the same,
A pallor wreathed the features of the patrons of the game.

A straggling few got up to go, leaving there the rest
With that hope which springs eternal within the human breast;
For they thought if only Casey could but get a whack at that—
They'd put up even money with Casey at the bat.

But Flynn preceded Casey, and likewise so did Blake,
And the former was a pudding, and the latter was a fake;
So on that stricken multitude a ddeathlike silence sat,
For there seemed but little chance of Casey's getting to the bat.

But Flynn let drive a single, to the wonderment of all,
And the much-despised Blakey tore the cover off the ball;
And when the dust had lifted, and men saw what had occurred,
There was Blakey safe at second, and Flynn a-huggin' third.

193

Then, the gladdened multitude went up a joyous yell;
It bounded from the moutain-top and rattled in the dell;
It struck upone the hillside and rebounded upon the flat,
For Casey, mighty Casey, was advancing to the bat.

There was ease in Casey's manner as he stepped into his place;
There was pride in Casey's bearing and a smile on Casey's face.
And when, responding to the cheers, he lightly doffed his hat,
No stranger in the crowd could doubt 'twas Casey at the bat.

Ten thousand eyes were on him as he rubbed his hands with dirt;
Five thousand tongues applauded when he wiped them on his shirt.
Then while the writhing pitcher ground the ball into his hip,
Defiance gleamed in Casey's eye, a sneer curled Casey's lip.

And now the leather-covered sphere came hurtling through the air,
And Casey stood a-watching it in haughty grandeur there.
Close by the sturdy batsman the ball unheeded sped—
"That hain't my style," said Casey. "Strike one," the umpire said.

From the benches, black with people, there went up a muffled roar,
Like the beating of the storm-waves on a stern and distant shore.
"Kill him! Kill the umpire!" shouted some one on the stand;
And it's likely they'd have killed him had not Casey raised his hand.

With a smile of Christian charity great Casey's visage shone;
He stilled the rising tumult; he bade the game go on;
He signaled to the pitcher, and again the spheroid flew;
But Casey still ignored it, and the umpire said, "Strike two."

"Fraud!" cried the maddened thousands, and echo answered "Fraud!"
But one scornful look from Casey, and the audience was awed.
They saw his face grow stern and cold; they saw his muscles strain,
And they knew that Casey wouldn't let that ball go by again.

The sneer is gone from Casey's lip, his teeth are clinched in hate;
He pounds with cruel violence his bat upon the plate.
And now the pitcher holds the ball, and now he lets it go,
And now the air is shattered by the force of Casey's blow.

Oh, somewhere in this favored land the sun is shining bright;
The band is playing somewhere, and somewhere hearts are light,
And somewhere men are laughing, and somewhere children shout;
But there is no joy in Mudville—mighty Casey has struck out.

AWAKEN

Lawrence Tribble
(18th century)[9]

One man awake,
Awakens another.
The second awakens
His next-door brother.
The three awake can arouse a town
By turning
The whole place
Upside down.

The many awake
Can make such a fuss
It finally awakens
The rest of us.
One man up,
With dawn in his eyes
Surely then
Multiplies.

FOUR THINGS

Henry Van Dyke
(1852-1933)

Four things a man must learn to do
If he would make his record true:
To think without confusion clearly;
To love his fellow man sincerely;
To act from honest motives purely;
To trust in God and Heaven securely.

LOVE BETWEEN BROTHERS AND SISTERS

Isaac Watts
(1674-1748)

What ever brawls are in the street
There should be peace at home;
Where sisters dwell and brothers meet
Quarrels shou'd never come.

Birds in their little nests agree;
And `tis a shameful sight,
When children of one family
Fall out, and chide, and fight.

Hard names at first, and threatening words,
That are but noisy breath,
May grow to clubs and naked swords,
To murder and to death.

The devil tempts one mother's son
  To rage against another:
So wicked Cain was hurried on,
  Till he had kill'd his brother.

The wise will make their anger cool
  At least before 'tis night;
But in the bosom of a fool
  It burns till morning light

Pardon, O Lord, our childish rage;
  Our little brawls remove;
That as we grow to riper age,
  Our hearts may all be love.

HOW DOTH THE LITTLE BUSY BEE

Isaac Watts
(1674-1748)

How doth the little busy bee
  Improve each shining hour,
And gather honey all the day
  From every opening flower!

How skilfully she builds her cell!
  How neat she spreads the wax!
And labours hard to store it well
  With the sweet food she makes.

In works of labour or of skill
  I would be busy too:
For Satan finds some mischief still
  For idle hands to do.

In books, or work, or healthful play
  Let my first years be past,
That I may give for every day
  Some good account at last.

THE SLUGGARD
Isaac Watts
(1674-1748)

'Tis the voice of the Sluggard. I heard him complain
"You have waked me too soon! I must slumber again!"
As the door on its hinges, so he on his bed,
Turns his sides, and his shoulders, and his heavy head.

"A little more sleep, and a little more slumber;"
Thus he wastes half his days, and his hours without number:
And when he gets up, he sits folding his hands
Or walks about sauntering, or trifling he stands.

I past by his garden, and saw the wild bryar
The thorn and the thistle grow broader and higher:
The clothes that hang on him are turning to rags;
And his money still wasts, still he starves, or he begs.

I made him a visit, still hoping to find
He had took better care for improving his mind:
He told me his dreams, talk'd of eating and drinking,
But he scarce reads his Bible, and never loves thinking.

Said I then to my heart, "Here's a lesson for me,"
That man's but a picture of what I might be:
But thanks to my friends for their care in my breeding:
Who taught me betimes to love working and reading!

OBEDIENCE TO PARENTS
Isaac Watts
(1674-1748)

Let children that would fear the Lord
Hear what their teachers say;
With reverence meet their parents' word,
    And with delight obey.

Have you not heard what dreadful plagues
    Are threaten'd by the Lord,
To him that breaks his father's law,
    Or mocks his mother's word?

What heavy guilt upon him lies!
    How cursed is his name!
The ravens shall pick out his eyes,
    And eagles eat the same.

But those who worship God, and give
   Their parents honour due,
Here on this earth they long shall live,
   And live hereafter, too.

I WANDERED LONELY AS A CLOUD

William Wordsworth
(1770–1850)

I wandered lonely as a cloud
   That floats on high o'er vales and hills,
When all at once I saw a crowd,
   A host, of golden daffodils;
Beside the lake, beneath the trees,
Fluttering and dancing in the breeze.

Continuous as the stars that shine
   And twinkle on the milky way,
They stretched in never-ending line
   Along the margin of a bay:
Ten thousand saw I at a glance,
Tossing their heads in sprightly dance.

The waves beside them danced; but they
   Out-did the sparkling waves in glee:
A poet could not but be gay,
   In such a jocund company:
I gazed—and gazed—but little thought
What wealth the show to me had brought:

For oft, when on my couch I lie
   In vacant or in pensive mood,
They flash upon that inward eye
   Which is the bliss of solitude;
And then my heart with pleasure fills,
And dances with the daffodils.

MY HEART LEAPS UP

William Wordsworth
(1770–1850)

My heart leaps up when I behold
  A rainbow in the sky:
So was it when my life began;
So is it now I am a man;
So be it when I shall grow old,
  Or let me die!
The Child is father of the Man;
And I could wish my days to be
Bound each to each by natural piety.

THE WORLD IS TOO MUCH WITH US

William Wordsworth
(1770–1850)

The world is too much with us; late and soon,
  Getting and spending, we lay waste our powers;—
  Little we see in Nature that is ours;
We have given our hearts away, a sordid boon!
This Sea that bares her bosom to the moon;
  The winds that will be howling at all hours,
  And are up-gathered now like sleeping flowers;
For this, for everything, we are out of tune;
It moves us not. Great God! I'd rather be
  A Pagan suckled in a creed outworn;
So might I, standing on this pleasant lea,
  Have glimpses that would make me less forlorn;
Have sight of Proteus rising from the sea;
  Or hear old Triton blow his wreathèd horn.

THE LAKE ISLE OF INNISFREE

William Butler Yeats
(1865-1939)

I will arise and go now, and go to Innisfree,
  And a small cabin build there, of clay and wattles made;
Nine bean-rows will I have there, a hive for the honey-bee,
  And live alone in the bee-loud glade.

And I shall have some peace there, for peace comes dropping slow,
  Dropping from the veils of the morning to where the cricket sings;
There midnight's all a glimmer, and noon a purple glow,
  And evening full of the linnet's wings.

I will arise and go now, for always night and day
  I hear lake water lapping with low sounds by the shore;
While I stand on the roadway, or on the pavements grey,
  I hear it in the deep heart's core.

THE SECOND COMING

William Butler Yeats
(1865-1939)

Turning and turning in the widening gyre
The falcon cannot hear the falconer;
Things fall apart; the centre cannot hold;
Mere anarchy is loosed upon the world,
The blood-dimmed tide is loosed, and everywhere
The ceremony of innocence is drowned;
The best lack all conviction, while the worst
Are full of passionate intensity.

Surely some revelation is at hand;
Surely the Second Coming is at hand.
The Second Coming! Hardly are those words out
When a vast image out of Spiritus Mundi
Troubles my sight: somewhere in sands of the desert
A shape with lion body and the head of a man,
A gaze blank and pitiless as the sun,
Is moving its slow thighs, while all about it
Reel shadows of the indignant desert birds.

The darkness drops again; but now I know
That twenty centuries of stony sleep
Were vexed to nightmare by a rocking cradle,
And what rough beast, its hour come round at last,
Slouches towards Bethlehem to be born?

HISTORICAL DOCUMENTS

PREAMBLE TO THE CONSTITUTION

We the People of the United States, in Order to form a more perfect Union, establish Justice, insure domestic Tranquility, provide for the common defence, promote the general Welfare, and secure the Blessings of Liberty to ourselves and our Posterity, do ordain and establish this Constitution for the United States of America.

THE DECLARATION OF INDEPENDENCE
In Congress, July 4, 1776

The unanimous Declaration of the thirteen united States of America, When in the Course of human events, it becomes necessary for one people to dissolve the political bands which have connected them with another, and to assume among the powers of the earth, the separate and equal station to which the Laws of Nature and of Nature's God entitle them, a decent respect to the opinions of mankind requires that they should declare the causes which impel them to the separation.

We hold these truths to be self-evident, that all men are created equal, that they are endowed by their Creator with certain unalienable Rights, that among these are Life, Liberty and the pursuit of Happiness.—That to secure these rights, Governments are instituted among Men, deriving their just powers from the consent of the governed,—That whenever any Form of Government becomes destructive of these ends, it is the Right of the People to alter or to abolish it, and to institute new Government, laying its foundation on such principles and organizing its powers in such form, as to them shall seem most likely to effect their Safety and Happiness. Prudence, indeed, will dictate that Governments long established should not be changed for light and transient causes; and accordingly all experience hath shewn, that mankind are more disposed to suffer, while evils are sufferable, than to right themselves by abolishing the forms to which they are accustomed. But when a long train of abuses and usurpations, pursuing invariably the same Object evinces a design to reduce them under absolute Despotism, it is their right, it is their duty, to throw off such Government, and to provide new Guards for their future security.—Such has been the patient sufferance of these Colonies; and such is now the necessity which constrains them to alter their former Systems of Government. The history of the present King of Great Britain is a history of repeated injuries and usurpations, all having in direct object the establishment of an absolute Tyranny over these States. To prove this, let Facts be submitted to a candid world.

THE US BILL OF RIGHTS

Congress of the United States
begun and held at the City of New York, on
Wednesday the fourth of March, one thousand seven hundred and eighty-nine.

AMENDMENT I

Congress shall make no law respecting an establishment of religion, or prohibiting the free exercise thereof; or abridging the freedom of speech, or of the press; or the right of the people peaceably to assemble, and to petition the Government for a redress of grievances.

AMENDMENT II

A well regulated Militia, being necessary to the security of a free State, the right of the people to keep and bear Arms, shall not be infringed.

AMENDMENT III

No Soldier shall, in time of peace be quartered in any house, without the consent of the Owner, nor in time of war, but in a manner to be prescribed by law.

AMENDMENT IV

The right of the people to be secure in their persons, houses, papers, and effects, against unreasonable searches and seizures, shall not be violated, and no Warrants shall issue, but upon probable cause, supported by Oath or affirmation, and particularly describing the place to be searched, and the persons or things to be seized.

AMENDMENT V

No person shall be held to answer for a capital, or otherwise infamous crime, unless on a presentment or indictment of a Grand Jury, except in cases arising in the land or naval forces, or in the Militia, when in actual service in time of War or public danger; nor shall any person be subject for the same offence to be twice put in jeopardy of life or limb; nor shall be compelled in any criminal case to be a witness against himself, nor be deprived of life, liberty, or property, without due process of law; nor shall private property be taken for public use, without just compensation.

AMENDMENT VI

In all criminal prosecutions, the accused shall enjoy the right to a speedy and public trial, by an impartial jury of the State and district wherein the crime shall have been committed, which district shall have been previously ascertained by law, and to be informed of the nature and cause of the accusation; to be confronted with the witnesses against him; to have compulsory process for obtaining witnesses in his favor, and to have the Assistance of Counsel for his defence.

AMENDMENT VII In Suits at common law, where the value in controversy shall exceed twenty dollars, the right of trial by jury shall be preserved, and no fact tried by a jury, shall be otherwise re-examined in any Court of the United States, than according to the rules of the common law.

AMENDMENT VIII Excessive bail shall not be required, nor excessive fines imposed, nor cruel and unusual punishments inflicted.

AMENDMENT IX The enumeration in the Constitution, of certain rights, shall not be construed to deny or disparage others retained by the people.

AMENDMENT X The powers not delegated to the United States by the Constitution, nor prohibited by it to the States, are reserved to the States respectively, or to the people.

SPEECHES AND PUBLICATIONS

THE GETTYSBURG ADDRESS

Abraham Lincoln
(1809-1865)
Delivered
November 19, 1863

Four score and seven years ago our fathers brought forth on this continent, a new nation, conceived in Liberty, and dedicated to the proposition that all men are created equal.

Now we are engaged in a great civil war, testing whether that nation, or any nation so conceived and so dedicated, can long endure. We are met on a great battlefield of that war. We have come to dedicate a portion of that field, as a final resting place for those who here gave their lives that that nation might live. It is altogether fitting and proper that we should do this.

But, in a larger sense, we cannot dedicate—we cannot consecrate—we cannot hallow—this ground. The brave men, living and dead, who struggled here, have consecrated it, far above our poor power to add or detract. The world will little note, nor long remember what we say here, but it can never forget what they did here.

It is for us the living, rather, to be dedicated here to the unfinished work which they who fought here have thus far so nobly advanced. It is rather for us to be here dedicated to the great task remaining before us—that from these honored dead we take increased devotion to that cause for which they gave the last full measure of devotion—that we here highly resolve that these dead shall not have died in vain—that this nation, under God, shall have a new birth of freedom—and that government of the people, by the people, for the people, shall not perish from the earth.

THE WAR INEVITABLE, *or* "GIVE ME LIBERTY OR GIVE ME DEATH"

Patrick Henry
(1736-1799)
Delivered
March 23, 1775

No man thinks more highly than I do of the patriotism, as well as abilities, of the very worthy gentlemen who have just addressed the House. But different men often see the same subject in different lights; and, therefore, I hope it will not be thought disrespectful to those gentlemen if, entertaining as I do opinions of a character very opposite to theirs, I shall speak forth my sentiments freely and without reserve. This is no time for ceremony. The question before the House is one of awful moment to this country. For my own part, I consider it as nothing less than a question of freedom or slavery; and in proportion to the magnitude of the subject ought to be the freedom of the debate. It is only in this way that we can hope to arrive at truth, and fulfill the great responsibility which we hold to God and our country. Should I keep back my opinions at such a time, through fear of giving offense, I should consider myself as guilty of treason towards my country, and of an act of disloyalty toward the Majesty of Heaven, which I revere above all earthly kings.

Mr. President, it is natural to man to indulge in the illusions of hope. . . . Let us not, I beseech you, sir, deceive ourselves. Sir, we have done everything that could be done to avert the storm which is now coming on. We have petitioned; we have remonstrated; we have supplicated; we have prostrated ourselves before the throne, and have implored its interposition to arrest the tyrannical hands of the ministry and Parliament. Our petitions have been slighted; our remonstrances have produced additional violence and insult; our supplications have been disregarded; and we have been spurned, with contempt, from the foot of the throne! In vain, after these things, may we indulge the fond hope of peace and reconciliation. There is no longer any room for hope. If we wish to be free—if we mean to preserve inviolate those inestimable privileges for which we have been so long contending—if we mean not basely to abandon the noble struggle in which we have been so long engaged, and which we have pledged ourselves never to abandon until the glorious object of our contest shall be obtained—we must fight! I repeat it, sir, we must fight! An appeal to arms and to the God of hosts is all that is left us!

They tell us, sir, that we are weak; unable to cope with so formidable an adversary. But when shall we be stronger? Will it be the next week, or the next year? Will it be when we are totally disarmed, and when a British guard shall be stationed in every house? Shall we gather strength by irresolution and inaction? Shall we acquire the means of effectual resistance by lying supinely on our backs and hugging the delusive phantom of hope, until our enemies shall have bound us hand and foot? Sir, we are not weak if we make a proper use of those means which the God of nature hath placed in our power. The millions of people, armed in the holy cause of liberty, and in such a country as that which we possess, are invincible by any force which our enemy can send against us. Besides, sir, we shall not fight our battles alone. There is a just God who presides over the destinies of nations, and who will raise up friends to fight our battles for us. The battle, sir, is not to the strong alone; it is to the vigilant, the active, the brave. Besides, sir, we have no election. If we were base enough to desire it, it is now too late to retire from the contest. There is no retreat but in submission and slavery! Our chains are forged! Their clanking may be heard on the plains of Boston! The war is inevitable—and let it come! I repeat it, sir, let it come.

It is in vain, sir, to extenuate the matter. Gentlemen may cry, Peace, Peace—but there is no peace. The war is actually begun! The next gale that sweeps from the north will bring to our ears the clash of resounding arms! Our brethren are already in the field! Why stand we here idle? What is it that gentlemen wish? What would they have? Is life so dear, or peace so sweet, as to be purchased at the price of chains and slavery? Forbid it, Almighty God! I know not what course others may take; but as for me, give me liberty or give me death!

"WE SHALL FIGHT ON THE BEACHES"

Winston Churchill
(1874-1965)
Delivered June 4, 1940

I have, myself, full confidence that if all do their duty, if nothing is neglected, and if the best arrangements are made, as they are being made, we shall prove ourselves once again able to defend our Island home, to ride out the storm of war, and to outlive the menace of tyranny, if necessary for years, if necessary alone. At any rate, that is what we are going to try to do. That is the resolve of His Majesty's Government—every man of them. That is the will of Parliament and the nation. The British Empire and the French Republic, linked together in their cause and in their need, will defend to the death their native soil, aiding each other like good comrades to the utmost of their strength. Even though large tracts of Europe and many old and famous States have fallen or may fall into the grip of the Gestapo and all the odious apparatus of Nazi rule, we shall not flag or fail. We shall go on to the end, we shall fight in France, we shall fight on the seas and oceans, we shall fight with growing confidence and growing strength in the air, we shall defend our Island, whatever the cost may be, we shall fight on the beaches, we shall fight on the landing grounds, we shall fight in the fields and in the streets, we shall fight in the hills; we shall never surrender, and even if, which I do not for a moment believe, this Island or a large part of it were subjugated and starving, then our Empire beyond the seas, armed and guarded by the British Fleet, would carry on the struggle, until, in God's good time, the New World, with all its power and might, steps forth to the rescue and the liberation of the old.

FAREWELL ADDRESS EXCERPT

George Washington
(1732-1799)
Delivered
September 17, 1796

FRIENDS AND FELLOW CITIZENS:

The period for a new election of a citizen, to administer the executive government of the United States, being not far distant, and the time actually arrived, when your thoughts must be employed designating the person, who is to be clothed with that important trust, it appears to me proper, especially as it may conduce to a more distinct expression of the public voice, that I should now apprize you of the resolution I have formed, to decline being considered among the number of those out of whom a choice is to be made.

I beg you at the same time to do me the justice to be assured that this resolution has not been taken without a strict regard to all the considerations appertaining to the relation which binds a dutiful citizen to his country; and that in withdrawing the tender of service, which silence in my situation might imply, I am influenced by no diminution of zeal for your future interest, no deficiency of grateful respect for your past kindness, but am supported by a full conviction that the step is compatible with both . . .

Interwoven as is the love of liberty with every ligament of your hearts, no recommendation of mine is necessary to fortify or confirm the attachment.

The unity of Government, which constitutes you one people, is also now dear to you. It is justly so; for it is a main pillar in the edifice of your real independence, the support of your tranquillity at home, your peace abroad; of your safety; of your prosperity; of that very Liberty, which you so highly prize. But as it is easy to foresee, that, from different causes and from different quarters, much pains will be taken, many artifices employed, to weaken in your minds the conviction of this truth; as this is the point in your political fortress against which the batteries of internal and external enemies will be most constantly and actively (though often covertly and insidiously) directed, it is of infinite moment, that you should properly estimate the immense value of your national Union to your collective and individual happiness; that you should cherish a cordial, habitual, and immovable attachment to it; accustoming yourselves to think and speak of it as of the Palladium of your political safety and prosperity; watching for its preservation with jealous anxiety; discountenancing whatever may suggest even a suspicion, that it can in any event be abandoned; and indignantly frowning upon the first dawning of every attempt to alienate any portion of our country from the rest, or to enfeeble the sacred ties which now link together the various parts.

For this you have every inducement of sympathy and interest. Citizens, by birth or choice, of a common country, that country has a right to concentrate your affections. The name of American, which belongs to you, in your national capacity, must always exalt the just pride of Patriotism, more than any appellation derived from local discriminations. With slight shades of difference, you have the same religion, manners, habits, and political principles. You have in a common cause fought and triumphed together; the Independence and Liberty you possess are the work of joint counsels, and joint efforts, of common dangers, sufferings, and successes . . .

Though, in reviewing the incidents of my administration, I am unconscious of intentional error, I am nevertheless too sensible of my defects not to think it probable that I may have committed many errors. Whatever they may be, I fervently beseech the Almighty to avert or mitigate the evils to which they may tend. I shall also carry with me the hope, that my Country will never cease to view them with indulgence; and that, after forty-five years of my life dedicated to its service with an upright zeal, the faults of incompetent abilities will be consigned to oblivion, as myself must soon be to the mansions of rest.

Relying on its kindness in this as in other things, and actuated by that fervent love towards it, which is so natural to a man, who views it in the native soil of himself and his progenitors for several generations; I anticipate with pleasing expectation that retreat, in which I promise myself to realize, without alloy, the sweet enjoyment of partaking, in the midst of my fellow-citizens, the benign influence of good laws under a free government, the ever favorite object of my heart, and the happy reward, as I trust, of our mutual cares, labors, and dangers.

"COMMON SENSE" EXCERPT
Thomas Paine
(1737-1809)
1776

These are the times that try men's souls. The summer soldier and the sunshine patriot will, in this crisis, shrink from the service of their country; but he that stands it now, deserves the thanks of man and woman. Tyranny, like hell, is not easily conquered: yet we have this consolation with us, that the harder the conflict, the more glorious the triumph. What we obtain too cheaply, we esteem too lightly: it is dearness only that gives every thing its value. Heaven knows how to set a proper price upon its goods; and it would be strange indeed, if so celestial an article as freedom should not be highly rated. Britain, with an army to enforce her tyranny, has declared that she has a right, not only to tax, but "to bind us in all cases whatsoever;" and if being bound in that manner is not slavery, there is no such a thing as slavery upon earth. Even the expression impious; for so limited a power can belong only to God . . .

I love the man that can smile in trouble—that can gather strength from distress, and grow brave by reflection. It is the business of little minds to shrink; but he, whose heart is firm, and whose conscience approves his conduct, will pursue his principles unto death. My own line of reasoning is to myself, as straight and clear as a ray of light. Not all the treasures of the world, so far as I believe, could have induced me to support an offensive war, for I think it murder; but if a thief break into my house—burn and destroy my property, and kill, or threaten to kill me and those that are in it, and to "bind me in all cases whatsoever," to his absolute will, am I to suffer it? What signifies it to me, whether be who does it, is a King or a common man, my countryman, or not my countryman; whether it is done by an individual villain, or an army of men?

INDEPENDENCE ORATION EXCERPT

Samuel Adams
(1722-1803)
Philadelphia,
August 1776

Contemplate the mangled bodies of your countrymen and then say, what should be the reward of such sacrifices? Bid not our posterity bow the knee, supplicate the friendship, and plough and sow and reap, to glut the avarice of the men who have let loose on us the dogs of war to riot in our blood, and hunt us from the face of the earth! If ye love wealth better than liberty, the tranquillity of servitude than the animating contest of freedom, go from us in peace. We ask not your counsels or arams. Crouch down and lick the hands which feed you. May your chains set lightly upon you, and may posterity forget that ye were our countrymen.

THE MAN IN THE ARENA

Theodore Roosevelt
(1858-1919)
From the "Citizenship in a Republic" speech at the Sorbonne, Paris, April 23, 1910

It is not the critic who counts: not the man who points out how the strong man stumbles, or where the doer of deeds could have done better. The credit belongs to the man who is actually in the arena, whose face is marred by dust and sweat and blood; who strives valiantly; who errs and comes up short again and again, because there is no effort without error or shortcoming; but who does actually strive to do the deeds; who knows the great enthusiasms, the great devotions; who spends himself in a worthy cause; who at the best knows in the end the triumph of high achievement, and who at the worst, if he fails, at least he fails while daring greatly, so that his place shall never be with those cold timid souls who know neither victory nor defeat.

I HAVE A DREAM

Martin Luther King, Jr.
(1929-1968)
Washington, D.C.,
August 28, 1963

I am happy to join with you today in what will go down in history as the greatest demonstration for freedom in the history of our nation.

Five score years ago, a great American, in whose symbolic shadow we stand today, signed the Emancipation Proclamation. This momentous decree came as a great beacon light of hope to millions of Negro slaves who had been seared in the flames of withering injustice. It came as a joyous daybreak to end the long night of their captivity.

But one hundred years later, the Negro still is not free. One hundred years later, the life of the Negro is still sadly crippled by the manacles of segregation and the chains of discrimination. One hundred years later, the Negro lives on a lonely island of poverty in the midst of a vast ocean of material prosperity. One hundred years later, the Negro is still languishing in the corners of American society and finds himself an exile in his own land. So we have come here today to dramatize a shameful condition.

In a sense we have come to our nation's capital to cash a check. When the architects of our republic wrote the magnificent words of the Constitution and the Declaration of Independence, they were signing a promissory note to which every American was to fall heir. This note was a promise that all men, yes, black men as well as white men, would be guaranteed the unalienable rights of life, liberty, and the pursuit of happiness.

It is obvious today that America has defaulted on this promissory note insofar as her citizens of color are concerned. Instead of honoring this sacred obligation, America has given the Negro people a bad check, a check which has come back marked "insufficient funds." But we refuse to believe that the bank of justice is bankrupt. We refuse to believe that there are insufficient funds in the great vaults of opportunity of this nation. So we have come to cash this check — a check that will give us upon demand the riches of freedom and the security of justice. We have also come to this hallowed spot to remind America of the fierce urgency of now. This is no time to engage in the luxury of cooling off or to take the tranquilizing drug of gradualism. Now is the time to make real the promises of democracy. Now is the time to rise from the dark and desolate valley of segregation to the sunlit path of racial justice. Now is the time to lift our nation from the quick sands of racial injustice to the solid rock of brotherhood. Now is the time to make justice a reality for all of God's children.

It would be fatal for the nation to overlook the urgency of the moment. This sweltering summer of the Negro's legitimate discontent will not pass until there is an invigorating autumn of freedom and equality. Nineteen sixty-three is not an end, but a beginning. Those who hope that the Negro needed to blow off steam and will now be content will have a rude awakening if the nation returns to business as usual. There will be neither rest nor tranquility in America until the Negro is granted his citizenship rights. The whirlwinds of revolt will continue to shake the foundations of our nation until the bright day of justice emerges.

But there is something that I must say to my people who stand on the warm threshold which leads into the palace of justice. In the process of gaining our rightful place we must not be guilty of wrongful deeds. Let us not seek to satisfy our thirst for freedom by drinking from the cup of bitterness and hatred.

We must forever conduct our struggle on the high plane of dignity and discipline. We must not allow our creative protest to degenerate into physical violence. Again and again we must rise to the majestic heights of meeting physical force with soul force. The marvelous new militancy which has engulfed the Negro community must not lead us to a distrust of all white people, for many of our white brothers, as evidenced by their presence here today, have come to realize that their destiny is tied up with our destiny. They have come to realize that their freedom is inextricably bound to our freedom. We cannot walk alone.

As we walk, we must make the pledge that we shall always march ahead. We cannot turn back. There are those who are asking the devotees of civil rights, "When will you be satisfied?" We can never be satisfied as long as the Negro is the victim of the unspeakable horrors of police brutality. We can never be satisfied, as long as our bodies, heavy with the fatigue of travel, cannot gain lodging in the motels of the highways and the hotels of the cities. We cannot be satisfied as long as the Negro's basic mobility is from a smaller ghetto to a larger one. We can never be satisfied as long as our children are stripped of their selfhood and robbed of their dignity by signs stating "For Whites Only". We cannot be satisfied as long as a Negro in Mississippi cannot vote and a Negro in New York believes he has nothing for which to vote. No, no, we are not satisfied, and we will not be satisfied until justice rolls down like waters and righteousness like a mighty stream.

I am not unmindful that some of you have come here out of great trials and tribulations. Some of you have come fresh from narrow jail cells. Some of you have come from areas where your quest for freedom left you battered by the storms of persecution and staggered by the winds of police brutality. You have been the veterans of creative suffering. Continue to work with the faith that unearned suffering is redemptive.

Go back to Mississippi, go back to Alabama, go back to South Carolina, go back to Georgia, go back to Louisiana, go back to the slums and ghettos of our northern cities, knowing that somehow this situation can and will be changed.

Let us not wallow in the valley of despair.

I say to you today, my friends, so even though we face the difficulties of today and tomorrow, I still have a dream. It is a dream deeply rooted in the American dream.

I have a dream that one day this nation will rise up and live out the true meaning of its creed: "We hold these truths to be self-evident: that all men are created equal."

I have a dream that one day on the red hills of Georgia the sons of former slaves and the sons of former slave owners will be able to sit down together at the table of brotherhood.

I have a dream that one day even the state of Mississippi, a state sweltering with the heat of injustice, sweltering with the heat of oppression, will be transformed into an oasis of freedom and justice.

I have a dream that my four little children will one day live in a nation where they will not be judged by the color of their skin but by the content of their character.

I have a dream today.

I have a dream that one day, down in Alabama, with its vicious racists, with its governor having his lips dripping with the words of interposition and nullification; one day right there in Alabama, little black boys and black girls will be able to join hands with little white boys and white girls as sisters and brothers.

I have a dream today.

I have a dream that one day every valley shall be exalted, every hill and mountain shall be made low, the rough places will be made plain, and the crooked places will be made straight, and the glory of the Lord shall be revealed, and all flesh shall see it together.

This is our hope. This is the faith that I go back to the South with. With this faith we will be able to hew out of the mountain of despair a stone of hope. With this faith we will be able to transform the jangling discords of our nation into a beautiful symphony of brotherhood. With this faith we will be able to work together, to pray together, to struggle together, to go to jail together, to stand up for freedom together, knowing that we will be free one day.

This will be the day when all of God's children will be able to sing with a new meaning, "My country, 'tis of thee, sweet land of liberty, of thee I sing. Land where my fathers died, land of the pilgrim's pride, from every mountainside, let freedom ring."

And if America is to be a great nation this must become true. So let freedom ring from the prodigious hilltops of New Hampshire. Let freedom ring from the mighty mountains of New York. Let freedom ring from the heightening Alleghenies of Pennsylvania!

Let freedom ring from the snowcapped Rockies of Colorado!

Let freedom ring from the curvaceous slopes of California!

But not only that; let freedom ring from Stone Mountain of Georgia!

Let freedom ring from Lookout Mountain of Tennessee!

Let freedom ring from every hill and molehill of Mississippi. From every mountainside, let freedom ring.

And when this happens, when we allow freedom to ring, when we let it ring from every village and every hamlet, from every state and every city, we will be able to speed up that day when all of God's children, black men and white men, Jews and Gentiles, Protestants and Catholics, will be able to join hands and sing in the words of the old Negro spiritual, "Free at last! free at last! thank God Almighty, we are free at last!"

OTHER MEMORY WORK

PLANETS

Mercury	Mars	Uranus
Venus	Jupiter	Neptune
Earth	Saturn	Pluto[10]

CONTINENTS
(Greatest to Smallest by Land Area)

Asia	Antarctica
Africa	Europe
North America	Australia
South America	

OCEANS
(Greatest to Smallest)

Pacific
Atlantic
Indian
Southern
Arctic

STATES AND CAPITALS IN ORDER OF DATE[11]

State	State Capital	Year Joined the Union
Delaware	Dover	1787
Pennsylvania	Harrisburg	1787
New Jersey	Trenton	1787
Georgia	Atlanta	1788
Connecticut	Hartford	1788
Massachusetts	Boston	1788
Maryland	Annapolis	1788
South Carolina	Columbia	1788
New Hampshire	Concord	1788
Virginia	Richmond	1788
New York	Albany	1788
North Carolina	Raleigh	1789
Rhode Island	Providence	1790
Vermont	Montpelier	1791
Kentucky	Frankfort	1792
Tennessee	Nashville	1796
Ohio	Columbus	1803

State	State Capital	Year Joined the Union
Louisiana	Baton Rouge	1812
Indiana	Indianapolis	1816
Mississippi	Jackson	1817
Illinois	Springfield	1818
Alabama	Montgomery	1819
Maine	Augusta	1820
Missouri	Jefferson City	1821
Arkansas	Little Rock	1836
Michigan	Lansing	1837
Florida	Tallahassee	1845
Texas	Austin	1845
Iowa	Des Moines	1846
Wisconsin	Madison	1848
California	Sacramento	1850
Minnesota	St. Paul	1858
Oregon	Salem	1859
Kansas	Topeka	1861
West Virginia	Charleston	1863
Nevada	Carson City	1864
Nebraska	Lincoln	1867
Colorado	Denver	1876
North Dakota	Bismarck	1889
South Dakota	Pierre	1889
Montana	Helena	1889
Washington	Olympia	1889
Idaho	Boise	1890
Wyoming	Cheyenne	1890
Utah	Salt Lake City	1896
Oklahoma	Oklahoma City	1907
New Mexico	Santa Fe	1912
Arizona	Phoenix	1912
Alaska	Juneau	1959
Hawaii	Honolulu	1959

STATES AND CAPITALS IN ORDER OF ALPHABET

State	Capital	Postal Abbreviation
Alabama	Montgomery	AL
Alaska	Juneau	AK
Arizona	Phoenix	AZ
Arkansas	Little Rock	AR
California	Sacramento	CA
Colorado	Denver	CO
Connecticut	Hartford	CT
Delaware	Dover	DE
Florida	Tallahassee	FL
Georgia	Atlanta	GA
Hawaii	Honolulu	HI
Idaho	Boise	ID
Illinois	Springfield	IL
Indiana	Indianapolis	IN
Iowa	Des Moines	IA
Kansas	Topeka	KS
Kentucky	Frankfort	KY
Louisiana	Baton Rouge	LA
Maine	Augusta	ME
Maryland	Annapolis	MD
Massachusetts	Boston	MA
Michigan	Lansing	MI
Minnesota	St. Paul	MN
Mississippi	Jackson	MS
Missouri	Jefferson City	MO
Montana	Helena	MT
Nebraska	Lincoln	NE
Nevada	Carson City	NV
New Hampshire	Concord	NH
New Jersey	Trenton	NJ
New Mexico	Santa Fe	NM
New York	Albany	NY
North Carolina	Raleigh	NC
North Dakota	Bismarck	ND
Ohio	Columbus	OH
Oklahoma	Oklahoma City	OK
Oregon	Salem	OR
Pennsylvania	Harrisburg	PN
Rhode Island	Providence	RI
South Carolina	Columbia	SC

CINDY'S ANTHOLOGY   OTHER MEMORY WORK

State	Capital	Postal Abbreviation
South Dakota	Pierre	SD
Tennessee	Nashville	TN
Texas	Austin	TX
Utah	Salt Lake City	UT
Vermont	Montpelier	VT
Virginia	Richmond	VA
Washington	Olympia	WA
West Virginia	Charleston	WV
Wisconsin	Madison	WI
Wyoming	Cheyenne	WY

PRESIDENTS

1. George Washington
2. John Adams
3. Thomas Jefferson
4. James Madison
5. James Monroe
6. John Quincy Adams
7. Andrew Jackson
8. Martin Van Buren
9. William Henry Harrison
10. John Tyler
11. James K. Polk
12. Zachary Taylor
13. Millard Fillmore
14. Franklin Pierce
15. James Buchanan
16. Abraham Lincoln
17. Andrew Johnson
18. Ulysses S. Grant
19. Rutherford B. Hayes
20. James Garfield
21. Chester Arthur
22. Grover Cleveland
23. Benjamin Harrison
24. Grover Cleveland
25. William McKinley
26. Theodore Roosevelt
27. William Howard Taft
28. Woodrow Wilson
29. Warren G. Harding
30. Calvin Coolidge
31. Herbert Hoover
32. Franklin D. Roosevelt
33. Harry S. Truman
34. Dwight Eisenhower
35. John F. Kennedy
36. Lyndon B. Johnson
37. Richard Nixon
38. Gerald Ford
39. Jimmy Carter
40. Ronald Reagan
41. George Bush
42. Bill Clinton
43. George W. Bush
44. Barack Obama
45. Donald Trump
46. Joe Biden

CIVICS QUESTIONS

Adapted from the US Citizenship and Immigration Services Civics Test.[12]

AMERICAN GOVERNMENT: PRINCIPLES OF AMERICAN DEMOCRACY

1. What is the supreme law of the land?

    the Constitution

2. What does the Constitution do?

    sets up the government

    defines the government

    protects basic rights of Americans

3. The idea of self-government is in the first three words of the Constitution. What are these words?

    We the People

4. What is an amendment?

    a change (to the Constitution)

    an addition (to the Constitution)

5. What do we call the first ten amendments to the Constitution?

    the Bill of Rights

6. What is one right or freedom from the First Amendment?

    speech

    religion

    assembly

    press

    petition the government

7. How many amendments does the Constitution have?

    twenty-seven (27)

8. What did the Declaration of Independence do?

    announced our independence (from Great Britain)

    declared our independence (from Great Britain)

    said that the United States is free (from Great Britain)

9. What are two rights in the Declaration of Independence?

    life

    liberty

    pursuit of happiness

10. What is freedom of religion?

    You can practice any religion, or not practice a religion.

11. What is the economic system in the United States?

    capitalist economy

    market economy

12. What is the "rule of law"?

Everyone must follow the law.

Leaders must obey the law.

Government must obey the law.

No one is above the law.

AMERICAN GOVERNMENT: SYSTEM OF GOVERNMENT

13. Name one branch or part of the government.

Congress or legislative

President or executive

the courts or judicial

14. What stops one branch of government from becoming too powerful?

checks and balances

separation of powers

15. Who is in charge of the executive branch?

the President

16. Who makes federal laws?

Congress

Senate and House (of Representatives)

(U.S. or national) legislature

17. What are the two parts of the U.S. Congress?

the Senate and House (of Representatives)

18. How many U.S. Senators are there?

one hundred (100)

19. We elect a U.S. Senator for how many years?

six (6)

20. Who is one of your state's U.S. Senators now?

Answers will vary. [District of Columbia residents and residents of U.S. territories should answer that D.C. (or the territory where the applicant lives) has no U.S. Senators.]

21. The House of Representatives has how many voting members?

four hundred thirty-five (435)

22. We elect a U.S. Representative for how many years?

two (2)

23. Name your U.S. Representative.

Answers will vary. [Residents of territories with nonvoting Delegates or Resident Commissioners may provide the name of that Delegate or Commissioner. Also acceptable is any statement that the territory has no (voting) Representatives in Congress.]

24. Who does a U.S. Senator represent?

all people of the state

25. Why do some states have more Representatives than other states?

(because of) the state's population

(because) they have more people

(because) some states have more people

26. We elect a President for how many years?

four (4)

27. In what month do we vote for President?

November

28. What is the name of the President of the United States now?

29. What is the name of the Vice President of the United States now?

30. If the President can no longer serve, who becomes President?

the Vice President

31. If both the President and the Vice President can no longer serve, who becomes President?

the Speaker of the House

32. Who is the Commander in Chief of the military?

the President

33. Who signs bills to become laws?

the President

34. Who vetoes bills?

the President

35. What does the President's Cabinet do?

advises the President

36. What are two Cabinet-level positions?

Secretary of Agriculture

Secretary of Commerce

Secretary of Defense

Secretary of Education

Secretary of Energy

Secretary of Health and Human Services

Secretary of Homeland Security

Secretary of Housing and Urban Development

Secretary of the Interior

Secretary of Labor

Secretary of State

Secretary of Transportation

Secretary of the Treasury

Secretary of Veterans Affairs

Attorney General

Vice President

37. What does the judicial branch do?

> *reviews laws*
>
> *explains laws*
>
> *resolves disputes (disagreements)*
>
> *decides if a law goes against the Constitution*

38. What is the highest court in the United States?

> *the Supreme Court*

39. How many justices are on the Supreme Court?

> *Nine (9)*

40. Who is the Chief Justice of the United States now?

> *Chief Justice John Roberts (sworn in as Chief Justice in 2005)*

41. Under our Constitution, some powers belong to the federal government. What is one power of the federal government?

> *to print money*
>
> *to declare war*
>
> *to create an army*
>
> *to make treaties*

42. Under our Constitution, some powers belong to the states. What is one power of the states?

> *provide schooling and education*
>
> *provide protection (police)*
>
> *provide safety (fire departments)*
>
> *give a driver's license*
>
> *approve zoning and land use*

43. Who is the Governor of your state now?

> *Answers will vary. [District of Columbia residents should answer that D.C. does not have a Governor.]*

44. What is the capital of your state?

> *Answers will vary. [District of Columbia residents should answer that D.C. is not a state and does not have a capital. Residents of U.S. territories should name the capital of the territory.]*

45. What are the two major political parties in the United States?

> *Democratic and Republican*

46. What is the political party of the President now?

47. What is the name of the Speaker of the House of Representatives now?

AMERICAN GOVERNMENT: RIGHTS AND RESPONSIBILITIES

48. There are four amendments to the Constitution about who can vote. Describe one of them.

    Citizens eighteen (18) and older (can vote).

    You don't have to pay (a poll tax) to vote.

    Any citizen can vote. (Women and men can vote.)

    A male citizen of any race (can vote).

49. What is one responsibility that is only for United States citizens?

    serve on a jury

    vote in a federal election

50. Name one right only for United States citizens.

    vote in a federal election

    run for federal office

51. What are two rights of everyone living in the United States?

    freedom of expression

    freedom of speech

    freedom of assembly

    freedom to petition the government

    freedom of religion

    the right to bear arms

52. What do we show loyalty to when we say the Pledge of Allegiance?

    the United States

    the flag

53. What is one promise you make when you become a United States citizen?

    give up loyalty to other countries

    defend the Constitution and laws of the United States

    obey the laws of the United States

    serve in the U.S. military (if needed)

    serve (do important work for) the nation (if needed)

    be loyal to the United States

54. How old do citizens have to be to vote for President?

    eighteen (18) and older

55. What are two ways that Americans can participate in their democracy?

    vote

    join a political party

    help with a campaign

    join a civic group

    join a community group

    give an elected official your opinion on an issue

    call Senators and Representatives

    publicly support or oppose an issue or policy

run for office

write to a newspaper

56. When is the last day you can send in federal income tax forms?

April 15

57. When must all men register for the Selective Service?

at age eighteen (18)

between eighteen (18) and twenty-six (26)

AMERICAN HISTORY: COLONIAL PERIOD AND INDEPENDENCE

58. What is one reason colonists came to America?

freedom

political liberty

religious freedom

economic opportunity

practice their religion

escape persecution

59. Who lived in America before the Europeans arrived?

American Indians, also known as Native Americans

60. What group of people was taken to America and sold as slaves?

Africans

people from Africa

61. Why did the colonists fight the British?

because of high taxes (taxation without representation)

because the British army stayed in their houses (boarding, quartering)

because they didn't have self-government

62. Who wrote the Declaration of Independence?

(Thomas) Jefferson

63. When was the Declaration of Independence adopted?

July 4, 1776

64. There were 13 original states. Name three.

New Hampshire	*Delaware*
Massachusetts	*Maryland*
Rhode Island	*Virginia*
Connecticut	*North Carolina*
New York	*South Carolina*
New Jersey	*Georgia*
Pennsylvania	

65. What happened at the Constitutional Convention?

> *The Constitution was written.*
>
> *The Founding Fathers wrote the Constitution.*

66. When was the Constitution written?

> *1787*

67. The Federalist Papers supported the passage of the U.S. Constitution. Name one of the writers.

> *(James) Madison*
>
> *(Alexander) Hamilton*
>
> *(John) Jay*
>
> *Publius*

68. What is one thing Benjamin Franklin is famous for?

> *U.S. diplomat*
>
> *oldest member of the Constitutional Convention*
>
> *first Postmaster General of the United States*
>
> *writer of "Poor Richard's Almanac"*
>
> *started the first free libraries*

69. Who is the "Father of Our Country"?

> *(George) Washington*

70. Who was the first President?

> *(George) Washington*

AMERICAN HISTORY: 1800s

71. What territory did the United States buy from France in 1803?

> *the Louisiana Territory*

72. Name one war fought by the United States in the 1800s.

> *War of 1812*
>
> *Mexican-American War*
>
> *Civil War*
>
> *Spanish-American War*

73. Name the U.S. war between the North and the South.

> *the Civil War, sometimes called the War between the States*

74. Name one problem that led to the Civil War.

> *slavery*
>
> *economic reasons*
>
> *states' rights*

75. What was one important thing that Abraham Lincoln did?

> *freed the slaves (Emancipation Proclamation)*
>
> *saved (or preserved) the Union*
>
> *led the United States during the Civil War*

76. What did the Emancipation Proclamation do?

freed the slaves

freed slaves in the Confederacy

freed slaves in the Confederate states

freed slaves in most Southern states

77. What did Susan B. Anthony do?

fought for women's rights

fought for civil rights

AMERICAN HISTORY: RECENT AMERICAN HISTORY AND OTHER IMPORTANT HISTORICAL INFORMATION

78. Name one war fought by the United States in the 1900s.

World War I

World War II

Korean War

Vietnam War

(Persian) Gulf War

79. Who was President during World War I?

(Woodrow) Wilson

80. Who was President during the Great Depression and World War II?

(Franklin) Roosevelt

81. Who did the United States fight in World War II?

Japan, Germany, and Italy

82. Before he was President, Eisenhower was a general. What war was he in?

World War II

83. During the Cold War, what was the main concern of the United States?

Communism

84. What movement tried to end racial discrimination?

civil rights (movement)

85. What did Martin Luther King, Jr. do?

fought for civil rights

worked for equality for all Americans

86. What major event happened on September 11, 2001, in the United States?

Terrorists attacked the United States.

87. Name one American Indian tribe in the United States.

Cherokee	*Apache*	*Arawak*	*Crow*
Navajo	*Iroquois*	*Shawnee*	*Teton*
Sioux	*Creek*	*Mohegan*	*Hopi*
Chippewa	*Blackfeet*	*Huron*	*Inuit*
Choctaw	*Seminole*	*Oneida*	
Pueblo	*Cheyenne*	*Lakota*	

INTEGRATED CIVICS: GEOGRAPHY

88. Name one of the two longest rivers in the United States.

    Missouri (River)

    Mississippi (River)

89. What ocean is on the West Coast of the United States?

    Pacific (Ocean)

90. What ocean is on the East Coast of the United States?

    Atlantic (Ocean)

91. Name one U.S. territory.

    Puerto Rico

    U.S. Virgin Islands

    American Samoa

    Northern Mariana Islands

    Guam

92. Name one state that borders Canada.

Maine	*Ohio*	*Idaho*
New Hampshire	*Michigan*	*Washington*
Vermont	*Minnesota*	*Alaska*
New York	*North Dakota*	
Pennsylvania	*Montana*	

93. Name one state that borders Mexico.

    California

    Arizona

    New Mexico

    Texas

94. What is the capital of the United States?

    Washington, D.C.

95. Where is the Statue of Liberty?

    New York (Harbor)

    Liberty Island

    [Also acceptable are New Jersey, near New York City, and on the Hudson (River).]

INTEGRATED CIVICS: SYMBOLS

96. Why does the flag have 13 stripes?

   because there were 13 original colonies

   because the stripes represent the original colonies

97. Why does the flag have 50 stars?

   because there is one star for each state

   because each star represents a state

   because there are 50 states

98. What is the name of the national anthem?

   The Star-Spangled Banner

INTEGRATED CIVICS: HOLIDAYS

99. When do we celebrate Independence Day?

   July 4

100. Name two national U.S. holidays.

   New Year's Day

   Martin Luther King, Jr. Day

   Presidents' Day

   Memorial Day

   Juneteenth

   Independence Day

   Labor Day

   Columbus Day

   Veterans Day

   Thanksgiving

   Christmas

SHAKESPEARE MEMORY PASSAGES

"THE QUALITY OF MERCY IS NOT STRAINED"
The Merchant of Venice
Act IV, Scene i
(PORTIA speaks)

The quality of mercy is not strained;
It droppeth as the gentle rain from heaven
Upon the place beneath. It is twice blest;
It blesseth him that gives and him that takes:
'T is mightiest in the mightiest; it becomes
The throned monarch better than his crown:
His sceptre shows the force of temporal power,
The attribute to awe and majesty,
Wherein doth sit the dread and fear of kings;
But mercy is above this sceptred sway;
It is enthronèd in the hearts of kings,
It is an attribute to God himself;
And earthly power doth then show likest God's
When mercy seasons justice. Therefore, Jew,
Though justice be thy plea, consider this,
That, in the course of justice, none of us
Should see salvation: we do pray for mercy;
And that same prayer doth teach us all to render
The deeds of mercy. I have spoke thus much
To mitigate the justice of thy plea;
Which if thou follow, this strict court of Venice
Must needs give sentence 'gainst the merchant there.

"TO BE OR NOT TO BE"
Hamlet
Act III, Scene i
(HAMLET speaks)
[*This is quite delightful with its odd words!*]

To be, or not to be, that is the question:
Whether 'tis nobler in the mind to suffer
The slings and arrows of outrageous fortune,
Or to take arms against a sea of troubles
And by opposing end them. To die—to sleep,
No more; and by a sleep to say we end
The heart-ache and the thousand natural shocks
That flesh is heir to: 'tis a consummation
Devoutly to be wish'd. To die, to sleep;
To sleep, perchance to dream—ay, there's the rub:
For in that sleep of death what dreams may come,
When we have shuffled off this mortal coil,
Must give us pause—there's the respect
That makes calamity of so long life.

For who would bear the whips and scorns of time,
Th'oppressor's wrong, the proud man's contumely,
The pangs of dispriz'd love, the law's delay,
The insolence of office, and the spurns
That patient merit of th'unworthy takes,
When he himself might his quietus make
With a bare bodkin? Who would fardels bear,
To grunt and sweat under a weary life,
But that the dread of something after death,
The undiscovere'd country, from whose bourn
No traveller returns, puzzles the will,
And makes us rather bear those ills we have
Than fly to others that we know not of?
Thus conscience does make cowards of us all,
And thus the native hue of resolution
Is sicklied o'er with the pale cast of thought,
And enterprises of great pitch and moment
With this regard their currents turn awry
And lose the name of action.

"FRIENDS, ROMANS, COUNTRYMEN"

Julius Caesar
Act III, Scene ii
(MARC ANTONY speaks)

Friends, Romans, countrymen, lend me your ears;
I come to bury Caesar, not to praise him.
The evil that men do lives after them;
The good is oft interred with their bones;
So let it be with Caesar. The noble Brutus
Hath told you Caesar was ambitious:
If it were so, it was a grievous fault,
And grievously hath Caesar answer'd it.
Here, under leave of Brutus and the rest–
For Brutus is an honourable man;
So are they all, all honourable men–
Come I to speak in Caesar's funeral.
He was my friend, faithful and just to me:
But Brutus says he was ambitious;
And Brutus is an honourable man.
He hath brought many captives home to Rome
Whose ransoms did the general coffers fill:
Did this in Caesar seem ambitious?
When that the poor have cried, Caesar hath wept:
Ambition should be made of sterner stuff:
Yet Brutus says he was ambitious;

And Brutus is an honourable man.
You all did see that on the Lupercal
I thrice presented him a kingly crown,
Which he did thrice refuse: was this ambition?
Yet Brutus says he was ambitious;
And, sure, he is an honourable man.
I speak not to disprove what Brutus spoke,
But here I am to speak what I do know.
You all did love him once, not without cause:
What cause withholds you then, to mourn for him?
O judgment! thou art fled to brutish beasts,
And men have lost their reason. Bear with me;
My heart is in the coffin there with Caesar,
And I must pause till it come back to me.

"ALL THE WORLD'S A STAGE"

As You Like It
Act II, Scene vii
(JAQUES speaks)

All the world's a stage,
And all the men and women merely players;
They have their exits and their entrances;
And one man in his time plays many parts,
His acts being seven ages. At first the infant,
Mewling and puking in the nurse's arms;
And then the whining school-boy, with his satchel
And shining morning face, creeping like snail
Unwillingly to school. And then the lover,
Sighing like furnace, with a woeful ballad
Made to his mistress' eyebrow. Then a soldier,
Full of strange oaths, and bearded like the pard,
Jealous in honour, sudden and quick in quarrel,
Seeking the bubble reputation
Even in the cannon's mouth. And then the justice,
In fair round belly with good capon lin'd,
With eyes severe and beard of formal cut,
Full of wise saws and modern instances;
And so he plays his part. The sixth age shifts
Into the lean and slipper'd pantaloon,
With spectacles on nose and pouch on side;
His youthful hose, well sav'd, a world too wide
For his shrunk shank; and his big manly voice,
Turning again toward childish treble, pipes
And whistles in his sound. Last scene of all,

That ends this strange eventful history,
Is second childishness and mere oblivion;
Sans teeth, sans eyes, sans taste, sans everything.

**ST. CRISPIN'S
DAY SPEECH**

Henry V
Act IV, Scene iii
(HENRY V speaks)

What's he that wishes so?
My cousin Westmoreland? No, my fair cousin:
If we are mark'd to die, we are enow
To do our country loss; and if to live,
The fewer men, the greater share of honour.
God's will! I pray thee, wish not one man more.
By Jove, I am not covetous for gold,
Nor care I who doth feed upon my cost;
It yearns me not if men my garments wear;
Such outward things dwell not in my desires:
But if it be a sin to covet honour,
I am the most offending soul alive.
No, faith, my coz, wish not a man from England:
God's peace! I would not lose so great an honour
As one man more, methinks, would share from me
For the best hope I have. O, do not wish one more!
Rather proclaim it, Westmoreland, through my host,
That he which hath no stomach to this fight,
Let him depart; his passport shall be made
And crowns for convoy put into his purse:
We would not die in that man's company
That fears his fellowship to die with us.
This day is called the feast of Crispian:
He that outlives this day, and comes safe home,
Will stand a tip-toe when the day is named,
And rouse him at the name of Crispian.
He that shall live this day, and see old age,
Will yearly on the vigil feast his neighbours,
And say 'To-morrow is Saint Crispian:'
Then will he strip his sleeve and show his scars.
And say 'These wounds I had on Crispin's day.'
Old men forget: yet all shall be forgot,
But he'll remember with advantages
What feats he did that day: then shall our names.
Familiar in his mouth as household words
Harry the king, Bedford and Exeter,
Warwick and Talbot, Salisbury and Gloucester,

Be in their flowing cups freshly remember'd.
This story shall the good man teach his son;
And Crispin Crispian shall ne'er go by,
From this day to the ending of the world,
But we in it shall be remember'd;
We few, we happy few, we band of brothers;
For he to-day that sheds his blood with me
Shall be my brother; be he ne'er so vile,
This day shall gentle his condition:
And gentlemen in England now a-bed
Shall think themselves accursed they were not here,
And hold their manhoods cheap whiles any speaks
That fought with us upon Saint Crispin's day.

"HOW SWEET THE MOONLIGHT"
The Merchant of Venice
Act V, Scene i
(LORENZO speaks)

How sweet the moonlight sleeps upon this bank!
Here will we sit and let the sounds of music
Creep in our ears: soft stillness and the night
Become the touches of sweet harmony.
Sit, Jessica. Look how the floor of heaven
Is thick inlaid with patines of bright gold:
There's not the smallest orb which thou behold'st
But in his motion like an angel sings,
Still quiring to the young-eyed cherubins;
Such harmony is in immortal souls;
But whilst this muddy vesture of decay
Doth grossly close it in, we cannot hear it.

"THE MAN THAT HATH NO MUSIC IN HIMSELF"
The Merchant of Venice
Act V, Scene i
(LORENZO speaks)

The man that hath no music in himself,
Nor is not moved with concord of sweet sounds,
Is fit for treasons, stratagems and spoils;
The motions of his spirit are dull as night
And his affections dark as Erebus:
Let no such man be trusted. Mark the music.

"FEAR NO MORE THE HEAT O' THE SUN"
Cymbeline
Act IV, Scene ii
(Song)

Fear no more the heat o' the sun,
Nor the furious winter's rages;
Thou thy worldly task hast done,
Home art gone, and ta'en thy wages:
Golden lads and girls all must,
As chimney-sweepers, come to dust.

Fear no more the frown o' the great;
Thou art past the tyrant's stroke;
Care no more to clothe and eat;
To thee the reed is as the oak:
The scepter, learning, physic, must
All follow this, and come to dust.

Fear no more the lightning flash,
Nor the all-dreaded thunder stone;
Fear not slander, censure rash;
Thou hast finished joy and moan:
All lovers young, all lovers must
Consign to thee, and come to dust.

No exorciser harm thee!
Nor no witchcraft charm thee!
Ghost unlaid forbear thee!
Nothing ill come near thee!
Quiet consummation have;
And renownèd be thy grave!

"WHEN ICICLES HANG"

Love's Labour's Lost
Act V, Scene ii
(Winter song)

When icicles hang by the wall,
    And Dick the shepherd blows his nail,
And Tom bears logs into the hall,
    And milk comes frozen home in pail,
When blood is nipped, and ways be foul,
Then nightly sings the staring owl,
        To-whoo;
To-whit, to-whoo, a merry note,
While greasy Joan doth keel the pot.

When all aloud the wind doth blow,
    And coughing drowns the parson's saw,
And birds sit brooding in the snow,
    And Marian's nose looks red and raw,
When roasted crabs hiss in the bowl,
Then nightly sings the staring owl,
        To-whoo;
To-whit, to-whoo, a merry note,
While greasy Joan doth keel the pot.

"TOMORROW AND TOMORROW AND TOMORROW"

Macbeth
Act V, Scene v
(MACBETH speaks)

Tomorrow, and tomorrow, and tomorrow,
Creeps in this petty pace from day to day,
To the last syllable of recorded time;
And all our yesterdays have lighted fools
The way to dusty death. Out, out, brief candle!
Life's but a walking shadow, a poor player,
That struts and frets his hour upon the stage,
And then is heard no more. It is a tale
Told by an idiot, full of sound and fury,
Signifying nothing.

"THY HUSBAND IS THY LORD, THY LIFE, THY KEEPER"

The Taming of the Shrew
Act V, Scene ii
(KATHARINA speaks)

Fie, fie! unknit that threatening unkind brow,
And dart not scornful glances from those eyes
To wound thy lord, thy king, thy governor.
It blots thy beauty as frosts do bite the meads,
Confounds thy fame as whirlwinds shake fair buds,
And in no sense is meet or amiable.
A woman mov'd is like a fountain troubled-
Muddy, ill-seeming, thick, bereft of beauty;
And while it is so, none so dry or thirsty
Will deign to sip or touch one drop of it.
Thy husband is thy lord, thy life, thy keeper,
Thy head, thy sovereign; one that cares for thee,
And for thy maintenance commits his body
To painful labour both by sea and land,
To watch the night in storms, the day in cold,
Whilst thou liest warm at home, secure and safe;
And craves no other tribute at thy hands
But love, fair looks, and true obedience-
Too little payment for so great a debt.
Such duty as the subject owes the prince,
Even such a woman oweth to her husband;
And when she is froward, peevish, sullen, sour,
And not obedient to his honest will,
What is she but a foul contending rebel
And graceless traitor to her loving lord?
I am asham'd that women are so simple
To offer war where they should kneel for peace;
Or seek for rule, supremacy, and sway,

When they are bound to serve, love, and obey.
Why are our bodies soft and weak and smooth,
Unapt to toil and trouble in the world,
But that our soft conditions and our hearts
Should well agree with our external parts?
Come, come, you forward and unable worms!
My mind hath been as big as one of yours,
My heart as great, my reason haply more,
To bandy word for word and frown for frown;
But now I see our lances are but straws,
Our strength as weak, our weakness past compare,
That seeming to be most which we indeed least are.
Then vail your stomachs, for it is no boot,
And place your hands below your husband's foot;
In token of which duty, if he please,
My hand is ready, may it do him ease.'

"BUT, SOFT! WHAT LIGHT THROUGH YONDER WINDOW BREAKS?"

Romeo and Juliet
Act II, Scene ii
(ROMEO speaks)

He jests at scars that never felt a wound.
JULIET *appears above at a window*
But, soft! what light through yonder window breaks?
It is the east, and Juliet is the sun.
Arise, fair sun, and kill the envious moon,
Who is already sick and pale with grief,
That thou her maid art far more fair than she:
Be not her maid, since she is envious;
Her vestal livery is but sick and green
And none but fools do wear it; cast it off.
It is my lady, O, it is my love!
O, that she knew she were!
She speaks yet she says nothing: what of that?
Her eye discourses; I will answer it.
I am too bold, 'tis not to me she speaks:
Two of the fairest stars in all the heaven,
Having some business, do entreat her eyes
To twinkle in their spheres till they return.
What if her eyes were there, they in her head?
The brightness of her cheek would shame those stars,
As daylight doth a lamp; her eyes in heaven
Would through the airy region stream so bright
That birds would sing and think it were not night.

See, how she leans her cheek upon her hand!
O, that I were a glove upon that hand,
That I might touch that cheek!

"THE LUNATIC, THE LOVER AND THE POET"

A Midsummer Night's Dream
Act V, Scene i
(THESEUS speaks)

More strange than true: I never may believe
These antique fables, nor these fairy toys.
Lovers and madmen have such seething brains,
Such shaping fantasies, that apprehend
More than cool reason ever comprehends.
The lunatic, the lover and the poet
Are of imagination all compact:
One sees more devils than vast hell can hold,
That is, the madman: the lover, all as frantic,
Sees Helen's beauty in a brow of Egypt:
The poet's eye, in fine frenzy rolling,
Doth glance from heaven to earth, from earth to heaven;
And as imagination bodies forth
The forms of things unknown, the poet's pen
Turns them to shapes and gives to airy nothing
A local habitation and a name.
Such tricks hath strong imagination,
That if it would but apprehend some joy,
It comprehends some bringer of that joy;
Or in the night, imagining some fear,
How easy is a bush supposed a bear!

"THEN YOU MUST SPEAK OF ONE WHO LOVED NOT WISELY"

Othello
Act V, Scene ii
(OTHELLO's death speech)

Soft you; a word or two, before you go.
I have done the state some service, and they know't;
No more of that;-I pray you, in your letters,
When you shall these unlucky deeds relate,
Speak of me as I am; nothing extenuate,
Nor set down aught in malice: then must you speak
Of one, that lov'd not wisely, but too well;
Of one, not easily jealous, but, being wrought,
Perplex'd in the extreme: of one, whose hand,
Like the base Indian, threw a pearl away,
Richer than all his tribe; of one, whose subdu'd eyes,
Albeit unused to the melting mood,
Drop tears as fast as the Arabian trees

Their medicinal gum": Set you down this:
And say, besides, that in Aleppo once,
Where a malignant and a turban'd Turk"
Beat a Venetian, and traduc'd the state,
I took by the throat the circumcised dog,
And smote him—thus.

"FAREWELL TO HIS GREATNESS"

Henry VIII
Act 3, Scene ii
(CARDINAL WOLSEY
speaks)

So farewell to the little good you bear me.
Farewell! a long farewell, to all my greatness!
This is the state of man: to-day he puts forth
The tender leaves of hopes; to-morrow blossoms,
And bears his blushing honours thick upon him;
The third day comes a frost, a killing frost,
And, when he thinks, good easy man, full surely
His greatness is a-ripening, nips his root,
And then he falls, as I do. I have ventured,
Like little wanton boys that swim on bladders,
This many summers in a sea of glory,
But far beyond my depth: my high-blown pride
At length broke under me and now has left me,
Weary and old with service, to the mercy
Of a rude stream, that must for ever hide me.
Vain pomp and glory of this world, I hate ye:
I feel my heart new open'd. O, how wretched
Is that poor man that hangs on princes' favours!
There is, betwixt that smile we would aspire to,
That sweet aspect of princes, and their ruin,
More pangs and fears than wars or women have:
And when he falls, he falls like Lucifer,
Never to hope again.

"GIVE THY THOUGHTS NO TONGUE"

Hamlet
Act I, Scene iii
(POLONIUS's famous
advice to LAERTES)

Give thy thoughts no tongue,
Nor any unproportioned thought his act.
Be thou familiar, but by no means vulgar.
Those friends thou hast, and their adoption tried,
Grapple them to thy soul with hoops of steel;
But do not dull thy palm with entertainment
Of each new-hatch'd, unfledged comrade. Beware
Of entrance to a quarrel, but being in,

Bear't that the opposed may beware of thee.
Give every man thy ear, but few thy voice;
Take each man's censure, but reserve thy judgment.
Costly thy habit as thy purse can buy,
But not express'd in fancy; rich, not gaudy;
For the apparel oft proclaims the man,
And they in France of the best rank and station
Are of a most select and generous chief in that.
Neither a borrower nor a lender be;
For loan oft loses both itself and friend,
And borrowing dulls the edge of husbandry.
This above all: to thine ownself be true,
And it must follow, as the night the day,
Thou canst not then be false to any man.
Farewell: my blessing season this in thee!

"THIS ROYAL THRONE OF KINGS, THIS SCEPTER'D ISLE"

Richard II
Act II, Scene i
(JOHN OF GAUNT speaks)

This royal throne of kings, this scepter'd isle,
  This earth of majesty, this seat of Mars,
This other Eden, demi-paradise,
This fortress built by Nature for herself
Against infection and the hand of war,
This happy breed of men, this little world,
This precious stone set in the silver sea,
Which serves it in the office of a wall,
Or as a moat defensive to a house,
Against the envy of less happier lands,
This blessed plot, this earth, this realm, this England,
This nurse, this teeming womb of royal kings,
Fear'd by their breed and famous by their birth,
Renowned for their deeds as far from home,
For Christian service and true chivalry,
As is the sepulchre in stubborn Jewry,
Of the world's ransom, blessed Mary's Son,
This land of such dear souls, this dear dear land,
Dear for her reputation through the world,
Is now leased out, I die pronouncing it,
Like to a tenement or pelting farm:
England, bound in with the triumphant sea
Whose rocky shore beats back the envious siege
Of watery Neptune, is now bound in with shame,

With inky blots and rotten parchment bonds:
That England, that was wont to conquer others,
Hath made a shameful conquest of itself.
Ah, would the scandal vanish with my life,
How happy then were my ensuing death!

"IF WE SHADOWS HAVE OFFENDED"

A Midsummer Night's Dream
Act V, Scene i
(PUCK speaks)

If we shadows have offended,
Think but this and all is mended,
That you have but slumber'd here
While these visions did appear.
And this weak and idle theme,
No more yielding but a dream.
Gentles, do not reprehend:
If you pardon, we will mend:
And, as I am an honest Puck,
If we have unearned luck
Now to 'scape the serpent's tongue,
We will make amends ere long;
Else the Puck a liar call:
So, good night unto you all.
Give me your hands, if we be friends,
And Robin shall restore amends.

SONNET 29

William Shakespeare
(1564-1616)

When, in disgrace with fortune and men's eyes,
I all alone beweep my outcast state,
And trouble deaf heaven with my bootless cries,
And look upon myself and curse my fate,
Wishing me like to one more rich in hope,
Featured like him, like him with friends possessed,
Desiring this man's art and that man's scope,
With what I most enjoy contented least;
Yet in these thoughts myself almost despising,
Haply I think on thee, and then my state,
(Like to the lark at break of day arising
From sullen earth) sings hymns at heaven's gate;
    For thy sweet love remembered such wealth brings
    That then I scorn to change my state with kings.

SONNET 18
William Shakespeare
(1564-1616)

Shall I compare thee to a summer's day?
Thou art more lovely and more temperate:
Rough winds do shake the darling buds of May,
And summer's lease hath all too short a date;
Sometime too hot the eye of heaven shines,
And often is his gold complexion dimm'd;
And every fair from fair sometime declines,
By chance or nature's changing course untrimm'd;
But thy eternal summer shall not fade,
Nor lose possession of that fair thou ow'st;
Nor shall death brag thou wander'st in his shade,
When in eternal lines to time thou grow'st:
    So long as men can breathe or eyes can see,
    So long lives this, and this gives life to thee.

READ-ALOUD BOOKS

There are so many wonderful books and many, many good choices are not listed here. These are some of our favorites that we have enjoyed in Morning Time with my own family and also with students I have taught. I have jotted down a few thoughts about each book.

THE ADVENTURES OF HUCKLEBERRY FINN
Mark Twain
(1835-1910)

This makes a great read-aloud, especially since you can avoid reading aloud the bad words, which I don't necessarily always do, but in this book there are a lot of N-words. While I understand why Twain used them, I would rather not hear them.

THE ADVENTURES OF TOM SAWYER
Mark Twain
(1835-1910)

This is the quintessential American novel and so much fun to read aloud more than once. It's not necessary to read this before *Huck Finn*, but if you can read it to your younger children, they will be glad to see Tom and Huck again when you read *Huck Finn*.

ALICE'S ADVENTURES IN WONDERLAND and THROUGH THE LOOKING-GLASS
Lewis Carroll
(1832-1898)

Every time I read these, I get a little more out of them. Someday I am going to read them super-slowly so as not to miss a thing—someday when I am super-smart.

AMERICAN TALL TALES
Adrien Stoutenburg
(1916-1982)

My new student and I listened to this book on audio. The narration was excellent and most of the stories were fun, too. A few of them bogged down, but in spite of that this is a great introduction to American stories. I don't often do audio with students, but I am happy we did with this book. The voice helped to make the book more compelling. We followed up many of the stories by watching cartoons of them on YouTube, mostly from 1940s Disney.

The last story, about Joe Magarac, was the least interesting, in my opinion.

THE ARTHURIAN TRILOGY
The Sword and the Circle
The Light Beyond the Forest
The Road to Camlann
Rosemary Sutcliff
(1920-1992)

There are so many Arthurian books to chose from! I recommend these for read-alouds even if you have already read the Howard Pyle Arthur. The language is rich, and possibly difficult at first, but once you get into it, it sings. Beautifully written by Sutcliff and oh, so English. You should follow this up in a year or so with *The Once and Future King* by T. H. White and *The Idylls of the King* by Alfred, Lord Tennyson.

BEAUTIFUL STORIES FROM SHAKESPEARE FOR CHILDREN
E. Nesbit
(1858-1924)

I finished reading this with my student over a two year period. He drew posters or pictures of the characters and plot while I read. He loves Shakespeare and this book helped a lot (along with my own love of Shakespeare).

My student wants to read all of the plays!

THE BLACK ARROW
Robert Louis Stevenson
(1850-1894)

Another excellent book set in the days of chivalry. Look for the Scribner Classic edition.

BLACK FOX OF LORNE
Marguerite De Angeli
(1889-1987)

A medieval tale of chivalry that we enjoy.

THE BLUE FAIRY BOOK (AND OTHERS)
Andrew Lang
(1844-1912)

This is a book of fairy tales collected by Andrew Lang and contains truly memorable stories to read aloud as part of a shared family culture. If fairy stories can't get a five-star rating then what is our standard? Five stars to Andrew Lang and his magnificent collection of multi-colored fairy stories. *The Blue Fairy Book* is the first in the series. *The Yellow Fairy Book* is one of my favorites.

**THE BOOK OF THE
ANCIENT GREEKS**
Dorothy Mills
(1889-1959)

This turned out to be my favorite book on ancient Greece ever. I have enjoyed many books in the past on this subject, including Edith Hamilton's great books, but this Dorothy Mills book made me feel that if all I did was study the Greeks for the rest of my life, I would not have wasted my time. Truth, beauty and goodness, oh, my!

CADDIE WOODLAWN
Carol Ryrie Brink
(1895-1981)

Carol Ryrie Brink is a family favorite author. This is one of those light, fun stories that subtly enter your family culture.

**CARRY ON, MR.
BOWDITCH**
Jean Lee Latham
(1902-1995)

This is a true story of a boy overcoming great odds in order to learn.

I enjoyed reading this with my eleven-year-old student. He wanted me to look up more details about Nathaniel Bowditch when we finished. I think we both expected a death at the end, even though I should have remembered it did not end like that. It was fun to discover that Nathaniel went on to have eight children.

**CHEAPER BY THE
DOZEN**
Frank B. Gilbreth,
Jr. (1911-2001) and
Ernestine Gilbreth
Carey (1908-2006)

True story of a large family. This is a great book to make your family feel a little more normal. One of the most humorous books around.

A CHRISTMAS CAROL
Charles Dickens
(1812-1870)

I listened to the audiobook, narrated beautifully by Tim Curry, in time for my December book club meeting. I also read it aloud to my students.

While I have friends who take umbrage at the book's theology, I still find myself filled with joy in Scrooge's change. Dickens captures all that infectious joy. Truly this is a short, brilliant work capturing the essence of Advent—the darkness before the light.

As to the rest of Dickens's works, I am an unapologetic fan. Yes, yes, he is wordy. Sometimes words are the thing. I find his delightful. I recommend *Bleak House*—the book, not the movie—if you need a starting place.

**THE COMPLETE
WINNIE-THE-POOH**
A. A. Milne
(1882-1956)

My favorite bear.
"Wherever I am, there's always Pooh!"
"A long time ago, about last Friday."
I recommend all four books. Do not skip the poems.

FAMILY GRANDSTAND
Carol Ryrie Brink
(1895-1981)

From the author of *Caddie Woodlawn*, this wonderful story which I inherited from my aunt will stick with you for a long time. The father is a college professor and the mom writes mysteries in the garret.

FARMER GILES OF HAM
J. R. R. Tolkien
(1892-1973)

My husband, Tim, and I listened to this on our trip home from visiting my parents. We have both read this aloud to our children, read it privately, and listened to it with Derek Jacobi on audio many, many times. Never gets old. We still laugh at the jokes, which are now just plain old friends, and we often call our dog Garm.

A true five-Star book with an exceptional audio narration by Derek Jacobi.

THE LORD OF THE RINGS TRILOGY
The Fellowship of the Ring
The Two Towers
The Return of the King
J. R. R. Tolkien
(1892-1973)

If you are brave and have the time, perhaps over a long winter or sunny summer, you can move from *The Hobbit* to *The Lord of the Rings* trilogy.

THE GOSPEL STORY BIBLE: DISCOVERING JESUS IN THE OLD AND NEW TESTAMENTS
Marty Machowski
(1963-   )

I read this once through to my youngest two children and again once through with a young student. All of them were engaged with the big Gospel themes and enjoyed the book. In addition, I also enjoyed the reading both times.

The best thing about this book is that it shows how the Gospel is tied to every Bible story. The Bible is a not a manual on how to be good; rather it is the story of redemption in Christ.

HANS BRINKER, OR THE SILVER SKATES
Mary Mapes Dodge
(1831-1905)

A book I brought with me from my own childhood. Another story of loss and gain, this one set in Holland, or the Netherlands, as we call it now. It is about a tragedy which changes a family interspersed with the joy of ice skating on the canals. I love this book.

HEIDI
Johanna Spyri
(1827-1901)

A tiny orphan girl left with her embittered Grandfather in the Swiss Alps in a story that misses being sentimental and at times reaches true greatness.

THE HIDING PLACE
Corrie Ten Boom
(1892-1983)

This is a deeply moving true story of World War II and the power of forgiveness.

THE HOBBIT
J. R. R. Tolkien
(1892-1973)

Not sure how many times I have read this. Of course, it never grows old.

"In a hole in the ground there lived a hobbit."

Wonder and mystery are all wrapped up in such an ordinary sentence!

HOUSE OF ARDEN SERIES
The House of Arden
Harding's Luck
E. Nesbit (1858-1924)

E. Nesbit's books are so wonderful that they were childhood favorites of men like C. S. Lewis. If you read this series, you will never, ever forget the Fifth of November. Of course, then you must go on and read all of Nesbit's books.

THE ILIAD
Homer
(c. 750-650 BC)
Translated by
Richmond Lattimore or
Robert Fagles

You can read retellings of this epic before high school and they will only enhance the enjoyment when you finally get to read the original. *The Iliad* is the beginning of so many other stories. "Sing, O Muse of the anger of Achilles." Your boys will love this. After I read *The Iliad* aloud to my youngest two boys, I wrote a review.

> Confession: This is the first time I have ever read the entire *Iliad* out loud. It was delightful. The boys began to look on the time as a refreshing break during our school days. That took me by surprise because they are not quite so accommodating with Shakespeare. For my older children, I just assigned the reading. I read a few chapters out loud from an old translation to them, but it felt like a struggle.

> I know people in-the-know have various opinions about translations, but for us the Fagles was pleasantly readable as a read-aloud. The readings seemed to flow.

> All in all, reading *The Iliad* aloud will go down as one of the best things I ever did with my children at home.

THE ILIAD AND THE ODYSSEY: THE HEROIC STORY OF THE TROJAN WAR AND THE FABULOUS ADVENTURES OF ODYSSEUS
Jane Werner Watson
(1915-2004)
Illustrated by Alice
Provensen and Martin
Provensen

When I read this to my students, we looked forward to it every day. My only complaint is that the Provensens left out Argos, the dog. In spite of that, I do believe this is the best children's Homer I have read. I love the chapter breakdowns, which are almost parallel to the poems. The Provensens never disappoint, do they?

JOHNNY TREMAIN
Esther Forbes
(1891-1967)

This is the gold standard for historical read-aloud fiction surrounding the American Revolution.

KIDNAPPED
Robert Louis Stevenson
(1850-1894)

Meet David Balfour! He shows up in this thumping good read and in its equally good sequel *David Balfour*. Go for the Scribner Classic edition.

KING ALFRED'S ENGLISH
Laurie J. White
(1950-2020)

I was a bit hesitant to read this, as I bought it on sale for Kindle and thought the Kindle version might be inferior, as so many other such books have been. But it turns out that it was surprisingly good.

We read it aloud during Morning Time and the short, interesting chapters made it ideal for this situation. My husband was listening in as we finished the book and he asked, "What book is that? I would like to read it."

The perfect Morning Time book.

THE KING OF IRELAND'S SON
Padraic Colum
(1881-1972)

This is a classic Irish fairy tale.

KOSHKA'S TALES: STORIES FROM RUSSIA
James Mayhew
(1964-   )

Previously published as *The Kingfisher Book of Tales from Russia*, I stumbled upon this at a book sale once and it quickly became a family favorite. Children absolutely love these tales. Five stars because I also could not get enough.

LASSIE COME-HOME
Eric Knight
(1897-1943)

This was one of the first books I read aloud when my children were small. It's a much richer, deeper novel of loss and gain than you would guess if all you know is the old TV show. It's a bit of a tear-jerker.

THE LAST OF THE MOHICANS
James Fenimore Cooper (1789-1851)
Illustrated by N.C. Wyeth

Cooper's books are made to enter and get lost in. They are not quick reads, but if you give them a chance, they pull you into their world and make you want to stay. Look for the Scribner Classic edition.

LITTLE BRITCHES SERIES
Ralph Moody
(1898-1982)

Truly amazing stories of resilience and familial love. Be prepared to cry. These are expertly told stories. Virtue is illustrated in all its glory and humility is pictured without ever once watching itself in the mirror.

LITTLE PILGRIM'S PROGRESS: FROM JOHN BUNYAN'S CLASSIC
Helen L. Taylor
(1818-1885)

I am not a fan of rewritings or abridgments and I *have* read the original *Pilgrim's Progress* several times, but I still can't help enjoying this retelling. It is to *Pilgrim's Progress* what E. Nesbit's *Beautiful Stories from Shakespeare* is to Shakespeare's plays.

As with the real *Pilgrim's Progress*, part one is better than part two, but there are nevertheless some wonderful highlights in the second half. We come to love Mercy, Great Heart, and the boys in part two.

It is the kind of writing that could quickly become insipid and trite, and yet it doesn't. This is not a book that will be loved by everyone, but it is a great introduction to a great classic for the ten-and-under crowd—and it is not painful for adults to read either.

LITTLE WOMEN
Louisa May Alcott
(1832-1888)

This was a favorite of mine as a girl. While it could be said to be a little bit mawkish, it still manages to ring true enough to life to make us return to it over and over again. It genuinely never gets old. My boys liked it, too.

LIVES OF THE NOBLE GREEKS AND ROMANS
Plutarch (c. AD 46-120)
Translated by John Dryden

I am a big fan of the Dryden/Clough Plutarch; the sentences are luxurious.

THE MARSH KING
C. Walter Hodges
(1909-2004)

This is an excellent story of the Christian King Alfred.

MEN OF IRON
Howard Pyle
(1853-1911)

Howard Pyle is a not-to-be-missed author. His rich use of language is almost on par with the King James Bible and his illustrations became a part of a whole new school of American illustration.

THE MERRY ADVENTURES OF ROBIN HOOD
Howard Pyle
(1853-1911)

Howard Pyle is one of my favorite read-aloud authors. This version of Robin Hood reads like a lyric ode to Sherwood Forest and the merry band of outlaws. It is the perfect book to read aloud to young poet-warrior hopefuls. It happened to be the last book I read aloud to the young man I had been teaching for almost four years, so the bittersweet ending of the book struck a remembrance in me of past readings with my own children. Look for the Scribner Classic edition.

Let us end here:

"Thus they rode slowly onward, talking about these old, familiar things; old and yet new, for they found more in them than they had ever thought of before. Thus at last they came to the open glade, and the broad, wide-spreading greenwood tree which was their home for so many years. Neither of the two spoke when they stood beneath that tree. Robin looked all about him at the well-known things, so like what they used to be and yet so different; for, where once was the bustle of many busy fellows was now the quietness of solitude; and, as he looked, the woodlands, the greensward, and the sky all blurred together in his sight through salt tears, for such a great yearning came upon him as he looked on these things (as well known to him as the fingers of his right hand) that he could not keep back the water from his eyes."

THE ODYSSEY
Homer
(c. 750-650 BC)
Translated by
Richmond Lattimore or
Robert Fagles

As with *The Iliad*, *The Odyssey* is a book to read in retellings and stories before hitting the big time. Fagles's translation makes for a great read-aloud.

THE OUTSIDERS
S. E. Hinton
(1948-   )

I did not expect to like this book as much as I did. Not knowing anything about it, I thought at first it was a New York City or New Jersey story and was surprised to discover that it took place in Oklahoma. For some reason this made it more believable. Of course, it is dated, but the themes are not. My twelve-year-old student was suspicious of the book at first but warmed to it greatly and I knew we would both miss Ponyboy, Darry, and Sodapop.

THE PASSION OF JESUS CHRIST: FIFTY REASONS WHY HE CAME TO DIE
John Piper
(1946-   )

This is the perfect Morning Time book since its chapters are very short and its concepts are basic. Piper is so good at clearly communicating truth and passion for Christ.

It only has fifty chapters, so technically we should have finished it much sooner than we did. It took us much longer than I anticipated as life threw us a series of curve balls. But we kept on reading when we could, a little bit at a time, and we did finish. This is not a great feat to brag about, but it is an example how Morning Time works by not giving up when things mess it up. Just pick up and continue where you last left off. No need to overhaul the whole thing because of every interruption in life.

THE PILGRIM'S PROGRESS
John Bunyan
(1628-1688)

The Pilgrim's Progress is a timeless classic allegory of the Christian life. While we can debate whether this is great literature or not, many of the metaphors have helped me through the dangers of being a Christian. Who doesn't find themselves in a Slough of Despond or a Castle Despair sometimes?

THE PRINCESS AND CURDIE
George MacDonald
(1824-1905)

I don't think this is quite as fun to read as *The Princess and the Goblin,* but it is still a wonderful book. Perhaps its deeper lessons take away from the joy of the story. Nevertheless, it is a wonderful book. My recent student was quite put out that the history of Gwynytystorm ended so dismally.

THE PRINCESS AND THE GOBLIN
George MacDonald
(1824-1905)

Here we see a boy, Curdie, struggling with his own self, all the while determined to behave honorably to the princess he befriends. This book is full of dark mines, evil goblins, magical grandmothers, scary journeys, and poetry. Did you know poetry could be a weapon? It is Curdie's weapon of choice against the goblins. My own sons have used poetry to get through some of the fiercest challenges available to young men and in running a few marathons, too. Curdie saves the princess, and he learns much about good and evil on his way to being a man.

ROLL OF THUNDER, HEAR MY CRY (AND SEQUELS)
Mildred D. Taylor
(1943-)

A tremendously beautiful story, by the time *Roll of Thunder, Hear My Cry* ends you feel like you know every single character. I hated to say goodbye to the Logans. This is a truly important book which continually made me ask myself, "Would I have done that if I had grown up in that culture?" It is a scary question.

THE SIGN OF THE BEAVER
Elizabeth George Speare (1908-1994)

For this category of book, a historical fiction novel written for mid-elementary to middle school students, this is a five-star book. It is a great one to give a child who needs reading practice, but likes good stories. I had my recent students read it aloud to me. It was perfect for that, also. I have read it several times yet still did not get bored this time around.

I would say this also qualifies as a book to include in the "Literature of Honor for Boys" list.

SMOKY THE COWHORSE
Will James
(1892-1942)

A western for boys who love horses and cowboys. Once again, go for the Scribner Classic edition.

THE STORY OF KING ARTHUR AND HIS KNIGHTS
Howard Pyle
(1853-1911)

One of my favorite King Arthur books. The Scribner Classic edition is my favorite. It's a great book to read before moving on to Rosemary Sutcliff's Arthurian trilogy.

THE STORY OF ROLF AND THE VIKING BOW
Allen French
(1870-1946)

A wonderful tale of heroism for boys (and girls)!

SWALLOWS AND AMAZONS
Arthur Ransome
(1884-1967)

Need a trip to the Lake District in England? These books will remind your children not to be duffers and remind you to let them explore sometimes.

TREASURE ISLAND
Robert Louis Stevenson
(1850-1894)

Join Jim Hawkins as he accidentally goes to sea with a band of pirates, led by Long John Silver, looking for buried treasure. The Scribner Classic edition is beautiful.

TREASURES OF THE SNOW
Patricia St. John
(1919-1993)

This is one of my favorite read-alouds. I picked it as the first book to read aloud to my granddaughters in our social distancing Morning Time during the 2020 Covid-19 pandemic. They both loved it and we read the last four chapters in one sitting, because we couldn't help it. Even though I have read this book many times, I still got very teary in parts. Also, I found it quite interesting that I related so much to the old grandmother this time.

If you ever wonder how a book can have a moral without moralizing, try *Treasures of the Snow*.

UNDERSTOOD BETSY
Dorothy Canfield Fisher
(1879-1958)

I loved reading this to my granddaughters on Zoom. It's full of great thoughts on over-parenting and education. It is about a little orphan girl who must leave the aunt who coddles her to go and live with her only other family on a farm, a family she has been taught to scorn and fear. I feel so blessed to have had an opportunity to read this again.

THE WHEEL ON THE SCHOOL
Meindert DeJong
(1906-1991)

One of the joys of teaching is getting to reread old friends. This one must be read in short sections, but it is a wonderful story of life in community.

THE WIND IN THE WILLOWS
Kenneth Grahame
(1859-1932)

The Wind in the Willows is a book I wish I could hug. Visiting these old friends is always a joy. As an adult, I love the wilder chapters where Grahame captures the essence of animal instinct. Warning: This is not an easy book to read the first time around. I gave up, too! I picked it up again a few years later and have never looked back. I sometimes read this just to myself for the joy of it. This is a top-five life book for me.

WITH WOLFE IN CANADA
G. A. Henty
(1832-1902)

Some people don't like Henty, but I found his books to be full of great historical stories, just the kind of books boys love at a certain age, and not too hard to read aloud either. This one is especially good. Find out how Wolfe died and how he loved poetry, all in a rousing good yarn.

THE WHITE COMPANY
Sir Arthur Conan Doyle
(1859-1930)

This is Conan Doyle's book of chivalry and it is one of the best examples of that sort of book. *The White Company* shows us what it means to be a gentleman both in manners and skill. It is the manliest of stories. One minute our hero is cleaving an enemy, and the next we find him deferring to a lady in the gentlest way. This is no one-sided view of chivalry. Our sons will not see that might makes right from this book. Instead, they will find full-orbed manhood which lays down its life for those weaker.

BELOVED BOOK SERIES

THE CHRONICLES OF NARNIA[13]

THE LION, THE WITCH, AND THE WARDROBE
C. S. Lewis
(1898-1963)

When you read a book over and over and over again, sometimes in the same month (though to a different student) and you never once become uninterested, then that book gets five stars. Forever and always, five stars to *The Lion, the Witch, and the Wardrobe.*

Also I am completely charmed and tickled to now have a granddaughter named Lucy and a grandson named Peter.

THE MAGICIAN'S NEPHEW
C. S. Lewis
(1898-1963)

Please read this after *The Lion, the Witch, and the Wardrobe*; that way there are more "aha" moments. There are many iconic, memorable scenes: Uncle Andrew and the animals, Digory ringing the bell, meeting Jadis for the first time, and then Jadis in the tree soiled by the fruit, Digory's terrible battle with hope and despair over the apple, the lovely creation of a beloved world, and the final amazing ending where it all comes together. It is so much fun to read this to a student and wait for the epiphanies to hit them. Remember not to steal them!

PRINCE CASPIAN
C. S. Lewis
(1898-1963)

Installment three (although it was the second Narnia book to be published) of the classic *Chronicles of Narnia*.

THE VOYAGE OF THE DAWN TREADER
C. S. Lewis
(1898-1963)

One of the best. From entering Narnia through a painting, to Eustace Scrubb deserving his name, to the Island where Dreams come true and Reepicheep the brave (and annoying) mouse, this simple book is chockful of evidence of being the "right kind of book" and then some. Who can forget Lucy looking through the magic book? And the Dufflepuds, a people I often resemble?

THE HORSE AND HIS BOY
C. S. Lewis
(1898-1963)

I'm always glad for an opportunity to read this aloud. Such fun.

THE SILVER CHAIR
C. S. Lewis
(1898-1963)

One of the best, sometimes my favorite. Puddleglum is, perhaps, my favorite Narnian character of all time.

THE LAST BATTLE
C. S. Lewis
(1898-1963)

"All shall be well, and all shall be well and all manner of thing shall be well," wrote Julian of Norwich.

Here is C. S. Lewis's attempt to comfort us with visions of heavenly truth. I think he succeeds. The first time I ever really desired Heaven was after reading this as a nineteen-year-old newly-married woman. Years later, as I finished reading it to my student, I felt my heart ache again longingly. I ache for that heavenly realty.

As I read of each character the children were finding in the "further up and further in" Narnia, Drake, my student, would jump out of his chair and hoot for joy. You gotta love a twelve-year-old boy!

I found myself happiest to see Puddleglum again.

I hope I am not saying goodbye to Narnia forever. I hope I can read them to my grandchildren.

LITTLE HOUSE BOOKS

The complete list of Little House titles is found on page 49.

LITTLE HOUSE IN THE BIG WOODS
Laura Ingalls Wilder
(1867-1957)

But Laura lay awake a little while, listening to Pa's fiddle softly playing and to the lonely sound of the wind in the Big Woods. She looked at Pa sitting on the bench by the hearth, the firelight gleaming on his brown hair and beard and glistening on the honey-brown fiddle. She looked at Ma, gently rocking and knitting.

She thought to herself, "This is now."

She was glad that the cosy house, and Pa and Ma and the firelight and the music, were now. They could not be forgotten, she thought, because now is now. It can never be a long time ago."

Simply the best passage of American prose. I have never once read it without tears. This morning my student said, "Miss Cindy, are you crying?" I was supposed to finish the book on Tuesday, but it was a rough day for me because of my dad's health situation. I knew better than to read the last chapter on that day.

FARMER BOY
Laura Ingalls Wilder
(1867-1957)

There was much wailing and gnashing of teeth this morning as we finished *Farmer Boy*. My student could not believe it was over! I'm not sure how many times I have read this, but I am thinking five.

I believe after *Little House in the Big Woods*, it is the best book in the Little House series. Goodbye, Almanzo. Not sure when we will meet again.

THE LONG WINTER
Laura Ingalls Wilder
(1867-1957)

While this is not the most compelling Little House book, it is a very important part of the story. I cannot imagine a better look at the character of the pioneers. To live with the Ingalls family through the long winter puts much of life's little frustrations in perspective.

When Laura says, "For shame, Grace," after months and months of suffering, and little Grace utters the first and last complaint of the whole book, it belies our own time and culture. No, it is not compelling to be confronted with one's own weaknesses, but this book is a vividly drawn picture of a life lived with gratefulness.

RESOURCES AND RECOMMENDATIONS

Various books and resources suggested in the text are listed here in the order they were mentioned. You can also refer to the Index and the Index of First Lines to help you find titles or authors.

FOREWORD
For the Family's Sake by Susan Schaeffer Macauley

A LITURGY OF LOVE
For the Children's Sake by Susan Schaeffer Macauley
Desiring the Kingdom by James K. A. Smith

ELEMENTS OF MORNING TIME
Grace Unknown by R. C. Sproul
Fifty Reasons Why Jesus Came to Die by John Piper
The Classic Hundred Poems by William Harmon
Beauty in the Word by Stratford Caldecott
The Complete Works of Shakespeare
Parents' Union Online—now known as AmblesideOnline (Amblesideonline.org)
Tales from Shakespeare by Charles and Mary Lamb
Beautiful Stories from Shakespeare for Children by E. Nesbit
Asimov's Guide to Shakespeare by Isaac Asimov
Lives of the Noble Greeks and Romans by Plutarch. Also refered to as Plutarch's *Lives*.
   Arthur Clough's revision of John Dryden's translation is recommended.

Towards a Philosphy of Education, Volume 6 of Charlotte Mason's series

Plutarch guides by Anne White: visit AmblesideOnline.org for Anne White's Plutarch guides, or consider buying the paperback or Kindle versions of *The Plutarch Project* books series from Amazon.com.

AmblesideOnline for composer and artists selections

Opal Wheeler's book series on composers

Hallelujah: Cultivating Advent Traditions with Handel's Messiah by Cindy Rollins

The Mother Tongue: Adapted for Modern Students by George Lyman Kittridge and Sarah Louise Arnold, adapted by Amy M. Edwards and Christina J. Mugglin, published by Blue Sky Daisies

Michael Clay Thompson practice books. See https://www.rfwp.com/pages/michael-clay-thompson/ for more information.

In Vital Harmony and *Know and Tell by* Karen Glass

Ideas Freely Sown and *Honest and Simple Souls* by Anne White

NOTES

1   Discover more at AmblesideOnline.org. Here is how AO describes their curriculum: "AmblesideOnline is a free homeschool curriculum that uses Charlotte Mason's classically-based principles to prepare children for a life of rich relationships with everything around them: God, humanity, and the natural world. AO's detailed schedules, time-tested methods, and extensive teacher resources allow parents to focus effectively on the unique needs of each child."

2   Charlotte Mason wrote, "Let us try, however imperfectly, to make education a science of relationships—in other words, try in one subject or another to let the children work upon living ideas. In this field small efforts are honoured with great rewards, and we perceive that the education we are giving exceeds all that we intended or imagined." Charlotte Mason, *School Education*, 163.

3   AmblesideOnline.org.

4   Reformation Day, October 31, commemorates the beginning of the Protestant Reformation. Martin Luther nailed the Ninety-Five Theses on the church door in Wittenburg, Germany, on October 31, 1517. In many church traditions, a Reformation Day party is held, which also serves as a Halloween alternative for families.

5   Stratfort Caldecott, *Beauty in the Word*, chapter 2 "Remembering."

6   Charlotte Mason, *Ourselves*, book 2, 72.

7   Charlotte Mason, *Towards a Philosophy of Education*, 185.

8   Ibid, 185-186.

9   Reprinted with permission from *The American Patriot's Handbook: The Writings, History, and Spirit of a Free Nation*. Grant, George. 2016, page 41-42. Not much is known about Lawrence Tribble, but that he was possibly a soldier in the Continental Army in the 1770s. This poem was discovered by George Grant, written on a slip of paper tucked into an antique 18th century Bible found in a bookshop.

10   Pluto was downgraded in 2006 to a "dwarf planet." You may still want to memorize it, however, since some still consider this a planet.

11   A good way to learn states and capitals is by labeling blank maps. Postal codes make this easier (see page 215). These lists are provided for your reference if you decide to do this during Morning Time.

12   Visit uscis.gov for the latest civics test.

13   The publication order of the Chronicles of Narnia is listed on page 49. I like to read them in the order shown on pages 249-250.

INDEX

INDEX OF FIRST LINES

ABOUT THE AUTHOR

For many years, Cindy Rollins blogged about her homeschool and "Morning Time." As her children grew up she began homeschooling for private families in her community using Charlotte Mason's timeless principles. This experience compelled her to share with others all that she had learned through implementing Morning Time, so that other families can enjoy it, too.

Cindy is the host of *The New Mason Jar Podcast* and also co-hosts *The Literary Life Podcast* with Angelina Stanford and Thomas Banks. She is a popular speaker, giving talks and workshops on Morning Time as well as personal and spiritual growth for mothers during the ever-changing seasons of life.

Cindy is the author of the beloved *Mere Motherhood*, an account of her mothering journey, *Hallelujah: Cultivating Advent Traditions with Handel's Messiah*, and *The Literary Life Podcast Commonplace Book Series*.

Find out more about Cindy's current workshops and speaking schedule at MorningTimeForMoms.com. Also visit TheNewMasonJar.com and TheLiterary.Life to discover more about her podcasts.

OTHER BLUE SKY DAISIES TITLES

GEOGRAPHY BOOKS
Elementary Geography by Charlotte Mason
Home Geography for Primary Grades with Written and Oral Exercises by C. C. Long

LANGUAGE ARTS AND GRAMMAR BOOKS
The Mother Tongue: Adapted for Modern Students by George Lyman Kittredge. In this series: Workbook 1 and 2; Answer Key 1 and 2
Exercises in Dictation by F. Peel
Grammar Land: Grammar in Fun for the Children of Schoolroom Shire (Annotated) By M. L. Nesbitt. Annotated by Amy M. Edwards and Christina J. Mugglin
The Literary Life Podcast Commonplace Books by Angelina Stanford, Cindy Rollins, andd Thomas Banks. Available in four designs, plus three children's versions.

THE COPYWORKBOOK SERIES
The CopyWorkBook: George Washington's Rules of Civility & Decent Behavior in Company and Conversation by Amy M. Edwards and Christina J. Mugglin
The CopyWorkBook: Comedies of William Shakespeare by Amy M. Edwards and Christina J. Mugglin

OTHER TITLES
The Birds' Christmas Carol by Kate Douglas Wiggin
The Innkeeper's Daughter by Michelle Lallement
Kipling's Rikki-Tikki-Tavi: A Children's Play by Amy M. Edwards
Hallelujah: Cultivating Advent Traditions with Handel's Messiah by Cindy Rollins

*These titles are popular with those inspired by Charlotte Mason and her educational philosophy.